A
WOMAN
IN REVOLT

A
WOMAN
IN REVOLT
A Biography of
FLORA TRISTAN

by
DOMINIQUE DESANTI

Translated by
ELIZABETH ZELVIN

Crown Publishers, Inc.   *   New York

Printed in the United States of America
Published simultaneously in Canada by General Publishing Company Limited

Designed by Jon M. Nelson

Library of Congress Cataloging in Publication Data

Desanti, Dominique.
    A woman in revolt.

    Translation of Flora Tristan, la femme révoltée.
    1. Tristan y Moscozo, Flore Célestine Thérèse
Henriette, 1803-1844.   I. Title.
HQ1615.T7D4613   1976   301.41'2'0924 [B]   75-43739
ISBN 0-517-51878-3

CONTENTS

Part I: Trying to Be

Part II: The Prophets' Fire

PART I

Trying to Be

1

A BASTARD UNDER
THE RESTORATION

On April 7, 1820, Flora Tristan is seventeen, in Paris. This
morning as usual, she goes downstairs into the Place Maubert to
empty the bucket and carry water back up to their attic rooms.
Street vendors from the nearby Pont Neuf clear their throats to
shout: "Chickweed . . ." "Water carrier . . ." "Ah, something you'll
like . . ."

The Rue du Fouarre and the narrow streets around it still look
the way they did then, a hundred fifty years ago, but the people who
live there have lately become middle-class.

Seventeen is not an easy age. Everybody expects you to behave
like a grown-up but obey like a child. You have your dreams, but
they echo your mother's. Flora knows what she looks like from the
mirror, crude compliments in the neighborhood, and her family's
praise. Nobody has yet drawn or painted her. In four years Niepce
will discover photography, but for a long time this will be only a
whim for the rich. Flora knows her own voice, as everyone does,
through her bones. Her insight into herself is that of her time.

Flora is small, though her long limbs make her look taller. Lithe,
slender, with breasts scarcely swelling, she is not sorry she fails to
conform to the fashionable notion of "beautiful women." They say

her eyes are Orient black "because her father was Peruvian," her manners elegant "because she is of good family." Her spelling is atrocious: no money, no schooling. Standing at the bookstalls of the Palais-Royal, she devours Benjamin Constant's *Adolphe* and Lamartine's *Meditations,* the year's sensation. She secretly sells the silver sugar tongs to buy the late Madame de Staël's *Corinne,* Sir Walter Scott, and Byron. She reads English and knows Spanish.

In the Latin Quarter, she admires the eccentricity of the students who let their hair grow and wear "stifled sigh" waistcoats under frock coats with "shawl" collars. These Tristan ladies rarely read newspapers: it's too expensive. But although they must be satisfied with rumors, Flora feels the nostalgic and irritable boredom that bathes the young. "The monarchy and the happiness of the middle class" have been restored, but thirty-five-year-olds tell of Napoleon's wars, and fifty-year-olds of the Revolution. In those days, at least, you lived, and what did it matter if you lost one or two members of your family . . . Flora has never heard of Fourier, nor of Saint-Simon, who will publish *On the Industrial System* the following year, she doesn't know that Victor Hugo is eighteen years old and George Sand sixteen, she doesn't know that two years from now in Germany a certain Karl Marx, whom she will never hear of at all, will be born . . . although he will know of her.

At home, Flora hears only about the past. She puts flowers before the portrait of her father, dead in 1808, dressed as the King of Spain's colonel, clean-shaven, with a face that she finds handsome because she looks like him: a mane of hair, sparkling eyes, a longish nose, a strong lower lip. Did he have her very white smile? Behind him in the picture is a man with dark skin and a dazzling necklace: it is Montezuma, ancestor of the Tristan de Moscoso family in the female line; he was king of the Indians and "surrendered" them, along with his daughter, to the Spaniards who conquered Mexico. Madame Tristan was born Thérèse Laisney. Her conversation is full of complex genealogies. The only other relative Flora knows, her uncle Commandant Laisney, furtively displays the "cross for bravery" that the Emperor pinned on his chest after Tilsitt. Uncle Laisney lives in Versailles, doesn't joke about morals, and doesn't like bluestockings, affectedly witty women, or female intellectuals. The Tristan ladies live on what he gives them every month. It's not

4

much; he is on half-pension; his situation will only be put right later on.

Madame Tristan is someone special to the shopkeepers on the Rue du Fouarre, the Rue Galande, and the Place Maubert. They listen to her describe Vaugirard, the house set in huge grounds where she lived with her husband. When he died in 1808, France was at war with Spain, he was a retired colonel of the King of Spain, and the house was seized as enemy property. Since then it had been impossible to obtain either compensation or restitution. Madame Tristan had lived in the country at first, then her son had died, she could no longer bear the solitude, and there they were in Paris. As for getting Flora well married. . . .

Do the neighbors believe this story? Or do they class it with the other hard luck stories of the Place Maubert: the homeless fat woman who sang at La Scala in Milan, the one-legged man with his tales of Austerlitz? Falsehood and truth get mixed together for these patter artists, these tightrope walkers, these on-stage mimes, and end up forming a unique neighborhood-truth, a Maubert chronicle. From their attic windows Flora can see the drunken playboys leaving the Red Castle, a tavern nicknamed "The Guillotine," where killers confront each other with switchblades. She loves to wander around the neighborhood, shuddering as she imagines brawls, seeing girls her own age wearing dazzling dresses with leg-o'-mutton sleeves, gauze turbans, warm furred pelisses. Bad women? . . . But, she tells herself, at least they don't have to count every log, or go to bed early to save lamp-oil, and you hear them shouting with laughter, you even see them, sometimes, arriving by carriage, in a berlin or a landaulet. . . .

"One day," her mother says, "your uncle Don Pio de Tristan de Moscoso, your father's younger brother, the richest man in Arequipa, Peru, will answer my letters, then you will have chinchilla pelisses, a maid to dress you, and a carriage with horses in fine trappings to take you to the Italian Theater. . . ."

Flora suffered her great blow at fifteen. She will write about it obliquely, then dressed up as fiction in a novel, *Méphis*: at thirty-five she will still remember that first day when the earth trembled, when she learned she was "not like other people." That she wouldn't be taken for what she was: a pretty girl, slim and healthy, with a lovely voice and many talents. That she was marked, damned, outlawed by an invisible flaw.

In 1818, Commandant Laisney offered her drawing lessons. At her teacher's, she met a good-looking boy of excellent family, a little older than herself. Puppy love: looks, scribbled verses, secret letters, furtive meetings. . . . The boy wanted to marry her. The family consented: these Tristan de Moscosos seemed to be of good family. . . . When the discussions became serious, Madame Tristan had to confess. She had met her husband in Spain, during the emigration, in Bilbao where he was garrisoned, and where she lived with her mother. Why had Madame Laisney, a lower-middle-class woman, emigrated? Panic, no doubt. In short, young Thérèse, sweet and easygoing, had been conquered by an officer old enough to be her father. Mariano de Tristan de Moscoso, Peruvian but a colonel in the royal Spanish army, was supposed to get the king's consent, that is, the high command's, if he wanted to marry. At the time, with the Terror over in France, everyone knew that the émigrés' return was near: the Spanish army didn't hold with these alliances. Or perhaps Thérèse didn't have the standard dowry?

In short, no consent. So Don Mariano de Tristan had the marriage performed by a French émigré priest . . . who had never had it registered. Madame Tristan had identity papers witnessed by ten Spaniards, but no marriage certificate. Flora was recognized by her father. She was born in Paris where the couple settled in 1802 when Don Mariano retired. They lived at Vaugirard until the colonel's death. And there it was. Flora de Tristan de Moscoso was a bastard. The young man's father promptly forbade her to enter his honorable family. At thirty-five Flora will write: "The young man for whom I had this feeling deserved it on all counts; but, lacking energy of the soul, he died sooner than disobey his father." Died, really? How did he die? Suicide? Tuberculosis at a time when it was rampant?

In short, from then on Flora knew herself illegitimate, a bastard. To measure the breakdown, the self-doubt, the sense of injustice and of being cursed that an adolescent could feel in 1818, let us remember that a notorious and emancipated Frenchwoman who died in 1972 entitled her memoirs, written at fifty, *The Bastard*. The critics of the late twentieth century seriously analyzed Violette

Leduc's bastardy complex, which had made her half-asocial. Let us remember that in 1971, when Parliament allowed recognized illegitimate children to share in their fathers' estates, French newspapers protested in the name of the sacred rights of the legitimate family, the nucleus of society. Flora—it is the flaw in her character, which doesn't lack "energy of the soul"—goes into a demented rage, reproaching her mother, in language out of Sir Walter Scott, Byron, and Chateaubriand, for "having brought her into the world for her unhappiness." The weak, tender mother, "Minette," weeps and the daughter stamps, beats her head against the walls, dashes their frugal china to the floor. All her life anger, even repressed, will make her tremble, shake with fever, render her breathless and speechless. The women of her time escape into vapors, fainting, and migraines; she spends herself in rage.

"Energy of the soul" gives her strength, the following year, to fall madly in love again. Twenty years later she will describe this man, much older than she—all her life she will be looking for a romantic father. "Irreproachably delicate" (in other words he left her virgin), but "one of those cold, calculating beings, in whose eyes a grand passion looks like madness: he was *afraid* of my love, he feared that I would love him *too much*."

Here is her life prefigured: she fights to escape a traditional woman's role; men look for companions who conform to the known model. The object of her grand passion must have decided that this exalted spirit would make a bad housekeeper. He won't be the only one.

So at sixteen she has taken the measure of what is possible. Her mother says they should be living like queens in Peru, but they live upstairs from hardened criminals. Society rejects you in the name of laws that contradict nature, of a past when you didn't exist; but it demands your respect and obedience. Love is the "breath of God" and woman's only important business; but if you love without restraint, you create a scandal.

So you can only blossom out into rebellion. Where can she find models? Women offer few. Men, then? Surely not sententious, narrow-minded Uncle Laisney. Her dead father, of course. And especially Simón Bolívar, her father's young friend who conquered glory and is much alive. He can't be followed even by telegraph; he goes too fast. When Flora is nine, he is exiled and puts out his manifestos for the liberation of Latin America: "War to the death with the Spaniards." When Flora is ten, he leads his armies 844 miles toward Caracas and in ninety days destroys five Spanish batallions, wins six battles, fifty cannons, three ammunition depots. After which he declares he will accept only one post: the post of danger at the head of his Indians and blacks. He is the *Libertador*, god of Venezuela and Colombia, this new entity called South America. . . . Napoleon succumbs when Bolívar triumphs. Soon he too is defeated by disunion. But Flora is not sixteen when he is up again, hires Irish to fight beside the Venezuelans, crosses the Cordillera of the Andes. Heroic combats "without shoes" (his orders of the day said it, in Spanish, before Hugo). In Bogota, he proclaims the Republic of Greater Colombia.

There is the image on which Flora wants to model herself: to conquer in order to give. More than the Libertador's victories, she loves the fact that he emancipated his slaves and sacrificed his fortune to the Cause. Her Uncle Laisney accuses "little Simón" of having executed 886 prisoners at the beginning of his career. Flora flares up: many more are killed in wars. Hands off her hero. . . . He never answered Madame Tristan's appeals for help? Well, maybe he never received the letters.

When Flora is seventeen, these ladies' condition verges on real misery: nothing left for heat or light. Everything of value has been pawned. Uncle Laisney grumbles that if his niece's spelling weren't so laughable, she could at least teach. What are they to do when the grandmother's little legacy is gone? Someone mentions an engraver who is looking for colorists for fashion and perfume engravings. He is the brother of a respected painter, Antoine Chazal, a disciple of the great Girodet.

The girl goes alone to the studio near the Bastille, a sort of shed where the smells of oil, acid, and glue mingle with the dusty stench of the coal stove. From the squalid odors of the Place Maubert, Flora will always be extremely sensitive to smells and noises; she can detect poverty with her eyes closed. Perched on a high stool, a languid girl in a stained smock is drawing lines. A man rises.

André Chazal is twenty-three. Neither tall nor broadly built, he tries to give character to his flabby face and weak glutton's mouth by letting his hair and side-whiskers grow. He makes his spindly body picturesque by dressing "artistically." He talks in long sentences full of fashionable phrases: social contract; sanctity of labor; sacred rights of passion . . . and equally sacred rights of the fatherland . . . André Chazal has the bad luck to be the younger brother of Antoine, whom everyone admires, who succeeds at everything, who has always been set up as an example for him. Until now, he used to console himself with drinking companions, and spent half the night playing cards in the taverns. But at twenty-three the time has come to get established and settle down. So there he is, a lithographer.

To look for a job, Flora has borrowed every elegant thing she could lay her hands on. A gauze turban on her long curls with their ripe Indian chestnut highlights. A Joan of Arc bag, a white velvet purse with a steel catch on it. Her only pretty dress, percale, with a sleeveless top of tobacco-colored lace. Chazal thinks this exotic beauty is a client and clears off the only armchair, bought second-hand and dating from the Old Regime.

"I'm told you're looking for a colorist. I can do that . . ."

Too late to change his tone and sound like a boss. Besides, he can't. A workingwoman, this queen? But still . . . He questions her, she answers with her ladylike air. Widowed mother. Impoverished. Father dead, a Peruvian gentleman, a Spanish colonel. "She aroused in me a violent passion," he will write angrily seventeen years later. From this first moment, he is sick with love. A poor and noble orphan, a damsel in distress, those eyes, those hands . . . What a romance! And her name? Flora Tristan, it rings like a poem.

He had asked for an "apprentice presented by her parents." He gets one to whom he must present himself, speaking of his brother. Since neither he nor she has accomplished anything yet, they define themselves by their families. He accompanies her to the Rue du Fouarre to meet Madame Laisney, on the excuse of discussing terms. The modesty of their lodging makes him overflow with compassion, he runs to get wood, oil, wine, something for dinner. Madame Laisney invites him to stay, and promptly begins to tell her stories of the past. Bolívar? She knew Bolívar? In the dullness of the Restoration the Libertador appears in the dreams of French youth, even though the newspapers seldom mention him.

Bolívar young? Madame Laisney goes to look for letters in a

drawer. These garrets are full of furniture from before the Revolution, the kind you find in secondhand stores, the kind fashionable people shove into the attic. . . . but the marvelous Andalusian lives in an attic.

Yes, Bolívar, the Tristans knew him in Spain, he wasn't twenty years old. He was an orphan, raised by a great scholar who was a disciple of Rousseau. To protect his pupil from frivolity, this Don Rodriguez dressed, fed, and housed him like a common workingman. They took endless walks together . . . until the day when the nineteen-year-old boy fell madly in love with the daughter of a marquis, a fragile adolescent, whose family didn't want her to marry so young. He abducted her. They got married, but this young beloved was dead in childbirth a year later, a fact the Tristans didn't know. One day in Paris Colonel Tristan sees that someone is advertising for him in the newspapers. He hurries toward a filthy rooming house and finds, in bed, a skeleton that he doesn't recognize: it's Simón Bolívar. Since his wife is dead, he refuses to live. The colonel brings him home, Thérèse cares for him, then they send him back to his tutor in Austria. Several years later he advertises for Don Mariano de Tristan again. This time his address is the most modern hotel on the elegant Rue Vivienne. On the way there, a dandy's carriage nearly runs them over; a giant dressed in the height of fashion seizes Thérèse in his arms. Dumbfounded, she asks how this transformation came about. He says, "I'll write and tell you."

Thérèse Laisney begins to read the letter to the fascinated André Chazal. . . . He was damned if he suspected that in hiring a colorist he would be practically rubbing shoulders with a South American hero. The future Libertador writes that his tutor didn't understand his sorrow, he was too busy with physics and chemistry. The young man fell into "such a state of consumption that the doctors declared I was going to die." Don Rodriguez, to hearten him, evokes all the careers that his beloved pupil could embrace. Simón answers that he could only accomplish something if he were rich. "Well, Simón Bolívar, you are rich! At this moment you have four million. . . ." For the tutor, spending nothing on himself or on his pupil, has increased the parents' fortune. "Rodriguez had thought to breed in me intellectual passions which, proud mistresses, would lead those of the senses as slaves." But Bolívar, as soon as he comes

10

into his fortune, goes dashing across Europe. "I went to London and spent 150,000 francs there in three months. Next I went to Madrid where I had a prince's retinue." In every city, under "the appearance of pleasures" he remains cold, and even Paris doesn't put an end to "the vague state of indecision that torments me." The present for him "is a complete void where even desire cannot be born."

"Ah!" says Flora, "how right his tutor was! Only great passions for learning, liberty, or love can give happiness...."

André Chazal believes himself transported into a dream: this garret housing a splendid creature who despises money but venerates passion.... And the secret of this Libertador who turns the world upside down because luxury bores him.... The loudmouth of the little cafés has never had such a time in his life. After dinner, Thérèse Laisney goes on reading and telling her story.

One evening in 1805 Bolívar gives a banquet to which he invites high-ranking officials and, in the most virulent terms, attacks the Emperor.

Thérèse remembers: "Everyone spoke at once but his resonant voice rang out, accusing Bonaparte of having betrayed the cause of liberty and blaming the soldiers of the Revolution for their complicity...."

After this dinner Bolívar no longer has any friends other than the Tristans. At their house, Vaugirard, with Florita on his shoulders, he walks with long strides through the garden, ravaging all the plants, apologizing: "I've scarcely broken the stem of a flower when it ceases to please me." Madame Tristan laughs at her memories: the Libertador also used to tear out the fringes of armchairs, he used to grab books and gnaw at them with his teeth while he talked.... Soon he goes off to transform a continent to appease his torturing need to make everything into something other than what it is.

To meet a beauty surrounded by such a romantic aura is too much for a neighborhood engraver. From the first evening, André Chazal is lost to everything but Flora. He spends his evenings in the Rue du Fouarre, seated near her coloring engraved labels. One evening when Madame Laisney has gone off to bed he throws himself on her and clasps her to him. For the first time she feels a man's body against her own ... and pushes him away, struggles, threatens to scream. . . . Love may be "the breath of God" but not this breath of wine and tobacco, this scent of acid and oil. . . . Is love, then, letting herself be mauled without a sound, with her mother sleeping behind the partition? So often imagined, this scene where the "gift" leads to supreme exaltation, is this what it is, then? This frail man, the clandestine horror, the coupling on the floor? Is life, then, always the murder of the dream?

"She saw my passion grow and yielded to it. I fought vainly against this passion." After eighteen years of hate the memory still holds its panting ardor.

Chazal finds allies in the mother and the uncle. A giver of employment; an honorable artisan-artist; the brother of a juror of the Salon? What more can one ask when one is at the end of one's resources: nothing left to sell, not a word from Peru?

Flora's interpretation will never vary: "My mother forced me to marry this man whom I could neither love nor esteem." She speaks of "legitimate prostitution" and says that in the face of Minette's disappointment and regrets, she forgave her in the end.

Chazal will claim that she loved him, but admitted that he took her against everyone's advice. "I fought vainly against this passion, according to my own observations and those of several people who said to me: this woman will never have the qualities that make a good wife and mother." But this "unequal character," these changeable moods were only because she "wasn't happy." In the popular language of the time, "not to be happy" denotes extreme poverty. Chazal hopes that his "modest competence" will sweeten Flora—he doesn't speak of irresistible passion. In court, he will produce letters that are probably apocryphal, except for one which is notable for its appalling spelling. A beautiful example of a romantic who gets carried away when she is pushed into a marriage of convenience. The letter is dated January 12, 1821 (three weeks before the marriage). She offers a collection of platitudes that one would guess— except for the spelling—were copied from some manual of love letters, and an unconscious anguish which, unlike the platitudes, rings true:

> I will tell you, my dear, that last nite that I wanted so, I wanted so for it to come, for I have terrable pains, espeshally when I walk, I think

I won't be able to take a dancing lesson, that's the bad part; but! also what happy momence! All nite I did nothing but think of you, I was always with you, I saw only you in all of nachure. Farewell, frend of my heart, ah how the morning struck the hart, I sawt you on my breast, on this brest which has known pleasure thru you alone. But farewell! I swear to love you always and to procure for you as much pleasure as I have given you pane, farewell! So lover of my soul, but I cannot leave you, ah . . . how it greeves me to bid you farewell.

Flora

P.S. Give a little wood to Armandine, its for her, becoz I don't need any, I dont urge you to look out for our interests, reason speaks for me, a thousand kisses of flame on your pretty little lips. Farewell.

This is the letter of a child playing lovers: when one has "given" oneself, one feels great impulses. This "pain" inflicted on the man does not indicate an idyll, however. The body protests: do these "terrable pains" come from remorse for the "fault" that makes menstruation more difficult? Or would Flora already be pregnant? (We don't have the first child's birth certificate.)

And so, persuaded by her mother and her uncle, this girl who dreams of Bolívar lets herself be pushed toward the only normal career for a woman: marriage. How could she realize, at less than eighteen, that with divorce abolished by the Restoration, she is getting herself into a trap from which there is no escape?

2

THE MARRIAGE TRAP

On February 3, 1821, at the mayor's office of the 11th *arron-dissement*, Flora becomes Madame André Chazal in a civil cere-mony. That year when her dreams die, Flaubert, Baudelaire, and Dostoievsky will be born.

The couple settles in the heart of the Latin Quarter, on the rue des Fossés-Saint-Germain (now the Rue de l'Ancienne-Comédie). Their first son, who will die in childhood, is soon born. Madame Tristan lives close by on the Rue de Copeau, across from the Jardin du Roy (now the Jardin des Plantes). Does she know that in May of that year the Carbonari establish their headquarters behind her house, on the Rue de la Clef? Flora is almost constantly ill; her body protests more and more. The studio, engraving, Chazal's conversa-tion interest her less and less. On the other hand, she mingles with the crowd around the Palais de Justice during the trial of the June 1820 rioters, the "accomplices" of the student killed by the police.

In May, Napoleon's death on St. Helena causes rumblings. In spite of the police, shop windows display pictures in which the famous cocked hat is raised toward the sun at Austerlitz, then overturned on the exile's rock. The crippled half-pay soldiers put on their "crosses for bravery" and even cautious Uncle Laisney sports his, humming Béranger's songs: *He is a little man.—All dressed in gray.—In Paris.*

They sing them from scaffolding in factory courtyards—to glorify the man who sent a whole generation to its death becomes a way of protesting against those in power. This becomes obvious and, in December, Béranger is indicted.

At the same time, there is news of Bolívar: in Peru, the Tristans' homeland, he fights and liberates; a republic is born wherever his horse prances. Flora feels she is living through Bolívar who detested Napoleon. But for her any unhappy hero becomes an object of love. She devours poems, reads Spanish and English—one day she will travel. One day—but when, and how? She recites *Corinne* to herself, identifies with Madame de Staël. But how can she reconcile the aspirations of a banker's daughter and the sordid daily life of an artisan's wife? She recites André Chenier: *I don't want to die yet....*

Chazal, at the beginning, tries to raise himself to the level of Flora's dreams. He takes her to the Salon, to his brother's master Girodet's studio, to the newly rebuilt Odéon Theater where crowds are flocking to see Mademoiselle George, and to the Café Procope next door to where they live. Flora's entrance there provokes a frank murmur of admiration.

When her first son is born, Flora thinks she must be a monster: this forced maternity has not released the burning maternal love that novels talk about. The fundamental mistake, her repugnance toward the only lover permitted, her legitimate lover, is underlined.

Only one refuge from his embraces is permitted: illness. Later Chazal will say: "I spared no expense" for this "long and costly illness." The young wife still tries to persuade herself that her husband is a victim of society, a fallen angel. When Vigny publishes *Eloa* in 1824, she will weep at great length, recognizing herself in the woman who gives herself to the demon in order to save him. Since childhood, she had decided to dedicate herself to "one of these men for whom great events attract great misfortunes." She has tried to convince herself that André was rejected by his family because of Antoine, the brilliant older brother, and that love could make him into a dark, inspired, glorious artist. The passing days reveal that his family judged well: André is a competent copyist, but there is nothing of the unrecognized genius about him. He uses the slang of art, but doesn't even understand the art of others. Géricault's *The Raft of the Medusa,* which brings a lump to his wife's throat, moves him less than the cold compositions of Girodet. He doesn't even have the stubborn drive which, for his brother, replaces talent. He bears the torments of an ambition which nothing justifies.

Flora flees this discovery through excitement about the events that are being talked about everywhere: in the Café Procope, in the nearby market. In February 1823 they booed a missionary; in the Law School, in a chemistry course in the Jardin du Roy, they booed some professors. In late September—the 21st—they execute the four sergeants of La Rochelle, Carbonari conspirators. In the market someone hands Flora an illegal pamphlet, still damp with printer's ink. It reports the execution. The great Lafayette—a friend of Bolívar—tried to bribe the prison director with secretly raised money: the affair was discovered. Thus the four martyrs die hero's deaths. Raoulx, the first called to the scaffold on the Place de Grève, asks permission to embrace his comrades, tears the blindfold from his eyes, cries, "Long live liberty!" The last to die, Bories, cries out to those who have come out of curiosity to watch him die, "Remember that it is your brothers' blood that they're shedding."

Flora actually gets sick with emotion, which doesn't much impress her mother, used to her excesses, but irritates Chazal.

The neighbors hear their quarrels, and will report them, later, to the judge of instruction.

"When I come home, nothing is tidy! Ah! my family was right: you'll never be a wife or a mother."

"The life you make me lead, a counter-jumper wouldn't offer to his girl. Me, the girl Bolívar carried on his shoulders. Oh! I'm dying of boredom in this stinking rooming house."

"Stinking? An apartment that costs six hundred francs a year? Have you forgotten the garret I took you out of, then? Look at this princess, will you."

"So now you blame me for having been ruined by social injustice?"

"I'm blaming you for being so high and mighty when, without me—"

16

"So you think that without you I wouldn't have had any better offers?"

"If anyone wants you, he's welcome to you."

Sobs, cries, the sound of crashing glasses—Flora's way of relieving her feelings—can be heard through the walls. André throws himself, weeping, at his wife's feet, imploring her pardon. Moved by her power over a man, Flora softens, draws him to her, promises to be patient, blames her "tropical violence."

Around them, while this is going on, the workers are stirring. First they find fault with the machines: Flora doesn't know that the year she was sixteen some weavers in Lyon were tried in the court of assizes for having attacked a cloth-shearing machine convoy, and that they were acquitted. The year of her marriage, the delegates from the old guilds met secretly in Bordeaux to get the guilds functioning again. Reserve funds and mutual aid societies in the building and jeweler's trades in Paris can boast more than eleven thousand members and are growing fast. A strike of Parisian tanners against the reduction of tariffs gets its leaders two years in prison.

On the other hand Flora is reading, during the long hours she spends in bed, *On the Industrial System* by Count Saint-Simon, who, on March 9, 1823, tried to commit suicide. She gets some formulas out of it. All those who contribute to the social wealth: bankers and workingmen, industrialists and artists, engineers and poets, all in short who don't live idle, those who work the soil or ideas, who make machines or minds or commerce function, are "producers." They have the right to credit. The State should be simply an apparatus for administering credit and production: it is economics that count, not politics. Flora is still too young, for the moment, to get more from this book than certain words: "credit," "industrial," "individualism."

In September 1823 she finds herself pregnant again. Disgusted by her state, she takes it badly. She spends more and more of her time stretched out on her bed, trying to look like the eternally beautiful and cold Madame Récamier on the sofa which already bears her name. They say in the Café Procope that Monsieur de Chateaubriand, a great writer but also, alas, Minister of Foreign Affairs, has taken the chill off the beauty of the century and made her fall in love. Flora dreams. . . . But where will her savior come from? She is a prisoner of marriage. On November 30 a comet is seen in the sky above Paris: is it a sign? And of what? The doctor, the druggist takes an interest in her, but she's not interested in them. At least they tell her the rumors which, as always, spread by mysterious paths, in spite of constantly increasing censorship—the opposition numbers only seventeen deputies. The Upper Normal School, the Law School, and Medical School have all been closed. In England, a law is passed giving the workers the right to strike in certain circumstances. This revolution in working-class life moves Flora much less than the piece of news that filters through the next day.

On Sunday, June 6, 1824, Chateaubriand arrives as usual at the Tuileries at noon. An officer warns him that a letter is waiting for him at the ministry, which he must read without a minute's delay. Astonished, Chateaubriand gets back into his berlin: the letter is a royal edict naming the Minister of Finance, Villèle, Minister of Foreign Affairs "as an interim appointment, to replace the Lord Viscount de Chateaubriand." An hour later, Villèle gets a note from the most illustrious writer in France: *Sir, I have left the office of Foreign Affairs; the department is at your command. Chateaubriand.* At the same time messengers are running through Paris notifying the guests at a dinner planned for that very evening at the Foreign Affairs office that the ministry kitchens have changed hands. That is how the affair becomes known.

Does Flora, chained to her bed by pains that she owes as much to her nerves as to her organs—psychosomatic illness existed before science gave it a name—dream of consoling Chateaubriand?

Three weeks later, on June 22, 1824, she gives birth to her second son, Ernest-Camille. This birth, like the last, gives her more distress than joy. Her "two puny and sickly children," for whom she has no milk, arouse a pitying tenderness, but also seal her slavery, "fruits of a union that ruined my life."

Already in her thoughts are what she will one day write:

> Woman is a pariah by birth, a serf by condition, unhappy by duty, and must almost always choose between hypocrisy and being branded.

This is what three years of marriage has taught her. Repulsed by his wife, Chazal starts spending his nights in the taverns again, drinking, gambling, losing the little he wins.

"Prisoner" becomes Flora's name for herself. When André, having happened to work for once, takes her to the theater to see the young Marie Dorval play a Sir Walter Scott role at the Porte Saint-Martin, she weeps so much that he is angry. Madame Tristan speaks of her daughter's "melancholy"; we would call it a nervous breakdown.

At the end of the year, a process-server and his men arrive before dawn to put seals on everything but the beds and kitchen utensils. In this manner she learns, as her lawyer will put it fourteen years later, that "Monsieur Chazal's affairs were in great disorder. Pursued by creditors whose good will he had overestimated, he had no other alternatives but flight or imprisonment before him. Naturally depraved, loose in his ways, he soon reached the last degree of degradation...."

That day Chazal, having run from his brother to his friends without being able to raise any money, suggests to his wife that after all she, who never helps him in any way, might well get them out of this predicament—the apothecary.... Flora remembers the fat man's look, fixed on her when she goes by, as he stands on the doorstep of his shop, his stomach sticking out in front of him in its light waistcoat crossed with gold chains. He never reminds her that she owes him for medicines. Yes, Chazal repeats, the apothecary.

Flora grabs the water jug and throws its contents all over him. Her fury mounts; she also grabs the wash-basin and throws it; the crockery breaks without hitting him.

"You will never touch me again. Never."

"I like whores better than phony princesses, you stuck-up bitch!"

Several frightful weeks pass. A prisoner in a marriage that has ruined her life. But, while restoring middle-class happiness, Louis XVIII abolished the already very limited law permitting divorce. What can she do? The law pursues a runaway wife. The man, head of the family, has all rights over his wife and child. André could beat her and she would have no right to leave him. In fact, he doesn't beat her: he torments her. "If you wanted to—the apothecary—or the doctor." Later Flora's lawyer will sum up: "He wanted to feed his passion for gambling by means of prostitution." Finally, on March 2—the children having been put out to nurse at Dammartin near Arpajon—she takes advantage of her husband's absence to cram her clothes into a wicker trunk and go to her mother's in the

Rue Copeau. (Chazal will say that she went "into public places," but she won't live in a hotel until much later. A decision made in despair: she has just realized that she is pregnant for the third time.

On May 19, 1825, Henri de Saint-Simon, the theoretician of "industry," dies amid his disciples on the Rue de Richelieu. The same day Chazal, who has had his wife followed and knows she has gone to see the nurse in Dammartin, has the mother and sons' beds sent to the Rue Copeau. Thus he can tell the neighbors that his wife, having ruined him by her extravagant spending (he will deny having said this), has not only left him but taken the furniture with her. Then he flees to the provinces, calling himself Monsieur André to put the creditors off the track.

On June 1, 1825, Saint-Simon's disciples found a limited partnership, "Enfantin, Rodrigues and Company," in which the banker Laffitte, model of the future "self-made man," buys ten shares at 1000 francs; this is the future Ecole Sociétaire, where Flora will hear of the Woman-Messiah for the first time.

That same day, or the day before, or the next day, Flora admits to her mother that she is carrying a third child. What should she do? Uncle Laisney storms: his niece is a lunatic, novels have turned her head, she is a pretentious fool who thinks she's Madame de Staël when she's only an artisan's wife. Madame Tristan weeps: why did she urge this marriage? Can a husband, then, instead of going to work, send his wife out to prostitute herself? The Commandant lays down the law: a wife who runs away from her conjugal home and takes away the fruits of the marriage has no place in society; she is a pariah.

"Well, then, I'll be a pariah!" says Flora. She knows very well—her pitiless lucidity already probes under the romantic dream, the highly colored, stormy vision—that her adventure recalls the melodramas of the Boulevard du Crime, stories of despoiled orphans and sold women. But a woman cannot deny her destiny on the ground that it is in bad taste.

3

THE PARIAH'S FIRST STEPS

Pariahs: the untouchables of India. . . . Standing before the oval mirror of a dressing table that dates from the splendors of Vaugirard, Flora sees that her pregnancy is becoming obvious. She must find work: coloring engravings won't give her enough to live on and pay the nurse.

She is going to leave the Rue Copeau. There has just been a last scene between the mother and daughter. Flora repeats again and again: "Better a pariah than a slave!"

She has shouted at her mother and uncle that they pushed her into selling *herself* forever to a man who wants to sell *her* like a whore. No, thank you. She wants to live. At twenty-one, she knows nothing of the world.

A small sign on a wall tells her that a confectioner on the Rue du Bac is looking for a saleswoman. With this belly, she can only present herself as a widow. The Widow Tristan Number Two; she deletes Chazal from her life. The confectioner hires her, moved to pity by the idea of her bearing a posthumous child, doing a good deed and good business at the same time: This very attractive young lady gives his shop distinction. The customers find her "far above her condition;" the customers are interested. . . .

On October 16, 1825, Flora once again feels herself being torn apart, reduced to unrestrained cries, plunged into bodily suffering. The last time, she vows. Besides, if she can't think of Chazal without trembling with disgust, all men, as if debased by him, repel her. Then she is told that she has a daughter. They put the daughter in her arms and an unknown joy, an incomprehensible melting feeling fills her, which her sons never gave her. Until now, she found newborns hideous, even her own. This one seems beautiful to her. She speaks to her: "I swear to you that I will fight for you, to make you a better world. You will be neither a slave nor a pariah. How? They say: drunkard's word, lover's word. Well, you have to keep your word to what you've just created, to what comes out of you."

During a convalescence that Madame Tristan wants to be long —young mothers of good family spend at least two weeks indoors—Flora reads avidly in English. *A Vindication of the Rights of Woman* by Mary Wollstonecraft. In barely thirty-eight years of life, this end-of-the-century Irishwoman wrote a great deal, gave birth to two daughters by two different fathers, and married the liberal philosopher Godwin. This last husband dedicated an astonishing book to her. Very poor, working as a governess, Mary meets an American; he becomes her lover; she refuses to marry him, on principle. When he leaves her, having given her a daughter, he wants to make her an allowance: she tells him: "I want nothing more from you. I am not humble enough to depend on your charity." She earns her living by literary work. Flora identifies with Mary much better than with Madame de Staël. She is amused to see that *A Vindication of the Rights of Woman* is dedicated to Talleyrand: Mary, of course, couldn't guess at the Duke of Otranto's future treasons. Do human beings, then, change totally in the course of life? In any case, she, Flora, is going to change. She will be another Mary Wollstonecraft. Ah! if only she hadn't married Chazal! The Irishwoman writes what Flora thinks:

> The principle is simple: if woman is not prepared by her education to become man's companion, she will arrest the progress of knowledge, for if truth is not common to all, it becomes ineffective and without effect on daily acts.

Forever after this "simple principle" will be central to Flora's ideas. Mary wanted the State to ensure an equal, coeducational education to girls and boys alike. Her book—Godwin tells the story—raised an atrocious scandal. Nothing in it attacked either marriage or religion, but Mary was declared immoral, subversive, an atheist. Yet what she writes, Flora has just lived: happiness is founded on an intellectual alliance, without which woman is merely man's plaything.

At last the pariah has found her feminine model. While waiting, she rocks her daughter to the sound of a liquid name: Aline. So maternity too can be voluptuous? This tiny body, already the image of hers, drinks and she feels as if she is at once mouth and breast. Man's mouth never filled her with this contentment. This carnal, possessive, total love that they call maternal invades her.

Soon her milk fails; a wet nurse is needed. Once more she must, above all, find money: this time for three children and herself. The confectioner's counter isn't enough.

Is it through friends or by advertisement that she meets some Englishwomen looking for a lady's maid? A lady's maid, at this height of British society, must pack, unpack, iron, dress her mistress, reserve seats in coaches, bargain with innkeepers, find hairdressers, guides, and merchants. The maid gets her full keep; her wages will pay for nurses and books. Besides, she will travel.

But a widow won't suit these ladies; they want a girl. Flora presents herself as an orphan, a poor but noble young lady, and is promptly hired. An impoverished Frenchwoman adds to their household ways a human touch that is very much in keeping: England is prospering from having defeated Napoleon.

The backstage of luxury is at least less sordid than the spotlight of mediocrity. From 1826 to 1828, the young woman will store up a great deal of experience in Switzerland, Italy, Germany, and England. We know nothing about these Englishwomen. Before the court, later on, Flora will swear that she destroyed all the documents of this period "out of foolish pride": to work in someone's home is, in Madame Tristan's milieu, the ultimate degradation.

Allusions in her novel and scenes in *Walks in London* show that she knew the aristocracy and the upper middle class from more than a few dinners in town or evenings at the theater in 1839. On her last trip, she will spend most of her time with the workers and the dregs of society. She must have seen high society from close up during the '20s. It is on high society above all, and most harshly, that the fugitive practices her gift for sarcastic observation and cruel wit.

London dazzles her with its "magic clarity of millions of gas lamps," the "beauty of the sidewalks" (there are hardly any yet in Paris), squares with severe iron railings "that seem to isolate the home from the mob," shops bursting with "masterpieces begotten by human industry." Decidedly, the London of Waterloo is far in advance, in technology and the level of middle-class life, of defeated Paris after the Treaty of Vienna.

Her masters live in the West End, with carriages and "dandies prancing on horses of the greatest beauty, and a mob of valets covered with rich livery and armed with long gold- or silver-headed canes." Does she have to wear a housemaid's uniform, a starched apron and little cap? Probably. She loathes the shopkeepers, these pureblooded John Bulls who amass great fortunes in dank shops. Class differences are more obvious here: they can be detected by accent, intonation, gesture. She finds the Londoner suspicious and inhospitable, but bold and reckless in business, the model of "fair play." She learns to loathe "*cant*, respect for the established thing," religion, and respectability, and laughs at the servility toward what is fashionable.

One senses a judgment on her masters in her allusion to the perpetual journeys where the Londoner "always drags along with him that deep boredom which so rarely lets a ray of sunlight penetrate his soul." From the emphasis placed on the distances, the extent of the city, the half a day spent in getting from one place to another, one can guess at the memory of interminable trivial errands.

Suffering from being a servant and also from being a Frenchwoman, one of the conquered, doesn't predispose her to sympathy, and England in 1820 presents a picture of almost unbearable self-satisfaction. It is success in hypocrisy, technical progress founded on an intense pauperism. In the most mechanized factories in Europe, and thus in the world, "a deathlike silence reigns, so greatly does the worker's hunger give power to the master's speech."

Other scenes from *Walks in London*, by their tone, date rather from the stay of the lovely servant, shy and much courted, than from the sociological journey of a woman writer of thirty-six. "The Englishman *sober is chaste* to the point of prudishness." But sometimes, away from home, he lets himself go in "low dives for *fashionables*" that are called "finishes." Places for the last drink, the nightcap at the end of a drinking bout. One can guess that the dandies offer to show London by night to the pretty French menial. Does Flora never decide to see, as it were, the world? To shake off the prejudices of her mother, that penniless snob? One can understand the incessant sense of degradation that the young woman feels, among the liveried valets, the uniformed governesses, the sons, brothers, friends, husbands who revolve around her with that English conviction that every Frenchwoman harbors a bottomless pit of delicious sin.

In the "finish," surrounded by homage which she repulses, hiding her disgust, she sees young lords

> get a girl so full of liquor that she falls dead drunk; then they make her swallow vinegar with mustard and pepper in it; this beverage almost always gives her horrible convulsions, and the jerks and contortions of this unfortunate girl provoke laughter and infinitely amuse the honorable company. . . . Each one threw glasses of wine and liquor on her lovely shoulders and magnificent chest. . . . The waiters of the tavern trampled her underfoot like a bundle of garbage.

These years of dependence give the future militant fuel for thought: her ideas will be kneaded from her experience. Flora needs to be moved by a thing before she can extract a law from it, accept it, and look for supporters for it.

Before her marriage, she felt and dreamed, she didn't think. During her "slavery," to fight off despair, she must have generalized from her own life. Asked herself questions about divorce, about legitimacy, then about woman's condition in general. As for education, trade, equality in work, the right to work, every day and every hour posed these problems for her. To the point of obsession. Dirty linen; dust; cold tobacco; dishes; the vulgarity of backbiting and desire when masters and servants relax and drop their masks.

In the Place Maubert, every sou was counted and no one spent more than he had. Now she sees hundreds of pounds thrown away for vanity's sake, for the sake of appearances, and tuppence out of the poor's wages disputed. They are spendthrift with money, and with feelings and impulses as well.

Avid for beauty, she finds the souls of the rich and the manners of the poor equally ugly. The working-class herd is ugly because they work from twelve to sixteen hours for one or two francs. For forty-five centimes, the machines give children of five to eight crooked legs and twisted spines, gnarled arms and scrofulous skin.

She examines herself in the mirror: beauty is nothing but easy circumstances; won't she grow ugly from wearing an apron, obeying, smiling because she must? To become or stay beautiful, you have to change the social order. Philosophy before the mirror.

She has read Saint-Simon, but—like Enfantin himself—surprised by the form, she misunderstood the meaning. The usual fate of books too far ahead of their time. Rereading it, she sees that he proclaims the equality of woman and man, and remembers his formula: "To each according to his abilities; to each ability according to its works." Here in England, Robert Owen is trying to improve the workers' conditions.

She is not yet interested in the fate of the exploited except by fits and starts.

Yet, in London, she reads Malthus, who revolts her: "When the worker's salary is insufficient to maintain his family, it is a manifest sign that the country has no need of new citizens." Flora copies the sentence in a notebook that she hides under her linen, in her trunk: experience teaches her how curious masters and servants are. She is revolted: What! She has three children, no means of raising them, and this clergyman of the Anglican Church, this Monsieur Malthus, this philosopher, can find no better solution? But her masters spend on a dinner party what they give her in two months. . . . The other fashionable philosopher, David Ricardo, a converted Jew, analyzes rent very well but proposes no remedy other than resignation. And Lord Brougham, that cannibal, suggests quite plainly to the House of Lords that "the population should be brought down to the subsistence level."

Around 1828, back in Paris, she is no longer a lady's maid. On May 3, the tribunal of the Seine pronounces a legal separation, establishing that she pays for the children's board and maintenance by herself. Chazal will say that his wife introduced that claim in the hope of collecting an inheritance. Nothing supports this thesis, except that the mother and daughter still hope for their fortune from Peru. Commandant Laisney sees Chazal arrive, trembling with rage, speaking of revenge for this humiliation: he is the husband! They'll see. What does Flora live on? The husband, or his lawyer, will claim—ten years afterward—that she "went to live with some other persons." Neither the lawyer nor his client can cite a single plausible name. Flora's existence reveals a profound contradiction between her idea of equality of the sexes and her attitude toward men. Such an incongruous set of habits, conventions, inhibitions, and fears bear on her conduct that resolution alone cannot free her.

The Pariah's great moments of exaltation come chiefly from amorous friendship. Highstrung, imaginative, her senses perhaps blocked, what she likes best is to exchange verbal "effusions," looks, squeezes of the hand, "innocent" kisses. Talking till dawn, sharing ideas, brotherhood of the spirit and sisterhood of the soul, all that will become the lot of Dostoievsky's Slavs is a supreme joy for Flora, the Paris Andalusian. Even this nickname, "Andalusian," which she bestows on herself rings like a false promise of sensuality. Did Chazal make her frigid? Probably. Feeling, emotion, confusion between friendship and love, between alliance and attraction, keep this passionate woman's existence under constant pressure. Did this much-desired woman herself ever experience satisfied desire?

During those years, so soon after escaping this husband of whom the mere sight or memory can make her shudder with disgust, her only feelings toward erotic love are fear and alienation.

To earn her living she has to resort—like many young people of today—to temporary jobs: reader, accompanist, translator, babysitter, in short, "reliable lady," and also, often, her old trade of colorist.

In 1829, she returns to Paris to bury her eldest son, the most sickly, the least wanted, the least loved. The child she was carrying when she realized she was trapped, when her unhappiness seemed overwhelming. Nobody expected this rickety little boy to live; he dies before he can be helped. Flora blames herself for feeling no more than a bearable grief and for weeping less over this sickly boy than she did over the horror of her marriage. Of the three children of her body, she feels a physical bond only with Aline, the fruit and sign of her liberation.

When she is in Paris, she takes Aline with her, renting furnished rooms and eating a *table d'hôte* meal once a day.

A provincial's Memoirs describe these places for us:

> The name *table d'hôte* in Paris is only a generic label covering all the stews that are eaten in common at a fixed time with whoever wants to partake of them, for a price which varies from 7 sous to 50 francs. There exist, indeed, places where for 7 sous (which is the price of a glass of sugar-water elsewhere) you can sate the most immoderate hunger . . . Thick soup, fried potatoes, as much water and bread as you want, such are the invariable sensualities of these tables without cloths. On top of that, instead of potatoes, you can see on some of them a piece of dry or stringy black meat. For 17 sous you can have the comfort of a tablecloth; for 22, you get a napkin and an Algerian metal fork, nay, even a silver one. Three sous more, and you reach the borders of luxury. For 25, indeed, the *table d'hôte* begins to dress itself up with the name of bourgeois cooking, the *soup* becomes broth, the boiled meat is called *beef*, and there is a *daily special*: veal or beefsteak, as the host says. The *table d'hote* proper begins at 40 sous and finishes at 4 francs. Above 4 francs, it's *dinner*, it's *supper*.

One evening, at a *table d'hôte*, a merchant marine officer turns around on hearing someone say "Madame Tristan." He's a red-faced fellow, stocky, blue-eyed and red-veined; he can be heard telling about his voyages with the glibness of a professional traveler. Stopping in mid-sentence, staring at her—she lowers her eyelids to Aline—he asks if she is a relative of Don Pio de Tristan, a Peruvian who has just spent several months with him in Valparaiso, as a political exile. Don Pio de Tristan de Moscoso. . . .

She must dissemble, show nothing of her emotion: Uncle Pio, the younger brother whom her father practically raised, who holds their fortune, who won't answer any of their letters. Forcing her voice to indifference, to a weary tone which to him sounds very "ladylike," she asks who this Peruvian namesake is. Is he amusing? Intelligent? Sensitive?

The officer—he introduces himself: Zacharie Chabrié from Brittany, a sailor, the son and grandson of sailors—plunges into a recital.

A charmer, this Don Pio, but what a tyrant, what a pirate! A real Marquis of Carabas: the sun never sets on his lands; the whole province of Arequipa is his: plantations, sugar mills, and even convents. He treats the Dominicans who live on his estate as servants responsible for the health of his soul. And if you wonder whether he gets his feudal rights, with all due respect, lovely lady! Nobody on his lands marries, travels, moves, or cuts down a tree without his permission. He treats the peasants like slaves, the slaves like objects, and his family like serfs. He has only one passion: money. And a taste for power, which he exercises on a tribe of widowed aunts, badly married sisters, and poor cousins. Listen, when the great Bolívar, the Libertador . . ."

Flora quivers: this man has seen Bolívar: her parents' young friend, her childhood hero? For him, he's not a myth, but a real being, whom one can cheer, whose hand one can shake. . . . Eyes and teeth sparkling, she looks at Zacharie Chabrié, and he falters, then goes on: "Yes, the great Bolívar, who sank his whole personal fortune in the escapade, asked for a tax on the landowners after having liberated Peru: doesn't the army have to be maintained? Those who refused, he taxed ex officio. Well, Pio de Tristan cried thief so loud that when those in power turned against him he went to spend a year in Valparaiso, until Bolivar left. He loves no one, Don Pio, not his wife nor his children. Only his mother, maybe, who is eighty-nine. . . ."

Thus, at this *table d'hôte* with cloth, Flora learns that her grandmother is still alive. And Don Mariano was the son she loved best. Hearing nothing more, motionless among the dirty plates and empty cups, she elaborates her plan. To write to her grandmother. And to her uncle. To get someone else to bring the letter to Chabrié, so that he won't know who the sender is, and will carry it on his next voyage. But what should she write?

In four years, she has learned what society accepts and what she must hide if she wants to be "recognized." An orphan, alone and poor: very good. A poor widow: not quite so good. A widow with children: people panic, it's too much. As for the picture of an unhappy wife fleeing with her children, good society draws aside, horrified. The Pariah. She mustn't mention her husband or children to her uncle: his brother's daughter. Her parents' marriage? He surely knows the story from elsewhere, the lie that wipes out Chazal and the little ones is enough. . . .

For several months, Flora hesitates. Already in revolt, she still has as yet no idea of social upheaval. Of course, divorce must be reestablished, and women given some instruction, a trade. Of course, the mother must win rights over her children. Of course, Mary Wollstonecraft is right. But she sees no means to act. Complex, contradictory like all young women, Flora wants at the same time to be "recognized," accepted by society, and to distinguish herself as an individual. She suffers too many humiliations not to aspire to the famous British respectability. Perhaps, if she hadn't worn her bastardy like a shameful tattoo, she would not have agreed to marry Chazal. After her two disappointments in love, she believed that no one would want an illegitimate child and that a *real* marriage would give her a class status again.

While she wavers about writing to her uncle, a chance encounter plunges her into an unknown world. A Polytechnic student—at another *table d'hôte*—starts talking about Saint-Simon. "Society would be renewed by 'association,' that is to say by combining all industrial works in the social interest. All the useful members of society will unite against all the idle." Flora knows by heart Saint-Simon's famous parable: if fifty great men—kings, princes, and dignitaries—died by accident, nothing would be changed. But if the fifty most distinguished talents in all fields were wiped out, France would take a long time to get over it. From the young man she learns that before he died the Master designated the Couple as the Social Individual, and declared woman not only equal, but superior, to man, since she can give life.

4

THE SAINT-SIMONIAN SCHOOL

Stimulated by this pretty lady's interest, the future engineer suggests that he take her to hear Prosper Enfantin, the greatest charmer in the Latin Quarter, whom none can resist. Himself a former Polytechnician, he was so poor when he was a student that he couldn't pay his board. Then he had a thousand jobs that took him as far as Russia. Some accuse him of mixing the Saint-Simonian doctrine with that of a very peculiar man, whom nobody has met, called Charles Fourier.

Flora has never heard of the latter. This Fourier dreams of perfect little societies, where each individual would blossom out according to his dominant passions, which would be applied for the good of all. Thus the total transformation of human relationships would be accomplished according to a model, with a rigorous time schedule. Harmonious association would replace imperfect civilization. A utopia? Flora wonders. Utopia: nowhere— The Polytechnician reads *The Organizer, a Journal of Progress and General Knowledge*. What knowledge? The study of societies: sociology. It is Enfantin's paper (soon he will subtitle it *a Journal of the Saint-Simonian Doctrine*). In this issue, it says: "The principle: respect for production and the producers, is infinitely more fruitful than this one: respect for property and property owners."

Curious, the young woman goes along with him to the Rue Taranne, across from the Church of Saint-Germain-des-Prés, in the old quarter with its unhappy memories. The Hotel Taranne, where political exiles, poets, and thinkers of all nations live, rents out lecture rooms. This is one of them, smoke-filled, badly lit, where, for lack of empty seats, they stay far back, near the wall. A man with a square face, seated behind a table, speaks without looking at anyone, his head motionless, his fingers playing ceaselessly with his snuffbox. His voice, low but very clear, enunciates:

"Politics should have no other goal but to better the lot of the producers. They will be classified according to their abilities alone, and rewarded according to them, according to their works. Every worker who contributes to the social good is a producer. The government has no other function than to coordinate, to make sure the producers are able to obtain credit without interest. . . ."

His glance passes over the audience.

His name is Armand Bazard. Behind him, leaning forward, is his wife Claire. Will she become the Mother, the female half of the Priest-Couple ruling the world?

Flora isn't listening. She has been literally transfixed by a glance: she can't turn away. His eyes, in contrast, glitter, they sparkle, above his long neck his face glows. He gets up for a moment: he seems immense, ready to pounce, like a hunting predator, on the room. Then he sits down again. That's him, that's Enfantin, her neighbor murmurs. The others on the platform? Claire Bazard is the only woman. Near her, Olinde Rodrigues, a mathematician and banker, the last intimate disciple of Saint-Simon. He brought Enfantin to the master who was getting over an attempted suicide. He subsidizes the School thanks to his banker friends: Laffitte, the Pereire brothers, and Gustave d'Eichtal, who, lost in his thoughts over there, has translated the Gospel. That other man, the very young one, is called Hippolyte Carnot, son of a member of the Convention, whose brother invented thermodynamics, a group of physical laws that can change industry and transportation. Very important: roads, bridges, canals, isthmuses. . . . That's just what Bazard is talking about. Steamboats and railroads are important; the telegraph, important; photography, discovered five years ago by Niepce, important: all this can permit peoples to communicate better, thus to know one another, thus to love one another. Wars and conflicts come from ignorance. In reality, Bazard states—and he quotes Saint-Simon—all peoples are equal and one day their conflicts will be settled by arbitration. A court above the nations, international, a society of nations where each one, weak or strong, will have the same rights, will rule on all difficulties. No more war, no more bloodshed: everyone's ambitions will be turned toward production, industry.

Polytechnic students out of uniform dominate the audience. A reservoir of engineers selected by the severest possible competition, this elite will give the new society that is being built its nucleus. Among the young men Flora sees here are some who will have great destinies, will direct banks, create—like Olinde Rodrigues—popular credit, or the French railway network. This hypnotic presence, this ecstatic wise man, this madman who subverts custom, in short, Prosper Enfantin, will direct the Paris-Lyon-Mediterranean railroads after beginning the Isthmus of Suez work in Egypt. On the other hand, that fine prophet's head, behind him, will become a famous vaudeville artist, who will make ladies in crinolines laugh: Léon Halévy. And this young man who's getting up, Michel Chevalier, will end up an influential senator of the Second Empire. Another, radiant, charming—a Polytechnician, of course—gives an account of the creation of groups in the provinces—the School's adepts are multiplying. "Our sisters want us, along with the proclamation of their equality, to emphasize the necessity of reestablishing divorce, the only possible base for happy unions. Without divorce, the most well-informed woman remains a prisoner of an error of feeling or the senses, or of some social pressure. Christ can't have wanted that. . . ."

In the audience, several simply dressed women. Who are they?

Saint-Simon and the elements of Fourier that these men include in their teaching—without ever citing him—still pass, at the end of the twentieth century, for reformers. To Flora all that she hears seems such a total upheaval that she doesn't know whether it's appealing or crazy. To read the master can uplift you. But to see and hear men full of energy, eloquence, an enthusiastic determination, proclaim that it's necessary to act without delay, to establish the model of a new society starting right now, is almost too much.

Shortly afterward, the providential Polytechnician takes her to the salons of the Ecole Sociétaire. The group has rented a floor of the Hôtel de Gesvres on the Rue Monsigny, near the Italian Theater. Above it are the offices of the *Globe*, a newspaper that they will soon buy back. The "Saint-Simons," as the columnists and cartoonists call them colloquially, have such a daring reputation that Flora doesn't tell anyone she is going.

The obvious eccentricity of their styles makes one forget how subversive their preaching is—at least on a first visit. Soon the government will see that what they have here is neither a stage show nor a harmless utopia. If Charles X, an absolute monarch, doesn't take them seriously, the bourgeois king, on the other hand, as soon as he is in power, will appreciate the danger of the little group, the radiance—the drive—of these eccentric young intellectuals, and on grounds of common law, finances, and corrupting morals will destroy them.

On this winter evening in 1830, in the huge salon of the Hôtel de Gesvres, a hundred men, almost all young, surround several women in ankle-length skirts (the cartoonists will draw them with skirts to mid-calf, shorter—what a scandal—than a petticoat). The women are crowded around the best-looking men: Prosper Enfantin and Abel Transon. Enfantin, the supreme Father, drives them mad, they say, to the point where some of them leave—or want to leave—their husbands to serve him "body and soul." That radiant creature, Aglaé Saint-Hilaire, has a recognized son by him; but he hasn't married her. So the Father has engendered a bastard? Flora is thrilled: no more legitimacy in the new society?

This other ardent girl is Désirée Véret, the acknowledged mistress of the handsome Abbé Transon. When he leaves Enfantin for Fourier, she will follow him, and fall in love with the Number One Fourierist, Victor Considérant; then her lover will marry Julie Vigoureux and she will become Madame Gay, go to England, and, with her husband, become a follower of Robert Owen; so she will have made the rounds of all the utopian socialists. In her ripe old age, Désirée Gay-Véret will figure among the founders of the International Working Men's Association, Marx's First International, thus helping inaugurate "scientific socialism." For the moment she is just an ecstatic young woman, followed by another workingwoman, Marie-Reine Gundorf, who will end her brief existence by suicide. And here is Suzanne Voilquin, the future author of the *Journal of a Woman of the People.* In 1833 she and Désirée Gay will found a short-lived paper, *The New Woman.* Suzanne Voilquin, of all these ardent women, will remain the most faithful to Saint-Simonism; she will follow the Father in his Egyptian epic, then join Clorinde Rogé, another worshipper of the Father, in Saint Petersburg. She and her husband will take Suzanne with them to America; the "woman of the people" will die, a sadly typical fate, in a workhouse in 1864.

Flora looks at these women and doesn't dare speak to them: the time has not yet come when, fully convinced, she will make speeches to passersby. Claire Bazard drifts royally from group to group, her daughter on her arm, this daughter for whom Enfantin will celebrate the first of the Saint-Simonian marriages.

The time comes to sit down to dinner. Flora notices that some of the others wear costumes in different shades of blue, lighter—she is told—as they rise in the School's hierarchy. Bazard and Enfantin are in "Flora blue," the color of a Mediterranean sky. The suits button in back: none can get dressed or undressed without the help of a "sister" or "brother."

Armand Bazard presides at one end of the table, between his wife and his daughter. At the other end, Enfantin, to whom everyone brings his plate for a helping of stew, very simple, with a few friendly words for each person. When Flora finds herself before him, his look rekindles her, his orchestral voice asks her: who is she? Out of habit, she calls herself a widow with children, but, to make up for this lie, she speaks of her illegitimate birth. He answers that only indissoluble marriage is contrary to nature, thus to the future order: isn't his own son born out of wedlock? All will be changed when the Priest-Couple rule the world. His look signifies that he is still looking for the Woman-Messiah and Flora trembles—so many are called—why not she?

Her dinner partner is an old Polytechnician, Fournel, a director of steel mills in Le Creusot, whose charming young wife, Cécile, contemplates her husband and Enfantin with equal adoration. Fournel points out to Flora two banker brothers, Isaac and Emile Pereire, the painter Raymond Bonheur, the musician Félicien

David. They talk about the necessary suppression of interest on money. A mortgage and loan bank will lend to all, asking only repayment of the principal, and inheritance taxes will pay for this credit. Thus industry will no longer be financed by capital belonging to individuals but by a registered working capital.

Suddenly Prosper Enfantin's voice is raised. All fall quiet. He dreams.

"Healthier, airier, better lit, cleanliness everywhere, aqueducts, handsome bridges, fountains, railroads, canals. For these things it's worth giving up tilburies, fine horses, the pleasures of the Stock Exchange and other gambling houses, and changing and ruinous fashions . . . it's even worth giving up the Gymnasium curriculum, the catechism of fashionable young widows and gallant colonels. It's worth romantic poetry, which is made for the idle, and gives nightmares to the unhappy poor. For all these things are for the masses who work, they are for the men who nourish, who enlighten, who inspire."

He speaks of true artists, true scholars who must be freed from the "pitiable patronage" of idle patrons.

These utilitarian views on art will be expanded, a century later, by the Russian Marxist followers of Lenin, under the name of "socialist realism." Flora will advocate them as early as 1838. Painting, she will say, was "societies' first instrument of intellectual progress," cave paintings came long before writing. She believes, like the Saint-Simonians, in a slow but continual progress since the Renaissance. Going further along Saint-Simon's track, she will note how ideology and customs lag behind the vanguard of thought: "when the masses are fighting for or against Roman Catholicism, the thinkers already no longer believe in it and the social leaders . . . *making use of religious beliefs as instruments* struggle for power." When she shows the influence on the creator of the dominant thought of his century, she will remember her short time among the Saint-Simonians.

Does she find it strange that these engineers, lawyers, scholars, artists trained in "positive" disciplines are so enthusiastic, share this excitement about what other people call "a utopia"? Having scientific and technical knowledge, these young men see its limits and seek to free the society of production from the limits of production. Defeated at the fall of the Empire, France has just undergone a period of semi-penury when the "new gentlemen" limit their ambition to producing and earning.

Flora is aware, through her Uncle Laisney with his limited views, of the nostalgia of men who still miss murderous but exciting wars. The officers of the Empire marched into countries and towns, welcomed as liberators by young people who could recite the Declaration of the Rights of Man and thought they saw in Napoleon the continuer of the revolution. A genuine ambiguity: he was a dictator, but established his code, which was more liberal than the laws of the German and Italian principalities or those of the countries ruled by Austria. When they find themselves poor and rejected after fifteen years of high tension, the men of the imperial generation feel bitter. A German poet, Heinrich Heine, the nephew of a Jewish banker from the Rhineland, is able to express the nostalgia of the "two grenadiers"; Béranger sings it in French. Heine is an unknown and Béranger is put on trial. For ten years, those who, back from exile, have not only "forgotten nothing and learned nothing," but understand nothing about the France they have come back to, have reigned. The new gentlemen construct, build, produce without faith or law, exploiting the poor who flock from the suburbs and the country at the will of supply and demand.

Young people listen to those who are nostalgic for glory and those who glorify money, and sink into a waiting made up of regret and impatience. From this comes the revolt of the best. From this comes this great trend toward the construction of model societies, parallel to the desire for political change. On one hand, behind Saint-Simon, Fourier, the neo-Babouvists * and, later, the anarchists, the young see the insufficiency of political changes. Flora will later be swept along in their wake. For them, the declaration of equality is nothing without the right to work. The declaration of brotherhood remains abstract if the relations between employers

---

* Followers of François-Emile Babeuf (1760-1797), who preached a form of communism.

and wage-earners, men and women, are not modified. Liberty remains utopian if it is not applied to a specific, spelled-out right to a decent existence: misery is the opposite of liberty, the worst side of inequality, the most total denial of brotherhood.

All these ideas are aired in the Saint-Simonian dining room, and Flora hears them and stores them away, perhaps without understanding them.

When dinner is over, other visitors arrive. A great fuss marks the entry of a nineteen-year-old Hungarian pianist of a luminous and unreal beauty. Franz Liszt, a former child prodigy and already famous in all the courts and salons of Europe, seems an apparition, an incarnation of moonlight. The women flock; hair to his shoulders, face boyishly smooth, he smiles, agrees to sit down at the piano, and attacks a waltz which a few couples follow. Then, having played a composition of Félicien David, he rises and passes around some cartoons: women in skirts to mid-thigh dancing with men in breeches but without stockings. Title: A Saint-Simonian Ball.

Enfantin says gravely: "It's a lot to have forced people to laugh at us: Thus we begin to exist for them."

In the groups, Flora hears the problems of freedom in love discussed. Freeing woman from conjugal and domestic slavery implies that she have the right to choose her companion or companions. Men and women can be categorized in two groups. The first—Fourier said it before Enfantin—are dominated by "flightiness," a passion for change, for multiple liaisons. The others, the steady ones, aspire to a single love. Why try to force two different types of human beings into a single mold?

Flora has never dared to think so far.

The following Wednesday she goes to the Rue Taitbout, to a hall where gaslight plays on the gilding and where public lectures of the Saint-Simonian school are presently being held. The hall is packed an hour in advance. She gets up to the first rows ("the Saint-Simons are good guys," even the jailers in their future prisons will sing), the men make way for her. Wearing "Father" written on a sleeveless, tieless vest under his half-open "Flora blue" habit, Enfantin pronounces maxims in a circle of women. Rumors fly. The two Fathers are quarrelling bitterly about sexual morality. Bazard, Olinde Rodrigues and several other direct disciples of the dead master are indignant at the role Enfantin assigns to woman. Liberation? No: a new kind of slavery if she serves as a toy for pleasure (later it will be "sex object") instead of serving as wife-and-mother; where is equality, and where is independence? She has changed a legal master for an illegitimate tyrant; what does she get out of it? Claire Bazard herself will protest "in the name of her sex" and, perhaps disappointed not to be chosen as the Mother, follow her husband in the agonizing rupture and retirement, to cause his death within a few months. But this evening all still pretend to be united. Enfantin recognizes Flora, catches her eye, and slowly smiles as if he were holding out his arms. As he goes by he murmurs: "I shall speak for you"; she doesn't know he says it to all of them in turn.

The court of Louis XIV can't have watched Bossuet mount the pulpit with more fervor than this audience. Yet before the Father can begin, a man gets up from the middle of the rows. Like an American at a revival meeting, he delivers an inspired harangue. Future society, golden age of the future; universal love, all doctrines mixed together: Saint-Simon and Fourier—even if the second treats the first as a charlatan—eclecticism nourished on social doctrine. Flora's neighbor, seeing her surprise, explains that inspirations are produced at nearly every public meeting—no doubt they're supernatural. If people weren't so inhibited, each one of them would be visited, possessed.

Another listener, rising, speaks by contrast on a very earthly subject: The Saint-Simonians should refuse to serve in the national guard: priests of all persuasions are exempted: "Why not extend the exemption to priests of the Saint-Simonian religion? We must fight to have our pastors recognized." It's just too bad about the forty-eight hours in jail that go with the refusal: he and his comrades offered to drink to their jailers, who sang:

> A Saint-Simon
> Is a good stout fellow
> When you're with him
> You're gay and mellow.

Floored by this mixture of prophecy and jest, Flora pulls herself together when Enfantin's voice rings out, effortlessly filling the hall: "The emancipation of women will mark the Saint-Simonian era.

They will contribute the most to its establishment and perfect it with the most love. Will woman be more powerful than man? Religiously, yes. Politically, no. But in fact yes, for strength has only been given to man to raise higher than himself all that wants to be loved."

He falls silent for a moment. He is making eye contact with friends among the audience. Flora is not aware that each word is heavy with allusions internal to the group, as with all closed sects. The leader's speech unfolds on two levels: one for simple listeners, the other for initiates. Flora thinks sadly that even the latter don't accept true equality: "Politically, no." Why? And how can they talk about the Woman-Messiah when they deny the mass of women political rights, however temporal?

But Enfantin, accused of being an autocrat, is justifying himself: "What I bring is not a dogma, but only one man's opinion. Moral law can be revealed in the future through woman alone. Until then, any act censured by the mores of the world around us would be immoral, because fatal to the doctrine." A shout assures him that they are with him unconditionally, idolators who accept his audacities and his restrictions alike. "Father! You are the living definition of Love! You are the sun of humanity."

And another voice, a woman's: "Father! I love you! Ah! It's still more than loving! From you, a single look of reproach could annihilate me!"

Inhaling adoration, exalted, beside himself, arms outstretched, head thrown back, Enfantin resumes his vision of the future.

"One day, when the Saint-Simonian society has come to be, you will see men and women united by a nameless love, a love that never cools or curdles to jealousy. Men and women will give themselves to several without ever ceasing to be to each other."

Suddenly, a great tumult. In back, they're breaking down the doors. Pushing through the crowd that streams toward the rostrum, a commissioner and a score of sergeants rush toward the orator, declaring the meeting closed in the name of public order.

5

THE UNCLE IN PERU

Does Flora find the courage to write to the uncle in Peru upon seeing men from the elite, a director of Le Creusot, financiers, scholars, and artists challenge this society, express more subversive boldness than she has ever dared to admit even to herself? Her desire to dedicate herself to the struggle for the new ideas gives her strength to fight her way out of an oppressive poverty. How can she teach herself and others when every month she must look for a new and miserable means of subsistence? If she were allowed her paternal inheritance (even the Saint-Simonians accept the handing down of goods from father to daughter) she could live at last, she could consecrate herself to the battle for the future society and—who knows?—found a newspaper. . . . So she writes.

To Monsieur Pio de Tristan

Sir,
    It is your brother's daughter, the child of that *Mariano* whom you held dear, who takes the liberty of writing to you. I like to believe that you are unaware of my existence and that of more than twenty letters that my mother wrote you, none reached you. Without a final piece of bad luck that has reduced me to the depth of misfortune, I would never have approached you. I have found a safe way to get this letter

to you, and I hope that you will not be insensible to it. I enclose my baptismal certificate; if you still have some doubts, the *great Bolívar,* the intimate friend of the authors of my days, can clear them up; he saw me being raised by my father, whose house he visited regularly.

The letter reveals a mixture of trickery by omission—not a word about the husband or children—and excessive naïveté. She believes her uncle knows about the nonvalidity of her parents' marriage. Her confused way of relating their meeting, the celebration and non-transcription of the union—one doesn't know if the ceremony took place in France or Spain—is disconcerting: Flora, at that time, and each time she acts without advice, is incapable of acting cleverly. One senses in this letter the juxtaposition of contradictory maternal tales. She gives many details on the loss of the sums sent by Uncle Pio to his brother, recalls that her father lived on an income of six thousand francs left him by an uncle who was Archbishop of Granada, tells the history of the house Vaugirard, not fully paid for and requisitioned by "the estate," and even gives the figure of the property transfer tax. Her mother's sufferings, her ten-year-old brother's death form a sad and confused litany. Later, in Peru, the president of the Court of Arequipa will tell Flora that, with this letter, she "cut her head in four."

She concludes:

> I don't wish, sir, that this glimpse of the misfortunes whose outlines I have feebly sketched for you may make you discover the details! . . . Your soul, sensitive to the memory of a brother who loved you like *his son,* would suffer too much upon measuring the distance that exists between my lot and what Mariano's daughter's ought to have been . . . this brother who, struck as by a thunderbolt by a sudden and premature death (a fulminating apoplexy), could only say these words: "My daughter . . . Pio is left to you. . . ." Unhappy child!
>
> Do not, however, believe, Sir, that, whatever the result of my letter may be for you, my father's shade can take offense at my murmurs, his memory will always be dear and sacred to me.
>
> I expect justice and kindness from you. I entrust myself to you in the hope of a better future. I ask for your protection and beg you to love me in the way that your brother Mariano's daughter has the right to expect.
>
> I am your very humble and very obedient servant,
>
> Flora de Tristan.

Eight years later, she makes fun of herself:

> After reading this letter, you can judge my sincerity, since I depicted my entire ignorance of the world, my belief in probity, that credulous confidence in good faith, that supposes others good and just as one is oneself.

The uncle answers in the fall.

Mademoiselle Flora de Tristan
Arequipa, October 6, 1830

Mademoiselle and my estimable niece,
I received, with as much surprise as pleasure, your dear letter of last June 2. I knew, since General Bolívar was here in 1823, that my beloved brother, Mariano de Tristan, at the time of his death, had a daughter; before that Monsieur Simon Rodriguez, known by you under the name of *Robinson*, had told me as much; but, since neither of them gave me any later news of you nor of the place where you lived, I was not able to keep you up on some business which concerned both of us.

There follows the detailed history of his search for the mother and daughter, and his surprise at having received none of Madame Tristan's letters. After these long details, Don Pio turns to serious matters:

> I have seen the baptismal certificate that you sent me, and I give it full and complete credit, as to your status as my brother's recognized daughter, although this document is not legalized and signed by three notaries who certify as authentic the signature of the priest who executed it, as it ought to be. As for your mother and her status as my late brother's legitimate spouse, you admit yourself, and you confess it, that the manner in which the nuptial blessing was given her is null and of no more value in that country than in all Christianity. Indeed, it is extraordinary that an ecclesiastic who calls himself respectable, like Monsieur Roncelin, should be permitted to perform such an act, without the appropriate powers with respect to the contracting parties. It is also quite meaningless that at the time of your baptism he declared that you were his legitimate daughter, as is equally meaningless the document that you tell me was sent from Bilbao by the intermediary of Monsieur Adam, and in which ten persons of the aforesaid town depose that they regarded and knew your mother as

Mariano's legitimate wife: This document proves only that it is out of pure and simple decorum that she was given this status, this title. I have, besides, in my brother's own correspondence, up to shortly before his death, something which I may use as rather strong, although negative, proof of what I advance; it is that my brother never mentioned this union to me, an extraordinary thing since we had never hidden anything from each other. Add also, that if there had been a legitimate marriage between my brother and Madame your mother, neither Prince Masserano nor any other authority could have put seals on the goods of a deceased person who left known legitimate descendants born in the country. Let us agree then that you are only my brother's natural daughter, which is no reason for you to be less worthy of my consideration and of my tender affection. I give you very willingly the title of my beloved niece, and I add to that even that of my daughter; for nothing that was the object of my brother's love can be other than extremely interesting [sic] * to me; neither time nor his death will be able to erase in me the tender attachment that I bore him and that I will preserve for him all my life.

Upon which he announces that his mother is still alive and is sharing out her goods in her lifetime, and that, on his entreaties, she is allotting 3000 pure silver piasters in cash to her beloved son's child. The uncle advises her to invest the sum so as to draw a half-yearly income. Being unable to transfer the piasters immediately, he is sending a draft for 2500 francs to his Bordeaux agent, Monsieur Bertera. And he invites his niece—rather halfheartedly —to come and embrace her family in Peru.

In the face of this refined Jesuitry, the castles in Peru crumble. The uncle says in passing: "There exist no funds whatsoever belonging to my late brother." At first Flora sees herself as definitively deprived of a future, then she pulls herself together and writes to her grandmother. Her uncle—she will learn much later—had never spoken of her to her eighty-two-year-old forebear, who will die just when her granddaughter is on her way toward her.

Between Flora's letter and Don Pio's answer, between June 2 and October 6, 1830, three days pass that shake France, and, according to Flora, Europe, the Glorious Three, July 27, 28, and 29, 1830. The revolution sweeps away the last unchartered king, but imposes on

---

* The French *intéressant* usually implies financial advantage.—Tr.

the victorious republicans another king. No longer "of France" like his ancestors, but only of the French, his contemporaries. A transition, but one that will last eighteen years.

Flora, never having seen a revolution, will magnify this one. Faced with the civil war in Peru, she will remember these days when she felt within herself the enthusiasm of a whole people. She will decide that no revolution, not even 1789, made thrones tremble so; they never recovered. The Glorious Three, according to her, definitively ensured "the progress of ideas."

6

A WOMAN DURING
THE GLORIOUS THREE

In 1830, Flora reads some verses published by a woman, Marceline Desbordes-Valmore, and *Hernani,* the groundbreaking play of romanticism. Only fashionable Paris attends the première on February 25 at the Théâtre-Français. She learns about the uproar through the gazettes and people's accounts.

The winter has been so harsh that it reminds Prosper Enfantin of winter in Saint Petersburg, where he was making his fortune in the twenties. There, they built ice castles on the Neva. A clever speculator, hearing him evoke this memory, promptly asks the prefect for authorization to build one on the Seine—but the authorization arrives the same day as the thaw.

After this hard winter Flora is reviving in the June sun, when the opposition gets two-thirds of the votes in the district elections. Joy: every sign of liberalization promises—could promise—the reestablishment of divorce.

Shortly after the Glorious Three, the Saint-Simonian College will be torn apart by dissension, Bazard will leave Enfantin and die of it. Claire, not long ago the Father's adorer, will refuse him access to her husband's deathbed. Abel Transon, Carnot, Pierre Leroux will secede. Finally Saint-Simon's cherished disciple, the group's financier,

Olinde Rodrigues, will leave with a great wrench. He will declare himself against free love, invoking as an example the singleminded love that unites him to his wife: Enfantin will exhibit a letter showing that Madame Rodrigues loved him, and throw the banker out on the spot. But as the rental of the Hôtel de Gesvres rested on his guarantee, the whole College must move out. Enfantin, having inherited a house in the village of Ménilmontant, establishes a phalanstery there, which will lead him to the Court of Assizes on August 27, 1832, and, for a whole year, to prison.

But in July 1830, the two Fathers are still coexisting.

France is undergoing what we would call a recession. In Lille, a third of the workers are on relief. Thousands of men from Limousin march toward Paris to work on construction sites and turn back to scratch their soil for lack of work. Flora, for months, has been having trouble finding the little jobs she lives on. But had someone told her that, at the end of July, Paris, her Paris, city of her birth and more beloved than any other, was going to rise, she would have shrugged her shoulders: people die but they don't rebel.

Summer flares up. The rich have already gone off to their country estates; neither Lafayette nor Chateaubriand is in the capital, the handsome townhouses in the Faubourg Saint-Germain and the Chaussée d'Antin are closed. Flora herself takes one of the costly but fast carts of the Laffitte Messenger Service to visit Minette and the children, but she doesn't stay long.

On the evening of the 27th—she is then living on the Rue Copeau, in her mother's empty lodgings—street rumors tell her that there are barricades near the Palais-Royal, that there's been shooting. She crosses the Seine: in summer she never takes the omnibus, it costs too much. The oil lamps are swaying on their ropes in the middle of the streets, in the breeze coming from the river. Sometimes, with a well-aimed stone, an urchin breaks the glass and the streetlamp goes out. The theaters disgorge their public: the show is in the street. Flora ends up going back home. Crowds everywhere. How can she sleep? As soon as day comes she follows the crowd from the neighborhood marching toward the Hôtel de Ville. At the head of the procession a tricolor flag sewn up in the night, with cloth bought by mail. As the sun rises, the crowd gathers in the square. They're selling doughnuts, pastry cones, and fruit. The sun rises higher in the sky. Flora refolds her shawl of imitation cashmere. She has put on her lovely dress of embroidered percale and a cabriolet hat adorned with fruit. People speak to her; she answers; it hardly matters today that one hasn't been introduced. "We don't want anything to do with the king's ordinances against liberty." Thus she learns that there have been ordinances. "We don't want anything to do with Minister Polignac." Neither does she. They relate, laughing, how a little while ago Polignac's carriage passed; they booed him; then they saw the Princess de Polignac and shut up. Respect for women. It's too much, isn't it?

The tricolor flag has been raised on the Hôtel de Ville, to great shouts. The tocsin sounds at Notre Dame, then all around, in all the churches. The sun beats down fiercely. They're singing:

> *What does a republican need?*
> *Iron, lead, and then some bread!*

"And what about divorce?" Flora thinks. But she doesn't dare say it. How could she believe that divorce won't be reestablished yet for another half-century? (The law will be passed in 1884.)

The crowd streams on and Flora lets herself be carried toward the Faubourg Saint-Antoine. Suddenly they stop: before them there is a barricade, but only the front rows see it. On the other hand, firing can be heard and Flora feels proud: the colonel's heredity, the memory of Bolívar? Her "nervous nature" trembles at any noise, but in the streets in revolution she feels happy, uplifted. Everyone talks to one another, telling truth along with falsehood. "The enemy has lost a third of its followers." Where, when, who, how? No one knows and Flora will never know that the news comes from an unknown named Auguste Blanqui who will be nicknamed "the shut-in" because he will spend two-thirds of his life in prison.

In the evening, the residents put lamps out on the windowsills to light those in the street. Still enclosed in the human net, the young woman comes back toward the Latin Quarter where the barricades are fattened with old bedding and furniture—how many slightly rickety Louis XVI armchairs met their end in this insurrection? In the middle of the night, returning to fall into bed, she meets Armand Bazard on the corner of the Rue de la Clef. This is where he founded the Upper Lodge of the Carbonari in 1824 and he comes, in desperation, to look there for his companion from those days whom he can't find anywhere: Lafayette. He wants to propose that he set up and preside over the Saint-Simonian society with the help of the two Supreme Fathers—Flora won't know about it, but when he eventually finds Lafayette the tired hero will say: "Everything, but not power."

The next day, the tricolor is everywhere and Lafayette is at the Hôtel de Ville; the street cries: "We're a republic!" How does it know? Flora crosses the Seine once more, nibbling—one doesn't think of eating—an *oublie,* a cone-shaped pastry already christened "the republican pleasure" by the vendor on the Pont-Neuf. At the Place de l'Hôtel de Ville, people take turns reading aloud to those who can't read a notice by Lafayette: "The confidence of the people of Paris calls me . . . I have accepted . . . the same as in 1789. . . ."

Does Flora, so inexpert, understand at once that, since the word republic is not pronounced, this revolution is doomed? It's not likely. They're selling *The Globe,* the opposition paper. "Paris has delivered France . . . Parisians, don't slack off . . ."

But they're already slacking off in their joy, and the mob peacefully invades the Tuileries, where, they say, no one remains; someone sits down on the throne. Under the sign *The public doesn't enter,* at the gate to the gardens, someone has written *Yes, sometimes.* (These words will become a ritual in each revolution: they'll be heard in 1848 and again during the Commune.) True story or false, Flora knows nothing about it. Insurgents in arms can no longer be seen. Is it over, then? And who, finally, has won? They say there are thousands wounded (there will be in all 1800 dead and, by official reckoning, 4500 hospitalized wounded).

In the evening Flora finds herself in the neighborhood of the Sorbonne, in the steep, narrow Rue Saint-Jacques, when suddenly a violin, a flute, a viol sound out. Amazed, she sees a student embrace a working girl. "Madmen!" she thinks, when a passerby offers her his arm: a waltz.

The next day, sure enough, it's all over: Lafayette commands the national guard. The bankers (Laffite and Ternaux, former Saint-Simonians, among them) will rule, with the Orléans branch as intermediary. If he is king "of the French," will Louis-Philippe reestablish divorce? Should she be happy or disappointed? She will choose definitively to believe that she was present at a major event in the history of France.

She gets out of it an unconscious liking for brotherly crowds. The dream of "all united," the idea that union indeed makes strength. Three days so magical that they will always be the Glorious Three; for her, the trinity of evocation, emotion, and hope. What she will be trying to find again all her life. What will allow her to believe herself capable of ambition for power in a faraway country, and will later push her along the road of apostleship, harder but more encouraging to illusions.

For the first time she verifies that the people, that is to say that indistinct crowd that participates in riots, feel happier and stronger for being beaten. But, she will know better at each insurrection, the disorganized masses' victory is always stolen by those who are united by self-interest. This time, it will be the bankers and factory owners, and not the "industrials" in Saint-Simon's sense, for the workers remain equally miserable and scarcely better armed.

Two years later, in Lyon, "two classes struggled against each other." The silkworkers' shop foremen will be accused of wanting to set up a "clandestine workers' government," and Jean-Claude Romand, author of the slogan *Live working or die fighting*, will be condemned to hard labor.

But in 1832 Flora is too busy with her own concerns to really vibrate to the silkworkers' rhythm.

7

THE PARIAH BURNS
HER BRIDGES

In March and April 1832, Paris is ravaged by cholera. Flora's elder son is dead, the other, Ernest, is boarded out near Arpajon. Madame Thérèse Tristan and her brother are at Bel-Air, near Versailles.

In 1832, the Chamber debates the law on divorce, which the lawyers assure Flora will be passed. In any case, she must be prepared. At the same time Chazal, who had disappeared, shows up again. Who told him about the Peruvian money? At any rate, he shows a sudden solicitude toward his children, learns by writing to the mayor's office in Arpajon that his son is there, and looks for Aline.

What happened between the couple at Bel-Air on April 1, 1832, is told by Flora in *The Peregrinations of a Pariah*, and also in her statement before the court of assizes in 1838, where she confuses Bel-Air with Versailles and "telescopes" her memories; besides these there is a memoir written by Chazal in prison. (If until now we have had to put together sentences from Flora's books, her letters, the sometimes unpublished memories of contemporaries, this scene, on the contrary, must be disentangled from conflicting testimonies.)

It is an uncontested fact that Chazal signed a statement:

> I declare and promise Madame Chazal, before her mother and her uncle, that I am ready to act by any means and to submit to every demand of the established law concerning legal separation, if she wants a legal separation, and that I will be equally willing, in all good faith and perseverance, when it comes to divorce; I declare in addition that, even if the law on divorce is not passed this year, but in two or three years, I will act at that time as I promise to act at present. I declare that I will be the one to request the divorce, and that to achieve my ends I will employ all possible means, even the most extreme, to obtain the separation or divorce, whichever it may be, after Madame Chazal has deposited the estimated amount of the legal fees with either her lawyer or mine and either of them has officially recorded the remittance.
>
> At Bel-Air, April 1, 1832
> Chazal

He will be told in court that he never paid for the children's board. He will answer: "It's true, but I didn't know where they were."

At any rate, on April 1, 1832, we find the husband at Monsieur Laisney's, "a captain, decorated, honorable" (he doesn't call him commandant anymore), with the mayor of Bel-Air and, evidently, a process-server or police officer. "I refuse to sign a paper claiming that I maltreated her and threw her out of my home."

Flora will say: "I was forced to entrust my son to him; that was his price for consenting to legal separation or divorce, if the law was passed."

Flora, on her side, promises in writing to "bear every humiliation, every outrage, with a courage and patience worthy of a better lot," adding that "I will even be obliged to him for it." This in view of the settlement, no doubt.

At all events, the couple meet in Commandant Laisney's apartment. Flora will say that the mere sight of her husband drove her mad, threw her into a state of agitation where she could no longer control herself.

Chazal's story: "She threw a plate at my head and hit me. To this anger I opposed the calm of strength; I only had an official report drawn up."

52

Flora's story: "I was very agitated; I was mad. A look, a gesture from my husband was enough to irritate me. A rather violent scene took place, and it is true that, Monsieur Chazal having taken a chair to beat me, I seized a plate and threw it, but it didn't hit him. My uncle came in, drawn by the noise. He doesn't understand the state the sight of Chazal puts me in. He believed that this scene was feigned because, during the day, there had been talk of staging such a scene to bring about our legal separation. I told my uncle in vain that what had just happened was extremely serious, he didn't want to believe it and reproached me strongly for having used his house to stage such an act. This idea of my uncle's, against which I protested with the greatest energy, made me furious. I left him angry, and I have not seen him since."

A good demonstration of those mad rages that deprived Flora of all self-control, all sense of her own interests. So there she is, angry with her uncle, her sole male protector.

She takes refuge at her mother's. In the *Peregrinations* she will tell how her uncle and her husband came to her there, and it was agreed that Chazal would take Ernest, his mother-in-law keeping Aline.

Here the versions diverge. He claims that they hid his daughter's address from him; Flora tells two different stories about what happened next.

In her written reminiscences, the husband's pursuit took place the next day, thus on April 2, 1832, while he was taking his son away. On the other hand, before the court of assizes she will no longer speak of Ernest, she will place the scene "another day." But the stories are still the same. Since Flora, upset and speaking without notes, gets several details wrong in her deposition, we shall follow the Memoirs, supplementing them with the husband's explanation.

After a trying night, with Flora having been unable to eat or sleep for three days—her "nervous nature" often brought on these attacks of anorexia—Madame Tristan goes with her daughter to the post-chaise.

No doubt Flora blames her mother once more for her disastrous marriage: Madame Tristan, as she is getting into the carriage, takes her hand: "You don't hold it against me?" "No, I've forgotten it all." Flora leaves the coach at the last stop, 8, rue des Fossés-

Saint-Germain-l'Auxerrois. She sees the travelers getting down from the back of the coach and suddenly, "what was my astonishment at finding before me . . . Monsieur Chazal! He wanted to provoke a scene . . . Heaven lit my way, I contained myself. . . ." Chazal explains that he wants to get his daughter's address at all costs and that Commandant Laisney had advised him to follow Flora. He claims to have said, before the crowd at the stagecoach stop: "You must obey the law and I call on you to come and live under my roof. Thus I will know what you have done with my daughter."

In no way did he want, he comments, to take up their life together again. According to him, Flora abuses him. She says, on the contrary: "Monsieur Chazal then insulted me in the most frightful way. He had me arrested and taken to the police commissioner's. This magistrate sent me away without wanting to listen to Monsieur Chazal."

Chazal: "The police commissioner merely said: 'If this woman is your wife, take her away.' 'But how? Tied hand and foot?' 'Take her away.' She went away."

Flora: "It was three o'clock. He followed me in the street, made several scenes, and took me into two guardhouses." (In the *Peregrinations* she will say: "He pursued me as far as the Rue Servandoni shouting: 'To the guard! to the guard!' ")

In both cases: "At the corner of the Rue Servandoni he grabbed me by my cloak and shoved me so hard that the clasp broke and I was going to fall on three students who were passing by. All four of us fell down. These young people were furious; they bitterly reproached Monsieur Chazal, who defended himself by saying that I was his wife and renewed his insults and attacks on me.

"I made the mistake of admitting before these gentlemen that Monsieur Chazal was my husband, and, as they were law students, they told me: 'If he's your husband, we can do nothing for you. If he hadn't been your husband, we would have avenged you promptly.'

"This horrible scene was witnessed by more than three hundred people."

They help her into a hackney carriage. Chazal will say that she went off to her lawyer's, damned soul that she was.

Flora can't take any more.

The next day she goes to see her mother and certainly makes a violent scene: "You lavished your tenderness on me, you took my hands affectionately. And you didn't tell me that while we were in the front of the coach my monster of a husband was in the back! And you exposed me to his outrages without any defense!"

This scene must have been much less articulate, accompanied by verbal violence, shudders, the usual convulsions of Flora in a rage.

Six years later, speaking on oath, before the court, she will recall: "My mother? I forgave her for the harm she did me then, but I can never forget it. That is why I broke off relations with my mother, and why I didn't let her know about my trip to Peru."

Her bridges are all burned. Alone in the world with a seven-year-old child, Flora no longer has a past. She wants to erase everything and begin again. But how?

Paris, a unique city for her, has become odious. She leaves. Every tragedy has its grotesque reverse side: it's even the rule, the mainspring of romanticism. Flora's departure takes place around April 20, the same day as the flight of the Duchess de Berry, who wants to rouse the faithful to put the miracle child, born after his father's assassination, on the throne. Three times they ask for Flora's papers. Her hair, her Andalusian look save her at once: the duchess is a blue-eyed blonde. Besides, how can they claim that tall Aline is a three-year-old boy in disguise? From city to city Flora flees, from rooms to random lodgings. The newspapers tell her that *The Globe*, the Saint-Simonian paper, has folded. Then about the incredible trial of Prosper Enfantin, from August 27 to 29, before the Paris Court of Assizes. Flora follows it eagerly.

The Court Gazette describes Enfantin: "His head is handsome; his long black beard, his hair floating on his bare shoulders, the quaintness, the elegance of his dress draw all eyes to him." By way of a profession, he calls himself "leader of the new faith," his followers call themselves "apostles." The president looks for the lawyers.

Enfantin: "We have no lawyers but advisers, there are mine." Cécile Fournel and Aglaé Saint-Hilaire stand up. But, the president objects, women aren't admitted to the bar.

Enfantin: "The cause is of special concern to women." Despite this insistence, they are not admitted. None of the witnesses wants to take the oath without the Father's permission, which President Naudin and the attorney general don't allow. So they soon get to the charges. "Disgusting doctrines . . . stomach turned with indignation . . . utter contempt. . . ."

When the accused are allowed to speak, the situation is reversed. The "virtue" and "morality" of this "civilized society" are pitilessly dissected. The violence of this public washing of the dirty linen of received ideas obliges the president to flee: he adjourns the trial.

The Court Gazette is full of Enfantin.

From the emotion that she feels, Flora can gauge how much this man she hardly knew has marked even her. Ten years later the leader of the new faith will have become a middle-class preacher. He will recommend, for example, a quasi-military conscription of workers in Algeria. The obscure pretty woman he caught a glimpse of in the Rue Monsigny and at his lectures will, by an inverse route, have abandoned her role of aristocratic pariah to become an apostle of the oppressed. She will judge him, after a bittersweet correspondence, without indulgence but without acrimony:

"Enfantin destroyed, obliterated forever that Saint-Simonian School to which such remarkable men rallied and which had such advanced views on every social question." But he proclaimed "rehabilitation, and the sanctity of manual labor, as the fundamental laws of the Saint-Simonian doctrine. This rehabilitation alone includes the radical change of society." She will also write, on the whole Saint-Simonian School: "Madmen in their contemporaries' eyes . . . [they] will be considered superior men having been the first to understand woman's advent. Honor to madmen, then!" Perhaps her experience with them, exterior and superficial as it was, made Flora what she was. She saw that nonconformity can bring together avant-garde minds, those whom the unenlightened call "madmen."

These ideas are already taking shape within her while she reads the account of the trial.

In court, the Father practices his famous eye-contact policy. Words—this tribunal has heard so many!—serve only to punctuate silences. Enfantin is a forerunner of the practices of "body awareness" that will spread from the United States to Europe in the last third of the twentieth century. The prophet interrupts his sentences with long moments of contemplation, turned now toward his judges, now toward the public. To the astonished president he explains: "I need to see who is around me and to be seen. I desire to teach Monsieur the Attorney General the powerful influence of form, flesh, the senses, and for that make him feel the influence of looks." Eye contact, which makes the jurors lower their eyes. The court and the spectators can hardly contain themselves. The accused's superb eye and childlike confidence make them—as he wanted—lose "the calm suitable to their role." Enfantin is amused: "Well now, you ought to find it natural that I talk to you about my face, since Monsieur the Attorney General has talked to you about my fatuity. If you loved me instead of hating me, you would understand the moral power of the flesh, the senses, and beauty."

Glad to have confused them, he will change his tactics in the afternoon and profess the new religion.

For the "Pariah," ill in desolate lodgings, these prophecies take on a seminal importance. Enfantin tells how, at first reading, Saint-Simon's form of expression surprised him so much that he didn't even understand the importance of the lesson. In the same way this sermon which she clips from the *Court Gazette* will long remain an obscure text for Flora, until she gives it a new meaning, transforming it by assimilating it. It is a "text" for future psychoanalysts that Prosper Enfantin proclaims before the judges, who are convinced he is more crazy than criminal:

> ... For if Jesus was sent to teach the world the Father's wisdom, I am sent by *my God, Father and Mother of all men and all women,* to make the world desire her Motherly tenderness. I said: *God, Father and Mother of all men and all women,* because these simple words contain our religious faith. ... When the sacred name of God is pronounced before you, what attributes does it recall to your minds, what virtues does it awaken in your souls? Isn't it man's attributes, the male virtues that, always and everywhere, your men's hearts deify? Well, think, I beg you, of the immense difference that exists between the man who sees in his God only the attributes and virtues of deified man, and he who sees there as well, poetically elevated to an infinite power, the graces and virtues of woman?

The cult of Mary? Enfantin still finds it male and "somber as solitude."

> I affirm to you that whichever of you will take the communion of hope and love with our God, who is not only good like a Father, but

who is also tender like a Mother, I affirm that *whichever of you will take communion with Him and Her will have donned, by that alone, a new life.* For his love, his mind, and even his flesh will be transfigured. And that is why we seem so strange to you. It's that we aren't living the same life as you, it's that our God is not yours, it's that—and I want the strangeness of my speech to engrave my thought in you—He is not only good like a Father. She is also tender like a Mother, for He is and She is the Father and the Mother of all men and all women.

These words will stick in Flora's memory to pop out again years later:

"To be sure, we have a political goal: to put an end to idleness and egoism, the double leprosy. God will only end these things through Woman and through Association. Thus must happiness, peacefully and progressively, be established."

For the Saint-Simonians, the Woman-Messiah is not simply a Universal Mother as for other sects. For them, God includes both sexes within him (Freud, at the end of the same century, will show that all humans possess a masculine component and a feminine component). Prosper Enfantin's God is not made solely in the eternal masculine image. Shortly before the trial, some Saint-Simonians tried to create a weekly paper called *The Free Woman.*

The accused men are sentenced to a year in prison, to Flora's despair. So those who show the way to come are all, and always, treated like pariahs? What can she do with her life, she who is bored by the well-adjusted middle class, self-content and fast asleep? Her grandmother's money scarcely allows her to subsist, and certainly not to devote herself to writing and apostleship. And if she went to Peru? A new letter invites her there more formally, and puts her onto her cousin de Goyeneche, in Bordeaux, who will take care of getting her onto a ship. Good: but what should she do with Aline? Take her along? Admit to the sordid marriage? That's courting failure: the Tristan de Moscosos will never accept a misalliance with an artisan who's languishing in prison for debt. She torments herself so that she falls ill, in Angoulême, where she happens to be, we don't know why. Suddenly fate offers her a way out. Sometimes it's chance that transforms dreams into possibilities. An educator,

Mademoiselle de Bourzac, becomes attached to Aline and the child doesn't want to leave her. Can she leave her daughter here, subject to payment of her board, and undertake a long journey? And what would happen if—crossings are so fertile with shipwrecks—she never came back?

"If by some misfortune she never saw you again, I would be a mother to her, she would stay with us," Mademoiselle de Bourzac assures her.

Flora gives Madame Tristan's address: not to be used unless news of her death reaches them. She has burned her bridges. Vowing anew that she will pave the way for a better life for her daughter, Flora takes the stagecoach for Bordeaux.

8

TOWARD SAD TROPICS

January 1833: she will be thirty in April. To the people she is going to meet this makes her an old maid. So since they don't know the exact date of her birth, Flora subtracts a few years from her age, a folly she will cling to until her death.

Her mirror reflects a surprising picture of youth. In this age of women who rapidly become fleshy, shriveled, swollen, this mother of three, this woman supercharged with anxiety, this penniless woman always in search of work hears herself called "pretty girl" in the street.

And yet, though her nerves sustain her, her health is fragile: too many emotions, too much *table d'hôte* food, too much insomnia and constant anguish. Besides, an obsession, fear of being recognized by someone who might call her Madame Chazal or speak of her children transforms each outing into a perilous test. She was recently in Bordeaux with Aline; the city seems to her full of dangers.

At the stagecoach stop, a thin, elderly man, with a bigot's shifty look but lordly manners, approaches. Mariano de Goyeneche, her distant relative, has a brother who is a bishop and a family that left Vizcaya to get rich in Peru. He shows an emotion that clashes with his air and manners: Ah! he would have recognized Flora among a thousand for her resemblance to his dear Mariano de Tristan, companion of his youth. Already he loves her like his own daughter.

Flora feels herself welcomed with a warmth that owes nothing to amorous plans. She's not used to it, and this sympathy consoles her for Aline's absence. The cousin installs her at a neighbor woman's: propriety doesn't permit him to lodge her in his house, however big, since he lives there alone.

Here, Flora enjoys comfort, and even elegance, for the first time in her life. Eight-tenths of her contemporaries are unaware of what will later be called "dwelling-place culture." She knows about it through her English masters, but if ladies' maids ensure luxury, they hardly profit by it. Now others bring up and pour out tubs of hot water for her, clean, iron her dresses and linen, and bring her well-brushed shoes.

The very first evening, delightedly handling crystal glasses and silver tableware, even happier with the decor than with the delicious food, Flora meets a pale young man with the aggressive melancholy of the Byronic dandy. He is called Philippe Bertera, takes care of Uncle Pio's business, will soon become the Peruvian consul in Bordeaux. His sad beauty attracts the young woman, suits her taste for heroic gloom and sister souls that bravely surmount great disappointments. He confides to her not many days later that he has been alone in the world since a family tragedy and reverses of fortune which, however, haven't completely stripped him. Philippe Bertera is a superb horseman, takes her out riding while the old cousin rests, goes with her to the outfitters who must equip her for the voyage and for Peru. It's he who chooses her satin brocade dress with balloon sleeves above the elbow. He who advises the warm cape with the scalloped border: sometimes it's very cold in Arequipa. But then sometimes the heat is terrific: she should also order this organdy dress, several hats, a Naples silk umbrella.

When they ride in a closed carriage, he takes her hand and confides, tears in his eyes: "Only duty toward God keeps me from putting an end to my life." Flora, her heart beating, forbids herself to confess: "With me, it's my duty toward my children." Her fear of being recognized has not disappeared and gives their escapades the spice of danger.

Does their tenderness stop, as Flora writes in the *Peregrinations*, at "a melancholic intimacy that, pious in its aspirations, did not touch the earth at any point"? Or has she veiled from her readers the outcome of her loves with the three men who, by her own admission, attracted her: Bertera, Commandant Chabrié, and the colonel-journalist Escudero? The hypothesis of frigidity, here again, would tend to make one take her word for it. And yet—as we shall see—for the third of these men, even her language is different, and allows one to believe in a brief shared passion.

In Bordeaux, pampered, surrounded, she ought to be happy, and yet is tormented to the point of spending the nights in tears. What if she confessed everything? If she begged Goyeneche to take her, with Aline, into his big empty house. Each time her decision is made, in the morning, examining the pious old bachelor, she draws back: no, he won't understand, this egoist, he will consider her a lost woman.

Soon—how fast these weeks have sped by—Bertera announces that he has found a ship's captain who is willing to be paid, as Uncle Pio demands, on arrival and in Peruvian money. The ship is called the *Mexican* and its commander Zacharie Chabrié . . . Flora stifles a cry: it's her *table d'hôte* companion, Uncle Pio's friend: he knows Aline, he thinks she is "the Widow Tristan" . . . She lets him come: with an obstacle before her she always knows how to face it. As soon as she is alone with him, she holds out her hand to him and speaks with tears in her voice: "Monsieur, I don't know you. However, I am going to entrust a secret to you and ask a great favor of you."

His answer shows that he has already understood. Moreover, all throughout the voyage, Flora will see ladies in distress whom Chabrié saved from ruin. This Breton is a real Saint Bernard.

She offers him the false confession constructed during the nights of insomnia. Experience has shown her the limits allowed by society: "Warmly welcomed as a widow or young spinster, I was always repulsed when the truth came to light." She also speaks of the "unfortunate Pariah whom people think they've done a favor when they don't insult her."

To Chabrié, who knows Aline, Flora presents herself as a girl seduced and abandoned. She hides her husband . . . who will comment: "To pass oneself off as a young spinster when one has a husband and children is a serious offense." (He will never have anything to condemn her with but the arguments she provides for him in the *Peregrinations*.)

Now that the sailor knows she is an unwed mother, can she hide it from the tender Philippe? Besides, now that her departure is set, fear of dying at sea and abandoning Aline gives her no rest. Should she tell Bertera everything? But he puts her on such a pedestal. . . . Is she going to lose caste in his eyes? She doesn't invoke this egoistic worry, but prefers to claim that she didn't want to distress her too-sensitive friend with the story of her misfortunes: "I made this sacrifice to the friendship that I had sworn to him." She gives him the same false confession as Chabrié. The idea of what his sweetheart has suffered overwhelms Philippe: he swears to take care of Aline if her mother disappears. For a long time he will help Flora with loans.

April 7, the day of departure, is also Flora's thirtieth birthday. The dawn of death or of renewal? Early in the morning Philippe takes her down to the docks in a cab. All that she is giving up seems divine to her: the dear trees in the public garden, the peasant women bringing milk, the mild breeze. So strong is the desire to stay that she clings to the Spaniard's hand but doesn't dare beg: "Keep me—" "I am saying farewell to my trees." Once on board, Chabrié growls: "Come on now, keep your chin up!" But his eyes are damp too (to tell the truth, he cries easily).

This world of men and water that Flora is now penetrating ought to frighten her. To the dangers of the voyage, to the April storms, is added the strangeness of this adventure. At the time, to accept the position of being the only woman on a ship, among twenty men, was tacitly to accept "dishonor." In good society, a woman of thirty sailing for months at a time without a chaperone among unattached males had lost her reputation before the anchor was weighed.

For the first time, this fatherless girl is going to spend four and a half months (and not, as anticipated, eighty days) in an exclusively masculine world. Fifteen officers and seamen; six passengers; twenty-one men around this "dejected beauty," quickly conscious of her charm.

Flora lives this new situation on two planes. First, as soon as she isn't grounded by seasickness, she notes down conversations, what her companions look like, the fluctuations of her own feelings, in her diary. Then, without her formulating it, all these observations ferment in her, acting as fertilizer for her future vision of the world. Flora's ideas, we shall see, are nourished by her experience. The poor adolescence, the deep wound that marriage inflicted on her sexuality, and the image she has of her role, sensitize her to the humiliations of wage-earners without a trade. For years, everywhere, she has known herself at the mercy of others. Right now on this boat she is Woman, the object of men's conscious or hidden desire. Socially, too, she is privileged, like all the passengers. They have none of the cares and labors that the three officers, the seamen, and the drudge of a cabin boy assume. In the ship's company, a gulf separates officers and workers of the sea. On this boat class differences appear in miniature, but Flora senses it without yet drawing any lesson from it.

Every period imposes a "spirit of the times." The most lucid project bold ideas: they are the avant-garde. But none can completely free themselves from it.

At thirty, Flora knows she is a pariah but would also like to be, like all women, accepted and admired. On the *Mexican*, the fighter for equality accepts her royalty gladly.

Tempests, fogs, errors in navigation, breakdowns—all that the sea imposed on ships before radio and radar—are her lot. Nobody is surprised that a voyage lasts twice as long as expected. Sick almost constantly—she can't stand the swell—Flora becomes more sensitive to the protections being offered her. She will draw striking portraits of her companions.

Alfred David, the mate, calls himself an atheist, believes man is wicked, and has no faith in love. A cabin boy at fourteen, he claims to love nothing but his cigar, good living, and the pleasure of the girls at every port. Flora argues with him. Chabrié takes the side of original goodness. The slender dandy with his eccentric sidewhiskers plays Voltaire opposite the bald, potbellied Rousseauist, whose fine tenor voice delights Flora. Another officer, Briet, an old sailor from Lorient, brings up his memories of the Hundred Days on the slightest pretext. Flora listens, argues, commiserates, questions. By the time she lands she will have greatly enriched her experience and, regarding the seamen, measured what destitution can achieve. Some of the men don't even have warm clothing. For lack of gloves, one of them had fingers so badly frozen that he let go of the mast and fell, breaking both his legs. The five who are well rigged out can take bad weather. The other four are subject to scurvy, fever, abcesses. "The true sailor must be a snail who carries all he possesses on his back. He lives only to see land. And I've seen lands. . . ."

Some of these "true" sailors, like Leborgne, give this woman on her way to win her inheritance a hard lesson in anarchism.

"The true sailor has neither homeland nor family. He boards ship after ship of every nation and deserts each time there's some advantage in it. When he gets into a port, he may, on a whim, abandon his ship, and also the salary due."

"Then he doesn't love anyone?" (Love is Flora's key word: love of a man, and, afterward, of humans.)

"A true sailor loves no one—not even himself."

"And when he can't sail any longer?"

"Well, then—he begs."

No, she will never forget this depth of human despair. Workers in the English blast furnaces, slaves in the Peruvian sugar mills, the unemployed shut up in the London poorhouses and the spinners and weavers of Lyon, their looks will always remind her of the face of this "true sailor," standing in rags at the foot of the mast on board the *Mexican*.

"Mind you, it's all lost now. There are hardly any true sailors left. They get married, they take along a well-filled trunk, so they desert less, so as not to lose their possessions or their money."

Every day, whether Flora is stretched out sick, or settled in her cabin reading and writing her diary, Chabrié comes to her bedside. He is going to stand his watch. He is going to suffer for four hours, with the rheumatism in his leg, his easily chilled body, his fingers full of chilblains. "Mademoiselle Flora, you are God, at least for me. One of your looks is enough and I go up there for four hours without feeling the cold." She puts on his gloves for him, slowly, finger by finger, smiling.

> I took his hand . . . often, even, while fixing his double cravats, to protect him from the cold, I kissed him on the forehead.
> "The friendship that I feel for you greatly surpasses, though it is of a very different nature, the love that other women have had for you." It pleased me to surround him with these attentions and caresses as if he had been my brother or my son.

We have already had intimacy that never comes down to earth

with Bertera; here is sisterly tenderness for a man who is quickly aroused, fiery, impulsive, a full-blooded, sentimental type, ready for every kind of madness when caught up in a quick passion. Chabrié is a version of the "true sailor" refined by culture and breeding. But the core of anarchy, the disdain for what people say, the taste for wide-open spaces and solitude is the same. He sometimes alludes to a deep emotional disappointment. Nothing could attract Flora more. He is suffering: a woman betrayed his confidence, proved unworthy. Does he still love her? Nothing is missing, not even the question mark, for "this crystalization" of love that Stendahl will be immortalizing during these same years.

Very Stendahlian, Flora will write five years later that this "material [century] will accuse of being unrealistic . . . the depiction of a true love on the one hand and a pure friendship on the other."

Frigidity? or caution in telling the story? She constantly assures us that she wants to become a "being of truth." As proof, she presents her Peruvian family and Chazal with the *Peregrinations*, which will allow them to accuse her of every perversion. But how can she break completely with her times? Militant egalitarian, future apostle of women's rights, she will say in the court of assizes, to justify her attitude toward Chabrié: "For five months, I was alone on shipboard among six men [we note that the crew doesn't count among the "men"]. If someone has traveled on board a ship, he will understand the importance of what I have just said. Monsieur Chabrié gave me proof of his friendship, I entrusted myself to it, I accepted his protection. Ah, my God, could I do otherwise? I was alone among six men, what dangers didn't threaten me?"

A passage in the *Peregrinations* also notes that she accepted his love "as much to keep him from despair as to assure me of his powerful protection." Moreover the elegant David affirms: "Men only love women amorously. They scorn feminine friendship. Women, not being engaged in any of society's employments, having only a very small number of professions, need the ties of friendship more than men do. But man puts on his friendship, his protection the price of love."

And Chabrié himself, the most generous of men: "There is no friendship in the world: there is only interest among the wicked and love among the good."

The bond of equality is so little accepted that Flora can dream of it but not, at this stage in her evolution, either assert it or impose it. She has the honesty to recall constantly, in 1838, the state of mind consigned to her five-year-old "journal": "In 1833, I was still very far from having the ideas that, since, have developed in my mind."

Thus the future internationalist will store away, at stops along the way and across Peru, the substance of her internationalism, but, at this time, "the name of France and everything connected with it produced almost magical effects on me."

Manila, La Praya, first stop in the Third World, as we would say. Flora is horrified by the misery "of the Negroes," and especially their odor: her hypersensitivity to smells, developed by the loathings of her adolescence among the fetid emanations of the Place Maubert, often masters her and bears witness to a natural sensitivity constantly checked. She confuses the smells and the degradation of beings deprived of everything, undernourished, subject to brutality and injustice, with a race. She is still not used to anything but Europe.

At La Praya, she discovers a destitution, a stupor that the slums in European cities don't come near. Soon the realities of slavery are revealed, and horror for the victims is inverted to hatred for their tormentors. A slave trader in the port "began to boast of his merchandise, turning this human being around on all sides as a horse-dealer might have done a young colt. This barbaric act brought vividly to my mind all the evils of slavery."

From the very first stage, sitting on a rock on the beach, Commandant Chabrié declares himself:

"Mademoiselle Flora, I don't expect to make you love me. I ask only to help you bear your sorrows." I thanked him with a smile, and showing him the sea: "My heart is like that ocean; unhappiness has hollowed out deep abysses in it. It's not any human power that can fill it."

"Then do you accord more power to unhappiness than to love?"

That answer made me tremble. At the time I could not hear the word *love* pronounced without tears coming to my eyes. Monsieur Chabrié hid his head in his hands. For the first time, I looked at him; I didn't know his features yet. He was weeping. I examined him attentively and abandoned myself with delight to the most melancholy thoughts.

He proposes marriage, life with Aline on the deserted California coast.

Here is a scene from romanticism, in the style of Chateaubriand or Sir Walter Scott, under which is sketched Flora's taste, already noted, for an unhappiness that her consolation can relieve. A taste for causing disappointments that give her vengeance on society, for the unhappy loves of her adolescence, for her failure with Chazal, and at the same time give her a complete feeling of her own power. Chabrié will be her revenge and her victim. She will make the sailor entirely given to each emotion undergo what life inflicted on her: uncertainty, hope, pain, and final disappointment. Sadism? The coyness of triumphant frigidity? An Amazon subjecting man to the pain of refusal, the usual lot of women of whom society demands passivity? Does Flora behave toward Chabrié like a "castrating female"? Is it the rebellion of a victim without hope of equality? An underhanded revolt? It is all these things combined. To the boat's idleness, to the continual discoveries, including the one, so important to her, that she can arouse a real passion, and to the fears she takes refuge behind, is also added the masque of her account of it all. The heroine of the *Peregrinations* conforms to the fashionable model: unfortunate, persecuted, adored, she remains pure and desires what life doesn't offer.

They spend almost two days virtually alone together, the others having stayed on shore. Native musicians come to play on board and the drums must have their usual effect on their nerves. They lie at night on the bridge, before the bay, bathed in full moonlight, and a violent, excited man tries to persuade, to conquer a lonely young woman. You can imagine whatever outcome you please. One day, in the cabin, kneeling against her, he dreams of their future happiness. Ashamed of deceiving him, Flora clasps his head against her and tells herself that once she was his wife perhaps she would love him more. She already told herself that at seventeen, with Chazal. Even the language, the words she uses confess involuntarily: "Gradually, his love pierced me with such admiration that I got the idea of marrying him, staying with him in California." Bigamy, then, a crime punished by all the laws of Christianity?

"What makes it a crime, if not the absurd law that establishes the indissolubility of marriage?"

This whole passage in the book on Chabrié's love will be read in the court of assizes: the lawyer, to justify the husband's fury, wants to demonstrate the wife's immorality. She will defend herself, always, with the same words: "In my unhappiness, I was beside myself, I was mad." "You did not take any steps to get married in California?" the attorney general will ask. "Never, sir."

Flora is far enough ahead of her time to throw back onto society the crime it burdens her with, but not enough to renounce the protections that a woman alone, in this period, cannot dispense with (and how many women, a century and a half later, make the same decision?). Knowing everything about the feminine condition, she never loses sight of her goal: freedom. Words like "You will be mine" (Chabrié pronounces them) revolt her. She won't allow "the heart's promises . . . to be assimilated to contracts that have ownership as an object." Her taste for freedom alienates her from the enamored Breton. Behind the passionate tirades, the moonlit avowals and plans, the embraces, "chaste" or not, she feels a new master peeping out. He is ready to fight over "an equivocal word or smile" from David or from a young passenger. He would rather she didn't take her legacy: through disinterestedness, but also so that she may depend more on him. With this paralyzed lover she risks becoming another kind of pariah: one who wouldn't have "the shadow of freedom."

To this sailor, this daredevil with the heart of gold, she owes the recovery of her self-confidence. The knowledge—even if she scorns it—that a haven is offered her.

She also owes him some political notions. Apart from Saint-Simon's ideas, she had thought very little about the form of governments. Chabrié, in endless discussions with David, talks about the republic of his dreams, which would be copied closely from the United States. David, out of dandyism, asks the legitimist: "Chabrié, do you want your Phrygian cap *?" He knows America well.

"The worker there is disgustingly insolent . . . they hold three million Negroes in slavery in the name of individual liberty. Oh, no . . ."

"I shall never understand how, at home, we call it justice to sacrifice the well-being of twenty-eight million proletarians for the

---

* A symbol of emancipation and liberty.—Tr.

greatest happiness of three or four million landowners. Look here, David, don't you want freedom of the press, then?"

"For visiting cards only," and the dandy pirouettes.

When, after four and a half months at sea, the *Mexican* sights Valparaiso, Flora realizes, humiliated, that she can no longer walk with her light grace: she has the rolling gait that is needed on a ship's bridge. Most of the two hundred French residents of Valparaiso are gathered on the quay to see the very lovely niece of that despotic charmer Don Pio de Tristan step ashore. The news, brought by the captain, that that perfect and penniless young lady has traveled alone among twenty men, is the only topic of conversation. Brawls, duels, or—who knows?—murders can be expected.

Scarcely arrived, she learns of her grandmother's death, which makes her coming, in a word, hopeless. Chabrié rushes up: "Your grief is there, on my old heart, like an anchor that buries itself in the mud by its own weight."

In the evening, with Briet and David, he comes into the room Flora has rented at a Frenchwoman's; they talk until past midnight. All Valparaiso whispers about it: from now on, Flora will constantly be coming up against this incomprehension. The heroine of a Russian novel displaced in time and space, she loves endless discussions in a circle of men, all charmed but none daring to make a move. These unusual relationships will each time be interpreted with the familiar keys. A multitude of lovers will be attributed to this high-strung, cerebral, repressed woman. But Chabrié becomes demanding. Flora knows now that he was "tortured by an unworthy creature" and that he can make a rich marriage in Bordeaux. So she decides to embark for Islay without waiting for him. Crushed, he announces that he will meet her in Peru. Their farewells would seem to indicate a physical relationship ... if Flora didn't constantly mix her registers, like a good romantic: "He didn't feel in his embraces that he was clasping only a cadaver, incapable of returning the slightest caress." The indication seems precise. When the boarding launch passes near the *Mexican*, the traveler is seized with trembling and lowers her veil.

9

GOLD AND BLOOD IN PERU

The voyage cuts Flora Tristan's life in half. Before Chabrié's love and the Peruvian adventure, she was a poor, déclassée Parisian (her mother says she has "forfeited her rank"), a fugitive wife. To avoid appearing at odds with the law, she has no choice but to call herself a widow or seduced girl.

After the crossing she feels herself to be a woman who is fawned upon, flirtatious, ruling over willing men—but also a "captain of adventure" coming to conquer, by force of seduction, the right to live free. Does she think of staying in Peru? In court, she will claim: "I left France with the idea of never coming back."

During this period, thousands of French are going to colonize Algeria. Others are exiled to the Americas, among whom, within fifteen years, can be found Fourierists with their phalansteries and Cabetians with their Icarian utopias.

At Islay, her father's homeland welcomes her—with an invasion of fleas. After which, riding with a mule train, she jounces along narrow paths bordered by barren precipices, dressed as if for an excursion around Paris. Fatigue, thirst, exhausting heat; she slows down the progress of the others who make her a saddle, lend her blankets and shawls. One of her companions goes on ahead to announce her coming while she collapses, thinking of Aline, blaming herself for coming to find death "four thousand leagues from home." At last, there comes a troop of horsemen galloping to meet her: a young cousin, Emmanuel de Rivero, with some companions, a fine saddle horse for her with all its gear.

A violent shock: this eighteen-year-old boy "looked so much like me that he could have been taken for my brother ... he speaks French as if he were born on French soil."

"Ah! my cousin, how did it come about that I was unaware of your existence? I spent four years in Paris without a friend!"

He initiates her into the family. Uncle Pio is residing at the moment on a country estate. The household in Arequipa is ruled by Cousin Carmen Pierola de Florez, "a woman of wit, but prudent and very circumspect." How can one be anything *but* when one is subject to Uncle Pio, that paternal tyrant? All depend on him: poor relations, bailiffs, employees, servants, slaves. The task of supervision is entrusted to the Dominicans housed on the estate, a high domesticity of the soul. Emmanuel, whose father went bankrupt before he died, shares with his mother an income that lets him vegetate here but not study in France, and his uncle ... "Our relatives are the kings of the land. Hard and petty as bankers, they are incapable of performing an action that lives up to the name they bear." So there she is, forewarned.

At nightfall, they arrive at the wall of the Rue Saint-Dominique, in Arequipa: at the end of the drive resin torches light up the house. At the head of the steps, surrounded by relatives and servants, dressed like a young girl but "ugly to the point of deformity," stands her cousin Carmen. Her face pitted from smallpox, she emphasizes her one beauty: a tiny foot. Everyone surges toward the lighted drawing rooms.

Then begins "the tyrannical hospitality of peoples in their infancy." Her skin burned by the desert, broken with fatigue, Flora must listen to the Dominicans read an elegy on her grandmother composed by their prior, and the others' dithyrambs. At last she gets permission to go and lie down without supper. All of them, monks included, escort her toward the vast uncomfortable cellars to which her uncle's avarice relegates his guests. Once her *samba* (a black and Indian half-breed) is asleep, Flora gets up again to "nose around" in the house where her father was brought up, caressing furniture and heavy chests. Confronting the real dwelling with the imaginary memories; the inevitable shrinking.

Etiquette is strict: a woman, newly arrived, must not go out for a month: people come to pay calls. After which she returns them. On Sunday, one must be "at home" from ten to one, then from five to eight. The ladies make an appearance, the men get bored, everyone gossips; "boredom makes for curiosity."

Flora declares flatly that she will not follow the custom. Cousin Carmen is admiring but alarmed: "How can you act so? Isn't woman the slave of laws and prejudices?"

"Real freedom exists only in the will."

Carmen is fascinated. Flora promptly becomes a mirage for her.

"In Europe you find women to whom God has imparted the moral strength to escape the yoke."

While the two cousins' intimacy is being knit, an earthquake takes place, destroying a nearby town, Tacna, with eighteen dead and twenty-five injured. In this atmosphere of dread, Carmen tells the story of her life. Flora doesn't tell us what she confided about her own: nothing, certainly, that could do her harm with her uncle. She knows that a being who is morally a slave can give way before the master to the point of treachery.

Carmen, an ugly daughter, destined for the convent, married a libertine who went through her money in ten years while tormenting her, making fun of her with his mistresses, who insulted her. "A handsome husband thinks he can do anything with an ugly wife; such is the morality that results from the indissolubility of marriage." Full of malignant contempt, Carmen becomes worldly: her wit assures her success in the drawing rooms. At the end of ten years, the libertine comes back, sick and penniless. Carmen then practices "a noble vengeance that exalts her superiority": she cares for this wreck for sixteen months; he never leaves his bed again; he is entirely dependent on her. Triumph of flouted virtue.

With the legitimate oppressor dead, she changes tyrants: for twelve years—she is close to forty—she has been vegetating in Uncle Pio's shadow.

Arequipa interests the Parisian enormously. There are 30,000 inhabitants, not counting servants and slaves. Everybody does business, without prejudice. The day is punctuated by three meals. At nine o'clock a luncheon of meat and chocolate. At three o'clock a dinner made up of a single dish, *olla podrida*, where everything is mixed together: this barbarity makes Flora indignant. Has she then forgotten the *tables d'hôte* for a few pennies that were her fare for so long? At eight o'clock in the evening, a supper of shrimp and meat. They drink water with, often, only one glass for the whole company. Everything is unclean. The customs—which include rites of participation, but Flora doesn't know it—disgust her. When one wants to do "a politeness" to someone, one sends him, by a slave who runs the length of the table, a dripping forkful of one's own food. The slaves are dirty. Dinner guests are rare because of the extreme costliness of everything. During the evenings, they serve tea, chocolate, and, the only dish that Flora appreciates, cakes baked by the nuns.

On October 28, she learns that Chabrié is riding toward her. Two days later, at eight in the evening, he arrives. The almost complete darkness of the drawing room conceals their emotion. At last, she can take him into her apartment. He weeps unrestrainedly. "I couldn't breathe. An iron chain constricted my chest. I pressed his head against me, but I could not find a word to say to him." For six days he pleads, begs, sobs, threatens. She promised him this Californian happiness; they must live it. But they are no longer between sea and sky. The future is agonizing, but she doesn't want to bury herself with him and decides to destroy the picture he has of her. Should she reveal the truth to him? He would only want to console her even more. So she demands that he get some missionary to make a false certificate of her parents' marriage, which will be antedated. Then she can get her legacy: a million. Flora knows Chabrié and his scale of values very well.

> Caught between honor and infamy ... the unfortunate man sat there, shattered, his elbow leaning on the table. He looked at me without speaking and like an innocent man on whom a death sentence had just been pronounced.

After which, of course, he storms to get in a good exit line: "I hate you as much as I loved you."

Before leaving Peru he writes an eternal farewell, promising that in case of a "fatal event" he will still take care of Aline.

Flora explains the episode in terms of an old-fashioned virtue which "required a more than superhuman strength." But if he had accepted her proposition, would she have played the deceitful game? It is unlikely: the uncle has her letter, where, "cutting her head in four," she puts down in black and white that her parents' marriage was not legal. Truthfully, in spite of her moral fatigue and yearning for peace, she doesn't have the slightest desire for a retired life, but a lofty one of great feelings . . . and in Paris.

So there is Flora with her retreat cut off on the eve of a battle which everyone predicts she'll lose. The head of one of her uncle's sugar mills in Camana, a typical pre-Revolutionary Frenchman, is smitten. "Dear Papa Crévoisier loved me to distraction." He tells her straight off: everyone is asking why this pretty spinster has come to Peru; they're complaining about her discretion; the people of Arequipa are boiling with impatience . . . Uncle Pio said beforehand that this "illegitimate child would have no right to anything and that his niece's illegitimacy was admitted in her own letters."

Flora declares that she has come simply to make her family's acquaintance. She scribbles notebooks full of observations. Already, she has decided to write.

She allies herself in friendship with a cousin by marriage, d'Althaus, a German by origin. He married a Tristan daughter, but has little time for family life: since the age of seventeen, he has known no trade but war and loved only France. He fought for Napoleon, but also for the Allies. In 1815, he finds himself back in Germany and lives three years there in peace: what intolerable boredom! So he quits the army and leaves for Peru to follow Bolívar. Ecstatic, Flora enriches the pictures she has of the Libertador. It was at Bolívar's side that d'Althaus came to Uncle Pio's, marrying his niece, Manuela, in 1826. Flora finds him romantic: he is supposed to be hard and has almost no friends.

At last, on January 3, 1834, at four in the afternoon, Flora, with d'Althaus, rides out to meet the gentleman on whom her fate depends. A whole cohort follows them: one has hardly any diversions, and the meeting of a petitioner from so far away and "the miser portrayed by Sir Walter Scott" should be entertaining.

I saw a rider coming at full gallop; I exclaimed: "There's my uncle!" I threw my horse forward, and in a moment found myself near him. What I felt then, I can only imperfectly express in words. I took his hand and, shaking it with love, I said to him:

"Oh! my uncle, how I need your affection!"

"My daughter, you have it in full. I love you like my child. And you are also my sister, for your father was like a father to me." He drew me toward him, I leaned my head on his chest, at the risk of falling off my horse, and stayed that way for quite a long time. I arose bathed in tears: was it from joy, happiness or memories?

Only then does she look at him. "My uncle doesn't have a European face." Yet he is pure Spanish, and the whole family look alike, except for him. Blue-eyed, he is slim and lordly in spite of having spent a quarter of a century among soldiers. Lively and charming. At sixty-four she finds him "more active than a Frenchman of twenty-five." This need to love that devours her, how she would like to pour it out on this man who ought to be her second father!

They ride toward the country house. One may ask where Flora, a Parisian without money, became an expert horsewoman: she can gallop for hours, stay in the saddle for whole days. And her uncle's grace on horseback charms her as much as his conversation.

The rest of the family await them. Flora finds her aunt cold. She is a woman of forty with black eyes, beautiful teeth, and a humble and submissive air. She has this talent for making one think she is nothing and knows nothing, seems affable and easily moved. But Flora distrusts people "whose gracious smile is not in harmony with their look" and her eyes remain cold and hard. There is no flash of sympathy.

This aunt, in other circumstances, could have been a peerless personage, "regent of a kingdom or mistress of a septuagenarian king," a Madame de Maintenon. But she is forced to model herself on "Peruvian ways." On the other hand she has a sister, Manuela, who immediately becomes Flora's friend. The mother of eleven children, she sparkles with vitality and "only seems happy from the happiness that she spreads . . . a model woman whom all envy and try to imitate." Generous to the point of prodigality, filled with madcap gaiety, following Paris fashions through the newspapers, she keeps her house perfectly, and in her home—rare exception—even the slaves are clean. "Made to live in the great capitals of Europe," she is satisfied with Arequipa and loves her husband, "contrasts sometimes harmonizing better than similarities."

Flora's feminism is real and not only theoretical: as soon as she meets a superior feminine character she admires and appreciates her.

As for her uncle, she judges him, this first evening when he sits enthroned, receiving homage, "one of those select men destined by Providence to lead others." Alas, all hope of moving him dies at the first serious discussion.

"Uncle, you are really persuaded that I am your brother's daughter?"

"Not a doubt, Florita: his image is faithfully mirrored in you."

"Uncle, my parents' marriage was public knowledge."

She pleads, weeps, clasps against her heart—a gesture familiar to him—the hand of this man who is so warm in words, so harsh as soon as gold is in question. He maintains his views: illegitimate, she must be satisfied with the 3000 piasters (15,000 francs) left by her grandmother. Five thousand francs income? But she wants to ruin him! He's not the man to soften: his hardness is as proverbial as his facility for changing camps from interest: a war hero, he was second in command of King Ferdinand's troops for two years. Then, when the republicans won at Ayacucho, he went over to their side, and the royalists declared him a traitor. He, "liking the old party by taste and the new by interest," soon finds the republicans costly. Bolívar, in his eyes, is only the man who "borrowed" 25,000 pesetas from him without returning them, plus 10,000 from General Sucre, his second in command. Yet he amassed plenty of gold in his plunderings: each one of the doughty royalist war lords has enough to have his spurs cast in gold. When Uncle Pio became prefect of Arequipa, he provoked so much hatred that he had to go into exile in Chile, where Chabrié knew him.

Flora isn't up to such an adversary. All the more so because he's bored right now, seeking diversion in endless tours of his estates. He missed the presidency of the Republic by five votes. He loves nothing, except power.

His niece pleases him; she adds the glamor of the unusual to his

renown. He has never met a pretty woman so intelligent, so cultivated, or so original. Let her stay and live here, near him.

He claims to have imposed, himself, this legacy of 3000 piasters,
which displeased the other legitimate heirs.

Up to this point in the conversation, Flora has contained herself,
reasonable, reasoning. But now one of her uncontrollable rages
seizes her, fed by all her privations, all her bitterness. They are in her
uncle's office, a vast vaulted hall facing the street. On the walls,
portraits of Spanish ancestors and one of Montezuma, king of the
Indians. For the first time, the poor pariah lives, in her father's
birthplace, as her family has always lived, surrounded by valuable
furniture and objects, with a horde of slaves. When her uncle says:
"But I will marry you richly, Florita," she explodes. That word
churns up the whole mire of the lie. "All human societies," in Peru
as in France, are "organized against her," then? So she will always be
a pariah, and a stranger everywhere? The French find her outland-
ish, "Andalusian," and the Peruvians call her "la Francesita."
Anyone can do anything against her, but she, a defenseless woman,
can do nothing.

They are alone. She strides across the vast room. She is experiencing one of those "moments when the soul communicates with a
superhuman power. Born with all the advantages that arouse men's
covetousness, they were only shown to me to make me feel the
injustice that stripped me." Finding her voice, she plunges into a
violent speech: "This very evening I shall leave your house, and
tomorrow the whole town will know . . ."

But where can she go? To Manuela's? Her cousin would be much
embarrassed by her presence; she too depends on her redoubtable
brother-in-law.

Flora takes refuge in her room where she has her meals sent up to
her. The next day, she consults the president of the court of justice.
He sighs: why did she "cut her head in four" by writing, herself, that
her parents' marriage wasn't recorded? Her uncle, with the strong
case this written admission gives him, will never yield, and she can
do nothing against him. How can she admit that she counted on
Don Pio's generosity and affection? A young merchant, a Frenchman, very handsome, advises her to leave the family home, which
would have greatly annoyed the proud gentleman. But how can she

78

risk this new break? What would she become in Arequipa, if not a miserable creature, despised by all? Having finally encountered comfort, and the sweet warmth of a family home, how can she resolve to become a pariah again? Proud Don Pio makes the first move: he doesn't want to lose his gold or his niece either. Seductive, disturbing with her mania for judging everything by Paris standards, priggish, but distracting and even touching, with a halo of mystery around her: what exactly does she want? what was her life? why, so beautiful and so eager to charm, has she not found a husband? Her uncle proposes to her—by letter brought to her room—an interview before witnesses. The cousins affirm that he indeed insisted on sending her a little money. She is moved; he says: "It wasn't a gift, it was a debt. Consider me as your proxy."

They embrace. No lawsuit, no scandal, the uncle has won. She stays. Not without a letter in which—as always—she asserts her right to respect in the name of her misfortune. "I came to find a father; I met a co-heir." So she abandons her claim, and without rancor. But let no one demand gaiety of her. What that means is that she spares herself, in the name of this mourning, the fastidious sessions in the drawing room. Her own room becomes, like her cabin on the boat, the place where the elect get together. Soon the Parisian is famous throughout Arequipa: what a brain! They say she has "soul." Even her anorexia passes for French elegance: coffee, milk, chocolate, fruit. They nickname her "Flower of the Air."

10

A REVOLUTION

One day, she is stretched out on her bed in her usual way, in an embroidered wool robe, chatting with Carmen and some others on "the emptiness of human things." Someone shoves the door open. It is Emmanuel, her favorite, the one who looks like her.

"Florita! It's revolution! massacre!" Her uncle comes in, agitated, pacing to and fro. What's to be done? Here Nieto, a colonel, has just seized power in the name of d'Orbegoso, the new president. So they're going to fleece the landowners, as in every coup d'état, as did the Libertador, his niece's cherished Bolívar. . . . And if, anticipating the appeal, he went and offered Nieto 2000 piasters? "It's not enough. Double it: it is eight o'clock; go quickly: they're going to publish their requisition decree, their *bando*, during the morning." Uncle Pio balks, then gives in.

Althaus shows up, still more excited: Nieto has asked him to be his chief of staff. He has even put on his uniform, on the off chance, but he still hesitates: what does his cousin, the only political mind in town, think of it?

Through him Flora finally understands what has happened. The coup comes from a woman, a diabolically ambitious one, General Pencha de Gamarra, wife of the deposed president.

Seeing that she couldn't keep her husband in power, she had Bermudez, whom she dominates, brought in as a candidate by her partisans. But her opponents alleged that the nomination was null, and, on their side, named Orbegoso. Then the troubles began.

As to the real causes, four years later Flora declares herself still incapable of explaining them. None, here, wonder on what grounds the candidates' rights are based. In Latin America, Europeans come to foment hatreds, provoke violence "not for principles, but for leaders whom they repay by pillage." The Saint-Simonians' and Fourierists' contempt for politics finds its confirmation here. England promoted the independence of "Spanish America" in the interest of her commerce, but she failed.

The feeling that was exploited to stir up these peoples to shake off the yoke of Spain was not love of a political freedom that they were still very far from feeling the need for, nor of a commercial independence that the masses were too poor to be able to take advantage of. What was put into play against the Spaniards was hate fed by the privileges they enjoyed.

"The prodigies that liberty hatched in North America" were hoped for. But, here, needs are limited "and beggary, the inseparable companion of Spanish Catholicism, is almost a trade here." Fortunes are made, not in land cultivation, but in civil service or mining. "The mass of the population is covered with rags and has not improved its lot." They lack liberal ideas. Gold acquired by commerce or legal pillage sleeps in cellars. In these countries "the miser is a public enemy who stops the circulation of money and makes work onerous or impossible." When power extorts this gold, the masses feel they are avenged.

Since the coup, Nieto, now a general, has been dominated by a thirty-six-year-old monk, Baldivia, an ex-Jesuit "turned lawyer, writer, journalist without ceasing to be a priest." He wants to replace with one of his friends the bishop—a brother of Goyeneche in Bordeaux—an abominable miser who is getting rich on the money meant for alms. Baldivia passes, among Don Pio's friends, for a "frightful revolutionary."

Leaning out the window, Flora sees a millionaire even richer than Uncle Pio arrive, barefoot and covered with rags. He is lugging a sack of gold and is trembling, literally mad with "misers' pain, the strongest of all." Carmen stirs up his suffering still more, while he rests, posing his sack on their window.

"Oh! señor, how hard it is to give these lovely coins to people who are going to circulate them!"

"Give them? Say that they're robbing me! But they've threatened to put me in prison and while I was there my wife would be able to steal this money, so I'm bringing it to them. Otherwise I would sooner have burned it."

Under her veil, this *manto* that leaves a single eye uncovered, Flora unsuccessfully hides a fit of uncontrollable laughter.

Later the third Goyeneche brother, Don Juan, shows up, also trembling with the fever of avarice, and, seeing her carefree, sighs: "Ah! Florita! How lucky you are not to have any possessions!"

She feels herself avenged. Especially the day Baldivia publishes a second *bando* and Uncle Pio must "lend" 6000 pesetas more.

Althaus comes privately to ask her advice. What should he do? He prefers Bermudez to Nieto's camp: with whom should he march? When Flora reveals to him that her uncle, out of caution, went to assure Nieto of his solidarity, the ex-soldier of Napoleon and the Austrian emperor decides: "If such a deep politician is lined up on his side, a soldier like me can accept the post he offers."

It's a good thing he does: on the requisition list he sees his wife's name: it's he who must execute the orders. He rushes to see the general, crying that his own wife has been assigned to him, and not the wives of the members of the government. But, says Baldivia, a niece of Don Pio . . . Althaus rattles his saber and clicks his spurs.

"Comrade, in this business, it's for you to make up the *bandos* extorting money from the middle class, and for me to execute them. My sword will be as useful as your pen. . . ."

"I was," Althaus adds, "as firm as at Waterloo." The next day, he laughs with all his European's contempt for "those people." For an army of 600 to 800 men, Nieto has bought 2800 sabers, "excellent tools for cutting turnips," 1800 guns not one of which has a chance of doing harm, grenadier's woolens from the Empire, thousands of belts but not one pair of shoes.

"You have to believe, cousin, that carrier pigeons brought the news of this revolution to these jokers, the French and English captains who came hurrying to litter Peru with all these shop rejects! The suppliers of the Grand Army gave the soldiers shoes that didn't last a week: General Nieto gives them three swords instead of a pair of shoes, and not a single shako. Cross-belts, but no cartridge-pouches ... Ah! Florita, when you describe these Peruvian antics to them in France, they'll think you're drawing an exaggerated picture!" (In fact, it's the Peruvians who will cry calumny when her book appears.)

"Absolutism was in Baron d'Althaus's soul, and the results he had before his eyes were hardly designed to convert him to the republican organization," Flora comments.

Another day, Althaus gives Baldivia credit: his demagogic speeches lure volunteers into the battalions christened "the Immortals." Otherwise, Althaus would have had the job of recruiting conscripts by force. And he doesn't see himself bursting into houses and tearing fellows from vociferous mothers and young wives in tears. Flora is touched.

"Althaus, I love you! You weren't meant for killing."

"Florita, yet I have never been handsomer than at Waterloo, and there I killed."

"For God's sake, don't talk to me about your Waterloo." He was on the wrong side for Flora, too French not to have wept at Napoleon's defeat. Later, writing on England, Flora makes her cousin's ideas her own. Convinced that the revolution established French superiority in Europe, she oddly relates Napoleon's defeat to the progress of libertarian ideas, forgetting on what ideology the "despot's" conquerors were based.

> The victory at Waterloo is a providential fact. Its consequences enfranchise the Irish peasant and the helot of English mills, and in France, where the proletarians are intellectually more advanced than anywhere else, it made forever impossible the return of despotism.

A surprising assertion from a Parisian who grew up under the Restoration. But Napoleon "after the Peace of Amiens reestablished slavery in Guadeloupe, in Cayenne and attempted, by a considerable armed force, to put the Negroes of San Domingo back into servitude."

She tells the story of the Glorious Three, "her" revolution, to whoever will listen, from Nieto or Althaus to the aunts, cousins, and visitors. This, she says, was the definitive triumph of "thought over might, in France." Her listeners' admiration reinforces the historic splendor:

> The three July days excited even more enthusiasm than the taking of the Bastille: the kings likewise were more frightened than at any other phase of the revolution.

These certainties make Flora condescending toward the Peruvian coup d'état.

Yet she goes on getting excited about it: "But how does your Baldivia get the recruits to come freely?"

"He calls them Alexanders, Caesars, Napoleons; he speaks to them in Greek and Latin. He says that the eyes of Europe are on them, that in Paris they'll be jealous of their valor! Do you know that they're organizing a national guard? Undoubtedly in order to please you? Since your arrival everything here is done the Parisian way, *al uso de Paris*. God! If my comrades from the Army of the Rhine saw me moving these Peruvian dolls around!"

"If you despise them why do you stay?"

"Because they owe me 15,000 piasters. Besides, my condition is to be a soldier, and they're fighting here. I'm too old to go and sign on under the Pasha of Egypt's banner, and besides the armies of the East don't make me laugh as much. Look, on Sunday you'll see the general—compliment him on his corps of 'Immortals.' He's very flattered when you're willing to talk about war with him. He often asks me what you think of this whole business. I sometimes feel like answering that you consider him the first among the ignorant."

"Althaus, wolves don't eat each other. On Sunday I'll tell him I've never seen anything so awe-inspiring in Paris."

"Don't worry: he'll believe it."

The cousins laugh a great deal. Flora has become a respected adviser, a political brain consulted by both the officers and the landlords. Only the monk Baldivia, no doubt conscious of her irony, remains stubbornly resistant to her charm: he hates to see her among his officers.

On the other hand, the general puts a fine horse at the Parisian's disposal so she may come often to his camp, one league from Arequipa. Around the tents improvised taverns or *chicherias* have sprung up, where the volunteers of the "battalion of Immortals," as well as the Chacareros, or countrymen, get drunk on *chica*, a liquor made from fermented corn. Flora has seen it being made in the country: where there is no corn mill, the women chew the grain and spit it into the vase where it will ferment. The foot-soldiers' living conditions arouse her indignation: their tents don't even keep the rain off them.

> The Peruvian people are antimilitary: they all abhor being soldiers: the Indian even prefers to kill himself sooner than serve. My uncle told me that during his twenty years of war in Peru, each time he had rivers to cross or precipices to skirt, he lost a great number of Indian soldiers who threw themselves into the rivers or over the precipices, preferring this dreadful death to a soldier's life.

Consequently the astute monk Baldivia begins all the articles in his newspaper with exhortations like: "Arequipans! the republic of Peru expects to find in you *defenders*, no longer wanting her noble cause to be defended by what they call *soldiers!*"

THE HEROIC PROVISIONERS

On the edges of the camp, Flora discovers "a new type of woman: the *ravañas*, Indian *vivandières*."

> In Peru, each soldier brings with him as many women as he wants: there are some who have as many as four. . . . The *ravañas* are armed; they load cooking pots, tents, all the baggage onto mules; they tow along after them a multitude of children of all ages, make their mules trot briskly, run along behind them, and that way climb high mountains covered with snow and swim across rivers, carrying one and sometimes two children on their backs. When they get to the place that they have been assigned to, their first job is to choose the best spot for camping. . . . If they are located not far from an inhabited place, a detachment of them descends on it to get supplies, throwing themselves on the village like famished beasts and demanding provisions for the army from the inhabitants. When they're given them with good will, they do no harm, but if anyone resists them they fight like lionesses . . . plunder the village, bring the spoils back to camp and share it with everybody.
>
> These women, who provide for all the soldiers' needs, who wash and mend their clothes, receive no pay and have as their only salary the ability to steal with impunity. . . . The *ravañas* are not married, they

belong to no one and are for whoever wants them. They are creatures outside of everything; they live with the soldiers, eat with them . . . are exposed to the same dangers and endure far greater weariness. When the army is on the march, it is almost always on the courage, the intrepidity of these women, who precede them by four or five hours, that their subsistence depends. When one thinks that while leading this life of hard work and perils they still have the duties of mother-hood to carry out, one is astonished that any of them can stand up to it. It is worthy of remark that while the Indian soldier would rather *kill himself* than *be a soldier*, the Indian women embrace this life *voluntarily.* . . .

I don't think one can cite a more striking proof of woman's superi-ority during a people's infancy; would it not also be the same among peoples more advanced in civilization, if a similar education were given to both sexes? One must hope that the time will come when the experiment will be tried.

The last lines show that nothing, neither the comfort of the paternal home nor the diversions of civil war, can deflect Flora from her line of thought: she uses the *ravañas'* example, picturesque as it is, as much for demonstration as for "ethnological notation," as we would say today.

These women with skin chapped by bad weather, husky voices, skirts to their knees, wear a sheepskin poncho, "their feet, arms, and heads are always bare." Sometimes "scenes of jealousy" are carried as far as murder. "It is without doubt that, in an equal number of men not constrained by any discipline and leading these women's life, murders would be much more frequent."

Miserable soldiers, incapable officers, diabolical gray eminence; only the *ravañas* ravaged by alcohol and sun, women outside the law of women, Amazons of misery, have Flora's sympathy. This "revolution" in which no one thinks of improving the masses' lot, and the ugliness of power from backstage, provide solid arguments for her pessimism. The future militant is serving her apprenticeship, here, in the world of political hustlers. And also in the pettiness of the middle class in an underdeveloped country, still more grasping, straining harder toward the maximum profit than the European bourgeoisie.

Arequipa represents the nerve-center of this civil war. The region constitutes Orbegoso's fulcrum and, for Señora Gamarra, the chief obstacle to imposing the rule of Bermudez, her candidate. Flora thus finds herself at the center of this struggle for power and therefore leads a "varied existence." But . . . "nothing in all that touched my heart." To observe without participating, what a "frightful void!" For an event to move her, she needs to play a part in it. Or to love. What foolishness to have believed she would find happiness in Peru! "I wasn't living, for to live is to love." But whom can she love in good conscience, aside from Aline? She goes as far as avoiding children of Aline's age who remind her of her absent little girl. What is becoming of her daughter? What if she's sick? What if she's dead? News takes months to get here. "I fell into a frenzied despair."

Forced to lie, she is suffocating from not being able to confide in anyone. Several men allude to a possible marriage. In provincial Arequipa, this woman who is so different sets romantic young people dreaming. But "I had to appear cold, indifferent . . . *stifle the beautiful nature* that God had put in me." If she repulses admiration, it is so as not to expose herself to scandal, but also for that intimate motive that she never admits to herself: man chills her, embraces terrify her except when an impulse takes hold of her and makes her forget everything. She imagines mad passions, but, if she no longer meets any obstacles, if everything becomes simple, she draws back, invents excuses, falls ill.

She is suffering from what we would call a nervous breakdown and what she terms "a somber melancholy." Toward children she feigns such coldness that they no longer dare come near her. Toward her family she feels humiliated, "the price of their hospitality was bitter to me." The "volcanic" air of Arequipa, food she can't eat except for coffee and oranges, Aline's absence, the future blocked everywhere. . . . Where can she find a solution? In France, the humiliating poverty of women without a trade; here the false comfort of tolerated parasites. "Florita, what wit!" She can always find a clever word to make them laugh, like Cousin Carmen, but these social successes don't console her for the emptiness. In the mirror yes, her body still has its grace, her eyes and teeth their sparkle. But in her heart, a chill that she will never get over. Where will she find a man who will love her like Chabrié and whom she will love like those transients of her adolescence, the dutiful son and the handsome Indifferent? She will never again experience that "divine breath," love, women's only goal, past and present prove it. So? "I had taken an aversion to life." Why shouldn't she help her weakness destroy her more quickly? What a lovely fantasy! Suicide. Uncle Pio's chagrin. Confessions: yes, she lied, there's the truth.... "In my last moments of agony, I could wrest [a promise] from him to take my children under his protection." Her sacrifice would buy Aline's and Ernest's peace of mind. An atrocious week haunted by the ghost of young Werther; she rereads Goethe.

Then—is it the air on a morning singing with birds and breeze? —the instinct of life triumphs. For Flora, an idea always foreshadows action. Meditation is carnal. This semi-invalid's body contains a political, a revolutionary's temperament.

Between February and March 1834 she pulls out of her crisis by sublimating her desire for love into social passion. She informs us of this in her book with that mixture of lucidity and naïveté that serves as a counterweight to her obligatory lie, to the mask she wears for others. She will never indulge in unmixed self-praise. Describing this change, she doesn't invoke the ideal, and shows herself as more of an opportunist than an apostle.

At this period, she no longer believes in a God of love, but only in Evil. On this phase, her analysis would satisfy the psychologists of the following century; she calls, without naming them, on Eros and Thanatos:

> I didn't see that suffering and delight are two inseparable modes of existence in life; that one inevitably leads to the other and that it is thus that beings progress; that all have their phases of development, through which they must pass. I thought that it depended on our will to shape us for any role whatsoever.

And robbed, repudiated, pariah, "I too resolved to enter the social struggle and after having long been the dupe of society and its prejudices, to try to exploit it in my turn, to live the way others did, to become like them grasping, ambitious, pitiless."

With severity, she shows herself in the middle of this society in revolution wondering what *part* she can play in it, what *instruments* she can use. Entering *into open revolt against the order of things*, she looks for a model.

To find her role, she must see what she can use of the roles of others. The monk Baldivia? No, she couldn't show his cynicism.

Althaus? Her German cousin seeks out "strong emotions": killing doesn't affect him, but it would plunge her into "horrible agonies." Don Pio? Her uncle with his perpetual changes is still incomprehensible to her.

Capable of acting by herself, but a woman, she must still find an arm, a "sword" to act in her place, in short, a man.

Her model, finally, is this mysterious Señora Pencha de Gamarra whom she has never seen but whom they talk about so much. Didn't she become the arbiter of the republic? To rule, in Bermudez's name, this woman of destiny wants to topple Orbegoso, a pure Castilian.

She, Flora, ought thus to muster Orbegoso's partisans and, for that, find an agent. "I felt an excessive pain at being forced to have recourse to another's arm when I felt myself capable of acting."

She looks for someone who can help her and, without telling us his name, finds "a military man." Is it Nieto? It's not impossible. He repels her, but he is in a position of power. She must "inspire him with love." And then at the last moment she gives up the idea. There are plenty of excuses. She invokes, first, one which, for a woman reduced to contemplating bigamy, seems laughable: he is married. Then she gives more likely, more general reasons: "I already saw rising up against me the shades of my slaughtered antagonists . . . I sought in vain to delude myself with the fine plans of public happiness whose dream I was building."

She also implies her distaste for using the old feminine tools: coquetry without love, seduction of a man to reduce him to a tool's role. But what other outlet does this society offer her?

This ambitious scheme will also be held against her at the strange tribunal that is supposed to judge her husband and will complacently leave her crushed.

Everything changes at the end of March 1834. It is announced that General San Remo, Gamarra's chief of staff, is going to attack. Uncle Pio panics, sends the women into two convents from which Flora extracts some amusing experiences. In one, her cousin the prioress regrets the ending of the Inquisition. In the other, the mother superior, also a relative, maintains her nuns in a mischievous and luxurious childhood and gives Flora, for the night, her own cell: the most exquisite bedroom she has ever seen. For one night, with

the deep joy of changing roles, Flora identifies with a refined prioress, directing souls and lives. Morning returns her to herself.

The ladies come back to town on April 1. For the holidays, Nieto
authorizes his troops to drink . . . and now they announce that, from
the heights of Cangallo, the enemy is going to launch its assault.

Flora climbs with her *samba* onto the flat roof, has a red sunshade
set up for her, and, through her uncle's telescope, observes the
volcano, the little valley, the distance beyond. Suddenly the *samba*
points: "Madame, here they are!" Two black lines zigzag on the
horizon, near the volcano, appear, disappear, look like flocks of
migratory birds. . . .

Suddenly she hears Althaus's voice below: "Cousin, these crazy
officers are so drunk they can't give an order, and their men are so
tight they can't hold a gun. If San Remo finds out, he'll be in the
town in two hours."

Families are pouring out of all the houses, carrying their dishes
and their silver chamber pots, blankets and provisions, and rush
toward the churches and convents where their gold and jewels have
long since been stored away. Never, in these civil wars, does the
victorious enemy plunder the numerous houses of God. Their
goods are hidden, but they themselves must find sanctuary. Which
Flora refuses to do, staying with her aunt in the house which has
become a center for news.

During these hours when she can't act, at least she feels she is at
the center of action. Spies come to say that San Remo, sure of
coming into a defenseless town, has not even brought along food
supplies or water. The soldiers are reduced to chewing on the
succulent desert plants, which retain water; the imprudent leader
weeps with rage.

Flora's disdain for these vain officers, who have no sense of their
responsibilities, is added to Althaus's judgments. She remembers
the Glorious Three, "but then it was an entire people who were
fighting." Muffled in her eternal cloak, she spends the night on the
windowsill in her uncle's study; the wounded, shaking with fever,
announce defeat. Then the voices of the assembled visitors heap
scorn on Nieto.

Uncle Pio paces back and forth through the vaulted hall, speaks,
exclaims, gesticulates. When a man lights his cigar, the flame shows,
in the shadows, the white robes of four Dominicans, who smoke

with one hand and play with their scourges with the other; the silver buckles on their shoes gleam. Emaciated by their loss of gold and the uncertainty of the times, three millionaires sigh. There is indeed something to fear.

This evening, Indians and blacks, believing their masters defeated, refuse to obey. "Cruel laugh, savage look," they resist, and the master no longer dares to beat them. Under their obsequiousness, Flora discovers a hate that shocks her. Why? Isn't she too a pariah? But, as all her life, she feels herself torn between the two camps, loyal to both—and to neither. The explosion of "wicked joy" of the oppressed when faced with the oppressor's unhappiness inspires in her "the deepest contempt for the human species"; the same contempt she feels for the generals and the bigwigs in the town hall who pile blunder upon blunder, and these indecisive rich men, and her aunt who "prays for the departed in both camps."

From outside, they learn that one of Nieto's officers fired on the Arequipan officers, taking them for the enemy. The assembled notables promptly begin to sing Gamarra's praises.

After two hours of sleep, Flora, in the early morning, goes up on the roof again and sees, on the neighboring terraces, on the galleries that run around the domes, the whole town, castes and races mingled, suddenly united in the same waiting: "Can unity exist among men only in the imminence of danger?"

She comes down from her observation post again to receive Althaus, covered with blood and dust, all elegance gone, all aloofness fallen away, his voice nearly gone, telling of the command's imbecilities: Baldivia let San Remo surround him, he authorizes the enemy to take a fresh water supply. Two days of parleying, during which the population remains shut up in the monasteries and some of the monks and nuns begin to get frightened. Nieto, white-faced, "the very picture of defeat," announces an imminent battle. Flora explodes: this man is mad, another general must be named. But her uncle, who could command, washes his hands of it: why compromise himself? From her observation post, Flora sees the atrocious rout of the wounded surge in, while her aunts and cousins fall to praying, kneeling in the courtyard. In tears, the women go to recognize their own. The hospital is revolting with its dirt and negligence; the wounded lying on the ground cry out more from fear than from pain: if the enemy gets in, they will be massacred. Nieto decides to abandon the town. He declares it open and has the precious munitions thrown into the river.

Flora runs to Althaus's, has a bed and a trunk loaded onto a mule "with the help of his Negro whom I was almost obliged to beat to be able to make use of him." (Brave confession: the miserable urchin from the Place Maubert will often, when she preaches the workers' union, be confronted with these lines from her book.)

While she is busy with this, the general and his staff gallop through the town; Baldivia carries away on his horse all that remains in the treasury. Flora kisses Althaus for the first time and he leaves, accompanied by Emmanuel.

Uncle Pio leads his family into the Church of Saint-Dominique, which adjoins the house. There, monks and laity vie in cowardice. "The age of convents is over! The soldiers will come to loot here because they know where the goods are and money is their only god."

The morning mass resounds on an unlikely hodgepodge in which men, women, children rub shoulders with dogs, chamber pots, and cooking braziers. "They said mass in one corner, ate and smoked in the other."

Three days later, the enemy is still on the outskirts of town when Gamarra's four hundred men arrive to join them. What a holiday, this meeting! The soldiers are all bathing together nude in the river when Nieto's army, regrouped, swoops down on them from the top of the hill. They soon learn that a certain Colonel Escudero is mustering the enemy soldiers, and despite Nieto's last foray he enters Arequipa.

Uncle Pio, who knows how to be on good terms with all parties, goes at once to invite the new chief of staff to dinner: this Colonel Escudero owes him a lot.

Flora, dressed in new clothes, overwhelmed by what she has seen, comforted that the killing is over, enters the drawing room. Colonel Escudero sees before him a very slender woman with long limbs and neck, thick chestnut hair, sparkling eyes. Amber skin like a local woman's, but Parisian manners, assured, free and easy. An air at once touchingly sweet and feverish. And suddenly she becomes animated, throws her whole self into the conversation, holding the officer with the depths of her eyes. As for Flora—five years later she describes him in flaming words.

92

Escudero is one of those adventurous Spaniards who left fair Spain to try their fortunes in the New World; very well informed, he is, according to the occasion, soldier, journalist, or merchant; he lends himself to every demand of the moment with astounding ease, and excels in every field on which he brings his prodigious activity to bear, as if that field were the specialty of his life. Escudero has a lively wit, inexhaustible imagination, gaiety, a persuasive eloquence; he writes with warmth and, nonetheless, has been able to make himself loved by all parties.

No doubt about it. That fervor that Chabrié didn't arouse—and the praises bestowed on him reveal it by their convinced yet reasonable tone—make the phrases vibrate.

This extraordinary man was the secretary, friend, adviser of Señora Gamarra; for three years he had occupied a position of intimacy with this *queen,* an object of envy for a crowd of rivals. He devoted himself to her cause, wrote to gain support for her plans, and repulsed the continual attacks directed against her; he fought under her orders, accompanied her in her adventurous courses, and never drew back before the audacious enterprises conceived by the genius of this woman of *Napoleonic* ambition.

Fascinated as Flora is by Pencha de Gamarra, that the dictatress's glory owes so much to him adds to Escudero the charm of the gallant knight and the prestige of the man capable of accepting and aiding in a woman's triumph. Mazarin?

In Uncle Pio's provincial and sumptuous drawing room, amid the compliments due to the victor, two free beings, unencumbered by prejudices, recognize each other before they speak.

From the first visit, I was bound to Colonel Escudero; our characters were in harmony; he showed great confidence in me and kept me informed of all that went on in Gamarra's camp.

Escudero is pessimistic about Peru, the prey of "men of blood and rapine." She asks him why he offers no remedy. It's because he hasn't the authority, he says: Señora Gamarra's ambition "constantly cuts across his plans for public happiness."

"I have heard that you have great influence over this lady?"

"More than anyone else, no doubt, but very little in reality. That woman has a will of iron. She would have been a great queen in a country where her will was never crossed."

This disenchantment, what a temptation for Flora! There he is, the arm she has dreamed of.

"Ah! Mademoiselle Flora, I bitterly repent having been swallowed up like that! In the three years that I have served Señora Pencha with my pen and my sword, I have not yet succeeded in making her adopt a single one of my plans. That makes me despair; and although her haughty and despotic character makes me unhappy, I would support her with resignation if I could arrive at doing good. However, that woman needs me too much for me to think of leaving her; I must work to make her recover an uncontested authority; if I succeed, I swear that I will give up the sword and the pen for the guitar, and will play it for three months without any cares whatsoever."

Their endless daily discussions thus lead them to reexamine even Escudero's future. That he is faithful to his Lady in unhappiness is, for Flora, the sign of his nobility. At the same time a temptation.

Flora presents the whole story of her relationship with Escudero as a plan arising from ambition. "He came to see me every day; we had long conversations together. I thought I saw that, if I inspired love in Escudero, I would have great influence over him." He was one of those men, indeed, who love to serve a lady, provided she leads them to adventure, provided she satisfies their taste for both action and power. And Don Pio Tristan de Moscoso's niece could have represented, for the bachelor, a very sure trump, an alliance with that local aristocracy of the Orbegoso clan that he had to have at this point in his career.

But there was more, surely: Escudero, enthusiastic, active, tired "of the yoke that his all-powerful mistress imposed on him," is ready to change not only camps but attachments as well. Flora attracts him. As for her, for the first time, she no longer claims insensitivity.

> Escudero pleased me. He was ugly in many people's eyes, but not in mine. He could have been from thirty to thirty-three years old, was of medium height, very thin, had tanned skin, very black hair, brilliant, languorous eyes, and teeth like pearls. His tender look, his melancholy smile gave his features a character of nobility, of poetry, that drew me to him.

94

Never has she been so carried away. In the upheaval of defeat, everyone enjoys great freedom; Flora goes out alone on horseback. Relatives and friends are too worried about their own survival to concern themselves with comings and goings and with the proprieties. What happens? Does Flora finally live that "divine love, the goal of life" whose model she has been constructing since childhood? Does Escudero, like the mysterious handsome Indifferent of her adolescence, take fright at an excess of passion? It is not very likely: in the mad atmosphere of this temporary victory that provokes in each one whatever he holds most secret, releases betrayals, sacrifices, and craziness, a mad passion is always welcome. Flora, a pretty woman of thirty, youthful, tense and gay, is attractive even to the glorious ones. Even to the conquerors' leader. For San Remo is not dead, as they said. Giving out that he was wounded in the thigh, which excused his defection in the last battles, he arrives in Arequipa, stealing Escudero's victory. They even call him "general" now. When Uncle Pio decides to go and pay his respects to him, he doesn't want Flora to accompany him at first: the freedom of his niece's language makes him tremble. Escudero insists, proof that he is conquered, for Flora doesn't mind talking about this "general who's so good at hunting that he ought to have commanded an army of hares."

There they are in a drawing room where a group of officers, all standing, are scattered about before them. Cautious, Uncle Pio goes out again, and has himself announced. When they are officially introduced, San Remo, in an armchair, leg stretched out—but not the right one—asks Flora to excuse him: he is unable to get up. She observes him with the eyes of her clan for whom whiteness is the criterion:

> Thirty years old, with an open, gay countenance, *but* his hair, his beard, and the color of his skin denoted that he had Indian blood in his veins, which made him very ugly to Peruvians of Spanish blood.

The conversation becomes a joust between the Parisian and the victor, "quite original, clownish and serious at the same time." In his subordinates' eyes San Remo commits an error by guffawing with laughter. Flora laughs with him, in spite of her uncle's withering look; she feels free, appreciated, independent and—it is her defect—cannot resist noting her advantage. She says she is happy to meet a man so dreaded.

"So the Arequipans are really afraid of me?"

"To the point where they have nicknamed you the Bogeyman."

He doesn't know this word; she explains it and he laughs.

"Ah! a charming comparison! Nieto is the nursemaid, the Arequipans the children, and me, I'm the man who eats them."

"You are going to eat them?"

"God forbid! I am going to restore tranquility, work, and commerce."

"A noble goal, but how will you go about it?"

"It is Señora Gamarra's system."

She again, this Catherine the Great of Peru! San Remo explains their system: it is protectionism: foreign trade is forbidden in the country, so necessary objects must be manufactured on the spot. Thus local industry, encouraged, brings gold out of its vaults, must create work, and, earning their living, the Peruvians will consume. Flora, internationalist and free-trader, answers, forgetting even the conqueror's new rank: "Colonel, manufacturers aren't trained like soldiers and factories aren't established like armies, by force."

It is Escudero she is addressing, it is "Señora Gamarra's system" she wants to discredit. But although San Remo lacks courage, he has a political mind. Peru has raw materials; they will get machines from England, and some workers from abroad, in order to learn. This country will be industrialized only if forced to. Flora, on the contrary, thinks that it is first necessary to create needs that the Peruvians are too poor to feel, and that this can only be done by importing goods in profusion. San Remo congratulates her on defending the interests of her country, France. She protests: "Peru is very dear to me," and refers to the extraordinary development of North America. She feels she is pitting a valid system against Señora Gamarra's: but the general has power; she, on the other hand. . . .

Resorting to the weapons of the weak, she deploys her seductiveness with great lucidity; Escudero listens. She wants to charm, and it's just too bad if her tool is a general for hares. Her memoirs, for once, lack modesty.

My gaiety and my gravity charmed the conqueror so much that, when I arose to leave, forgetting his broken thigh, he stood up at the same time to escort me back. . . .

She doesn't resist the malice of begging him to spare himself and he begins to limp again. This revenge on the conquering man would be worthy of the most aggressive twentieth-century feminists; but the use of charm remains an age-old tactic.

That evening, Escudero comes to call her to account, reproaching her for her malice: "Your gazelle's eyes whose power you know so well made San Remo forget his thigh. It's not generous to laugh at him."

"Eh, you're laughing at him too?"

"Oh! me, I laugh at everything. And I didn't make a conquest of the conqueror. He told me: 'If I were free, I would ask for that young lady in marriage. I can't conceive how you boys can let her get away.' "

Marriage, to that Indian? He would have proposed to her, a Tristan de Moscoso? Flora suddenly feels the family pride is very much a part of her.

"He is overconfident."

"Since his victory he thinks everything must succeed for him."

Just a heartless, calculating love, Escudero? just an ambitious scheme?

He certainly wanted to marry her. Very probably they loved each other fully. Flora's explanations seem to be justifications after the fact: "I was then tormented anew . . . the idea of allying myself with this witty, audacious, and devil-may-care man appealed to my imagination. . . . What does it matter to me, I told myself, if I don't succeed, since I have nothing to lose?"

The reasons she will give for her resistance to "the strongest temptation" of her life are not convincing. The "moral depravation" that power breeds? The danger of becoming "despotic, hard, even criminal" like people in power? Fear of becoming the enemy of that uncle whom, despite everything, she still loves? . . . To these reasons must be added a stronger one, fear that the truth will come out. To be a bigamist in the Californian desert would excite neither envy nor curiosity. But the wife of Colonel Escudero, if he succeeded in winning power, would indeed be exposed to investigation. Scandal was almost inevitable: they would know in France whom the colonel had married . . . and then Chazal would pop up. Impossible to confess to this Spaniard that she is married, to confess to her uncle that she deceived him, equally impossible to run this risk. Nothing to lose? No doubt, but what dishonor to be driven away, perhaps even imprisoned, as a bigamist, as having claimed a false civil status. Isn't she "Chazal's wife," three times a mother? This freedom from institutions that she has stolen, this pariah's status that she can only rid herself of in appearance, not in reality, pursues her here. If her cousin Dominique, who ran away from the convent, is still a nun, what would they say about her? She renounces Escudero because he wants to marry her, because her uncle would undoubtedly have consented joyfully, liking to have ties in every camp. The wrench is very hard.

> With this man, it seemed to me that nothing would have been impossible. I have the deepest conviction that if I had become his wife I would have been very happy. In the torments arising from our political position, he would have sung me a ballad or played the guitar with as much freedom of spirit as when he was a student at Salamanca. It required again, this time, all my moral strength not to succumb to the seductiveness of this prospect . . . *I feared myself,* and I judged it prudent to protect myself from this new danger by flight. I therefore resolved to leave at once for Lima.

Uncle Pio seems quite content to be rid of this entertaining but worrisome niece. He promises to go on paying the income of 2500 francs a year. So Flora begins her farewell visits and thus can weigh the disasters of the civil war. At the Goyeneches', the sister has gone crazy, the bishop has fallen into a deep depression, sitting with his eyes fixed on his episcopal ring. When his sister tells him that Florita is going to see their brother in Bordeaux again, the prelate groans: "Our brother is happy. He lives. Us, here, they're going to kill us, kill us, kill us. . . ." Upon which the mad sister begins to scream. On that image of the horrors of war, dressed in lace, Flora leaves her father's town and family. Never to return.

11

THE FREEST WOMEN
IN THE WORLD

Lima, population 80,000, an abundance of churches, multi-colored houses, broad streets. It's winter, flowers give a festive air. Relatives introduce Flora into a "good society" where none find her eccentric, except in her speech. The women of Lima, she says, are more intelligent, healthier, more active and even—relatively—stronger than the men. Sad as she is, her cousins draw her into their frivolity. Hips wrapped tightly in the pleated *saya*, head and bust hidden by the *manto*, with a single eye uncovered, they go out. The *manto* must be black, or you would be taken for a streetwalker. Your wealth can be seen in the fineness of your embroidered light satin shoes, the refinement of your handkerchief. You are *disfrazada*, disguised, and etiquette forbids friends to recognize you.

"There is no place on earth where women are more *free*, exert more authority than in Lima. They rule there without sharing, it's from them, at any rate, that the impulse comes."

From this comes Señora Pencha de Gamarra's power. Are they beautiful? White-skinned in any case, in the aristocracy, their lips naturally red, their hair and eyes black, speaking easily with gesture of mimicry, with "an indefinable expression of wit, pride, and languor." Beautiful figures, "magnetic charm in their glance." "The women of Lima rule the men because they are far superior to them in intelligence and moral strength." But without any education, for lack of schools. Many scarcely read; some not at all. They lead an entertaining life, bullfights, theater, walks and balls. They go alone, talking to whomever they want, having fun baffling friends, sometimes their brothers and sometimes even their husbands, by managing to remain unrecognized. But as gold is the only measure of all things in this society, they also take it for the love one bears them. To give the idea of a violent love they say: "He gave her bags full of gold; he completely impoverished himself for her." It's as if we said: "He killed himself for her." Flora claims that the richest woman accepts this gold, "even if she gives it to her negresses; for her it is a proof of love."

After what she has just lived through, the beguiling frivolity of the Liman women enchants Flora. Undoubtedly she generalizes from the customs of an aristocratic and limited circle. But these women show a refined casualness whose equivalent she won't find in Paris, even at the masked ball at the Opera where she will go to play Liman women. Here she takes the measure of English cant, French *comme-il-faut* and their hypocritical limits. Her cousins drag her off to listen to two or three masses a day: isn't church the ideal meeting place? At the Church of the Infant Jesus, there are cages near the altar with dozens of birds whose twittering often covers the celebrant's voice. After which the ladies take a walk on the Paseo del Agua, on the bank of the river. They make their way there slowly, in a light carriage, then they get down and sit on a bench, holding up their skirts. Her aunt spends four or five hours there and Flora amuses herself by listening as she spiritedly tears the passersby to shreds. Or else, when spring comes, they take the air on the great avenues leading to the mountains, among the *amancais*, yellow flowers with green leaves. In spite of the wind and the sand which the horses sink into, they go, they stop, they make an appearance and rest in tents.

Arequipa, with a volcanic climate, was a doubly provincial town: far from any port, therefore far from Europe, the center of reference. Lima has an almost colonial frivolity: for the lovely ladies' prestige, their lovers must be foreigners. Flora's apprenticeship has been fruitful: she has learned that great, fond oaths—her uncle's— can conceal the worst kind of pettiness. That to be a bishop, general, mother superior implies neither charity, nor courage, nor austere stringency. That one can, like Althaus, be generous, daredevil, but utterly cynical. Or, like Escudero, be dedicated while knowing that one will fail. But above all she has become aware of her own charm. Not only does she know that men find her beautiful—Europeans had already shown her that—but that she impresses them through intelligence and wit, and can influence powerful men: her uncle, her cousins, Nieto, and even San Remo, the enemy. Finally, Escudero proved to her that a victorious and powerful man can want to spend his life at her side, and raise her to the first rank.

But what does she learn of the deep cultures of this country, the Indians and the Blacks, except for the *ravañas* and their lesson of willing risk in order to be free?

Perhaps, in a sugar mill, this cell:

> I entered a cell in which two negresses were confined. They had killed their children by depriving them of milk: both of them, completely nude, were huddled in a corner. . . . [One of them,] young and very beautiful, turned her big eyes on me; her look seemed to tell me: "I let my child die because I knew that he would not be free like you; I preferred him dead to a slave."

This "indomitable" woman arouses in Flora what lies deepest: the oath sworn to Aline to prepare for her future a different world, in which woman will no longer be a "serf by condition."

She will also remember her conversations on slavery with an "old planter," a Frenchman. In essentials it resembles the discussions around 1960 between the descendants of this type of colonialist and the supporters of African independence. Monsieur Lavalle, sugar planter, owner of a superb house, confesses that on his estate "three-quarters of the young blacks die before they reach twelve years of age," but says nonetheless: "Mademoiselle, you don't know the blacks; it's because they're lazy that they let their children die and one can't get anything out of them without the whip. I don't believe that man, whatever his needs, can be made to work regularly without being forced to. It's only by means of corporal punishment that our missionaries succeeded in getting the Indians they got together to cultivate a little land. It's the same with the blacks; and you French made the experiment in San Domingo. Since you freed your slaves, they no longer work. . . . In Roman times, Europe was covered with slaves. Mademoiselle, you talk about the blacks like a person who only knows them through the fine speeches of your soapbox philanthropists."

Flora warns the sugar-cane planter against beet sugar. He answers: "Your beets are a joke." She, with a sure sense of evolution, guarantees that the decline of sugar in the colonies will oblige them all to abolish slavery in the long run. He laughs. "All these lovely dreams are superb for poetry. But for an old planter like me, I'm grieved to tell you, not one of your fine ideas is realizable." Yet Monsieur Lavalle, Flora states clearly, "gentle and affable in character," is the one who deals the best with these questions. She gets excited about the idea of the league of English ladies "who forbid themselves the consumption of sugar from the colonies": and take "only sugar from India although it is more expensive" . . . which made Parliament, she thinks, adopt the emancipation bill.

Flora brings back from the Third World what she can understand without knowing the enslaved peoples' past. The family milieu doesn't facilitate the awakening of her conscience. In France and England she led the life of a poor pariah, a servant, a humble person. In Peru, for the only time in her life, she takes part in luxury based on slavery. Wishing for upheaval, she has nonetheless known the status of a white in the colonies.

The sum of all this is a profound disenchantment, a pessimism crossed with mystic hope. And what about the women? The *ravañas* seemed admirable to her; the Liman women, prestigious in their frivolous freedom. Just before leaving she will meet her maleficent alter ego, what she didn't want to become, the regent of Evil: Señora Pencha de Gamarra, of whom she draws too vivid a portrait to be summarized.

Escudero has one last conversation with her.

"Ah! since you left I have often thought of you; you were right and I'm beginning to believe it, I could do something better than stay in America; maybe, without these last events in Arequipa, I would even have gone back to Europe with you on this ship. I thought of it more than once, but . . . the poor president has been driven out everywhere, her cause is lost since she has no resources, her cowardly husband has gone to seek refuge with Santa Cruz, and most certainly he is going to succeed in losing the little chance that he may have. I cannot abandon this woman. . . . We fled Arequipa by night, like thieves; it was by night too that we got her on board, we feared so for her life from the murderous hate that pursues her. Santa-Cruz not wanting to receive her in his States, she is being deported to Chile; as for me, I am perfectly free. Nieto begged me to stay with him, and Santa-Cruz asks for me in every letter; but you appreciate, Florita, that Señora Gamarra, in misfortune, has the right to my devotion."

... At that moment, Escudero seemed magnificent to me!

I was going to go on, when Señora Gamarra appeared on the bridge. "Ah! mi señorita Florita, how glad I am to see you! ... I'm impatient to know you. Do you know, lovely young lady, that you have made a conquest of our dear Escudero? He talks about you at every opportunity. As for your uncle, he only acts *under your inspiration.* Ah! wicked girl, I was very angry with you when I learned that you had left Arequipa two days before my arrival. What! you wanted to see San Remo and your curiosity didn't go as far as the *wild,* the *ferocious,* the *terrible* Doña Pencha! But it seems to me, dear Florita, that if you thought the Arequipans' *bogeyman* deserved to appear in your journal, the great *bogeywoman* of Peru could surely find a place there too?"

While talking in this way, she led me to the end of the poop, made me sit down beside her, and dismissed with a wave of her hand the importunate ones who would have liked to follow us. A prisoner, Doña Pencha was still president: the spontaneity of her gesture showed how conscious she was of her superiority. Not one person remained on the poop, although, the tent being up, it was the only place where one was assured of protection against a burning sun. ...
She examined me with great attention, and I regarded her with no less interest: everything about her proclaimed an outstanding woman, as extraordinary in the power of her will as in the great range of her intelligence. She might have been thirty-four or thirty-six, was of medium height and strongly built, although she was very thin. Her face, according to the rules by which they claim to judge beauty, was certainly not beautiful; but, judging by the effect she had on everybody, she surpassed the most beautiful. Like Napoleon, the whole empire of her beauty was in her look: what pride, what boldness and penetration! with what irresistible ascendancy it imposed respect, swept along wills, captivated admiration! The being to whom God has given such looks has no need of speech to command his peers; he possesses a power of persuasion to which one submits without dispute. Her nose was long, the tip slightly tilted; her mouth large, but expressive; her face long; her bone structure and muscles were strongly pronounced; her skin very brown, but full of life. She had an enormous head adorned with long, thick hair falling very low on her forehead; it was a deep chestnut, glossy and silky. Her voice had a dull, hard, imperative sound; she spoke in a brusque and jerky manner. Her movements were quite graceful, but constantly betrayed her mental

preoccupation. Her fresh, elegant, and most elaborate dress made a strange contrast with the hardness of her voice, the austere dignity of her look and the gravity of her personality. She had an Indian silk dress, in a bird of paradise color and embroidered in white silk; pink silk stockings of the greatest richness and white satin shoes. A wide shawl of flame-red crêpe de Chine, embroidered in white, the loveliest I had seen in Lima, was thrown carelessly over her shoulders. She had rings on every finger, diamond earrings, a most beautiful necklace of fine pearls, and above it hung a dirty and well-worn little scapular. Seeing my surprise on looking her over, she told me in her abrupt tone: "I am sure, dear Florita, that you, whose style is so simple, find me quite ridiculous in my grotesque outfit; but I think that, having judged me already, you ought to understand that these clothes are not mine. You see my sister there, so gentle, the poor child doesn't know what to do but cry: it's she who brought them to me this morning; she begged me to be so good as to put them on to please her, as well as my mother and others. These good people imagine that my fortune could be rebuilt, if I would agree to dress myself in European clothes again. Yielding to their entreaties, I put on this dress in which I am uncomfortable, these stockings which make my legs cold, this big shawl which I'm afraid of burning or getting dirty with the ash from my cigar. I like clothes suitable for horseback riding, standing the fatigues of a campaign, visiting camps, barracks, Peruvian ships: those are the only clothes that suit me. For a long time I have traveled through Peru in all directions, dressed in wide trousers of coarse cloth made in Cuzco, where I was born, an ample long coat of the same material with gold embroidery, and boots with gold spurs. I like gold; it's the Peruvian's most beautiful ornament, it's the precious metal to which this country owes its reputation. I also have a big cloak which is a little heavy, but very warm; it came to me from my father and has been very useful to me among our mountain snows. You admire my hair," this eagle-eyed woman added: "dear Florita, in the career in which my conduct, my audacity, and my muscular strength often failed my courage, my position several times was compromised; I had to preserve my attractions, to compensate for the weakness of our sex, and use them to arm myself, according to need, with men's strength."

"Thus," I cried involuntarily, "this strong soul, this high intelligence, had to yield, in order to rule, to brute strength."

"Child," the ex-president said to me, squeezing my hand hard enough to kill me, and with an expression that I will never forget, "child, know well that it's because I could never submit my indomitable pride to brute force that you see me a prisoner here; driven out, exiled by the same people whom I commanded for three years. . . ."

At that moment, I penetrated her thought; my soul took possession of hers; I felt stronger than she, and dominated her with my look. . . . She perceived it, turned pale, her lips lost color; with an abrupt movement, she threw her cigar into the sea, and her teeth clenched. Her expression would have made the boldest tremble; but she was under my spell, and I read clearly all that was happening within her; in my turn, taking her hand, which was cold and bathed with sweat, I said to her in a serious tone: "Doña Pencha, the Jesuits have said: 'He who wills the end wills the means'; and the Jesuits have ruled the powerful ones of the earth. . . ."

She looked at me for a long time without answering, she too sought to penetrate me. . . . She broke this silence with the accent of despair and irony.

"Ah! Florita, your pride abuses you; you think you are stronger than I; absurd! you are unaware of the ceaseless budding struggles that I had to keep up for eight years! the humiliations, oh! the bitter humiliations that I had to bear! . . . I begged, flattered, lied; I used everything; I drew back from nothing . . . and yet I still didn't do enough! . . . I thought I had succeeded, finally reached the point where I would gather the fruit of eight years of torture, pain, and sacrifice, when, by an infernal blow, I saw myself driven out, lost! lost! Florita! . . . I shall never come back to Peru. . . . Ah! glory! how much you cost! What madness to sacrifice the happiness of existence, one's whole life to obtain you! It's only a flash, a puff of smoke, a cloud, a fantastic let-down; it's nothing. . . . And yet, Florita, the day I lose all hope of living wrapped in this cloud, this puff of smoke, that day, there will be no more sun to give me light, nor air for my chest, I shall die."

Doña Pencha's bleak expression matched the prophetic tones of these last words: her eyes were sunk in their sockets and as if suspended in a globe of tears. She looked at the serene blue sky above our heads and, wholly given to her celestial vision, already seemed no longer of this world. I bowed before this superior soul, who had suffered all the torments reserved for beings of her nature in their passage on earth. I was going to continue the conversation, but she rose abruptly, in two bounds was at the bottom of the poop, called her sister and two ladies, telling them: "Come, I feel ill."

Escudero came to me, and said to me: "Excuse me, mademoiselle, I'm afraid Doña Pencha is having one of her attacks *; and, at these times, only I can care for her."

---

* Madame Gamarra suffered from epilepsy. The attacks she underwent put her in a dreadful state: her features were contorted, her limbs twisted, her eyes remained wide open and unmoving; she sensed the approach of the moment when she was going to have one. If she was on horseback, she quickly threw herself to the ground; if she was in some public place, she retired. When she had a seizure, her hair stood on end; she crossed her hands on her head and uttered three cries. Escudero told me he had seen her have as many as nine attacks in a day. If she had lived in other times, she could, like Mohammed, have made her infirmity serve her ambition, and give her words the authority of revelation.

"Colonel, I am going to leave; I shall come back tomorrow; go quickly to that poor woman's side; she has great need of your services and your affection."

"Don't worry, Florita, I'll do everything I can."

*　　*　　*　　*

The impression with which my conversation with Señora Gamarra left me disturbed me so much that I could not sleep that night. What a crowd of thoughts assailed my mind! I had, by a power of fascination, read into the soul of this woman I had envied so long and whose life, so seemingly brilliant, had nonetheless been so miserable! I couldn't think without shuddering that, for a time, I had planned to occupy Señora Gamarra's position. What! I said to myself, such, then, were the torments reserved for me if I had succeeded in the venture I was meditating? I too would have been a prey to sufferings, humiliations, anxieties. Ah! how preferable, how much more noble my poverty, my obscure life with freedom appeared to me! I had a feeling of shame at having been able to believe for an instant in happiness from ambition as a career, and that there could exist any compensation in the world for the loss of independence.

I returned to Callao; Señora Gamarra had left the *William Rusthon* and boarded another English ship, the *Young Henrietta*, which was leaving that day for Valparaiso. When I got there, I found Escudero looking pale and dejected. "What's the matter," I said, "poor friend, you seem ill?"

"It's true, I am, I had a very bad night. Doña Pencha had three dreadful attacks . . . I don't know what you talked about with her but, since you left her, she has been in constant agitation."

"It was the first time I've seen Doña Pencha, and it's possible that in my ignorance my words, instead of calming her grief, increased its bitterness; if so, I'm terribly sorry."

"It's possible that in your ignorance, as you put it, you wounded her pride, which is extremely sensitive."

I had been chatting with Escudero for scarcely fifteen minutes when he was called; he rushed into the cabin, and I remained alone. I went over again in my memory what I had said during the previous day's conversation, put my words to the test, to discover those that might have hurt Doña Pencha; but the vulnerable spots of lost power can only be fully understood by those who have possessed power themselves and experienced its intoxication, so my research was futile. I was sorry that I had not been more reserved with a suffering that was beyond the common run of afflictions.

I was interrupted in my reflections by Escudero; he tapped me on the shoulder and told me, in a tone that sickened me: "Florita, poor Pencha has just had the most violent kind of attack; I thought she was going to expire in my arms; she has revived now, and wants to see you. I beg of you, be careful what you say to her; a single word that hurts her feelings would be enough to give her another fit."

As I went down into the cabin, my heart was pounding . . . I entered the captain's cabin, which was large and very handsome, and there found Doña Pencha half dressed, stretched out on a mattress that they had put on the floor; she held out her hand to me, and I sat down beside her.

"You are not unaware, no doubt," she said, "that I am subject to a terrible disease and . . ."

"I know," I interrupted; "but is medicine powerless to heal you, then, or don't you have confidence in the help it offers?"

"I have consulted all the doctors and do exactly what they prescribed; their methods have been without success: the older I get, the more the disease advances. This infirmity has greatly hindered me in all I wanted to undertake: any strong emotion promptly gives me an attack; you must judge by that what an obstacle this illness must have been to my career. Our soldiers are so ill-trained, our officers so cowardly, that I resolved to command myself in all important business. For ten years, and long before I had the hope of making my husband president, I attended every battle, to accustom myself to being under fire. Often, in the heat of the action, the anger I felt at seeing the inertia, the cowardice of the men I was commanding made me foam with rage, and then my attacks came on. I only had time to throw myself on the ground; several times I was trampled under horses' feet and taken up for dead by my servants. Well! Florita, would you believe that my enemies used this cruel infirmity against me, so as to discredit me in the army's mind: they proclaimed everywhere that it was *fear*, the noise of the cannon, the smell of powder that attacked my nerves, and that I fainted like a little drawing-room duchess. I wanted to make them see that I was not afraid of blood nor of death. Each reverse made me more cruel, and if . . ." She stopped, and, raising her eyes toward heaven, seemed to converse with a being that only she could see; then she said: "Yes, I am leaving my country never to return, and, in less than two months, I'll be with you." Only something that did not belong to earth could give her the expression she had as she pronounced these words. I considered her then. Ah! how changed I found her since the day before! Her cheeks were so wasted, her complexion so livid, her lips so pale, her eyes sunken and brilliant as flashes of lightning! Her hands were so cold! Life seemed ready to abandon her. I dared not say a word to her, I was so afraid of doing her more harm. My head was resting on her arm, a tear chanced to fall on it; this tear had on this unhappy woman the effect of an electric spark. She came out of her vision, turned toward me brusquely, looked at me with blazing eyes, and said to me in a hollow and sepulchral voice: "Why do you weep? Would you pity my lot? Do you think me exiled forever, lost ... dead, in fact ... ?" I could not find a word to answer her; as she had roughly pushed me away from her mattress, I found myself on my knees before her; I crossed my hands mechanically and went on weeping as I looked at her. There was a long moment of silence; she seemed to grow calmer and said, in a heartrending voice: "You weep, you? Ah! God be praised! You are young, there is still life in you, weep over me, who have no more tears ... over me, who am nothing anymore ... over me, who am dead." With these words, she fell back on her pillow, crossed her hands on top of her head and gave three weak cries. Her sister rushed up, Escudero came, all hastened to lavish on her the fondest attentions; and I, standing, near the door, regarded this woman: she made not the slightest movement, no longer breathed, her eyes were brilliant and wide open.

The captain tore me away from this sad spectacle by announcing ... that they were raising the anchor. Mr. Smith came to take me back, I pencilled two words of farewell to Escudero, and left.

As we were about to get into the carriage, we saw the *Young Henrietta* drawing away from its anchorage. I made out on the poop a woman wrapped in a brown cloak and windblown hair; she stretched out her arm toward a launch, waving a white handkerchief. This woman was the ex-president of Peru. . . .

I returned home ill. This woman was still before my eyes; her courage, her heroic constancy, amid the countless sufferings that the unfortunate woman had had to bear, made her seem greater than nature to me. . . .

To have done with Doña Pencha's story, I will say that on reaching Valparaiso she rented a very handsome furnished house, where she established herself with Escudero and her numerous servants, but not one lady in town went to visit her. The foreigners who had something to complain about all cried out against her. If two or three officers out of her old companions had the courtesy to go and see her it was a lot. This woman, proud and haughty, must have suffered cruelly in this universal abandonment, in this isolation to which hatred confined her. Condemned to immobility, it was, with the activity of her soul, being thrown alive into a tomb. Having received no letter from Escudero before my departure from Lima, I cannot specify what her sufferings were; but seven weeks after leaving Callao, she died: here is what Althaus wrote me about it:

The Gamarra woman died in Chile six weeks after she got there; they say it was from an internal illness, I think it was from fury at no

108

longer being general in chief; *the poor woman ended very sadly; her only companion was Escudero, who has returned to Peru to rejoin Gamarra so he can get up to his old tricks.*

Doña Pencha justifies Flora for having rejected the temptation of power (which, in her case, could only have led to a rapid and devastating scandal). A fine demonstration of the inconsistency of political ambitions. If royalty does not confer on her an indisputable power, the hard trade of ruling is complicated, for woman, by the need for finding a middleman; she can inspire but not assume power. Does Flora have an inkling that once accorded legal rights the lag in customs will perpetuate this state of things, in precisely the most advanced countries? Peru teaches her that customs can be, in a backward and superstitiously Catholic country, more liberal than in the land of enlightenment and revolutions. But this middle class which is tolerant of feminine loves still reserves to males at least the appearance of authority. For not having respected this rule, Doña Pencha got herself hated and trampled down. Since pleasure is just a ladies' game,* the lovely masquerader can play it. But let a Peruvian woman decide to turn her mind and her vitality toward government, and the coalition of men annihilates her. Besides, the tradition that refuses visible authority to women is so ancient that those who rebel lose control of themselves and sink into delusions of despotism. Pencha de Gamarra, her epilepsy, her courage, her ephemeral success and her abuses symbolize the impulses and dangers of reform.

But Flora has still not lost any of her irresistible urge to accomplish something. The simple life, the haven of love—myths of too ardent characters—plunge them into boredom as soon as they are no longer myths. Flora knows it when she refuses Chabrié. Her own life cannot be enough for her: she must make it radiate outward in works and acts that can influence other lives. Her physical weakness, by sharpening the anguish of death, urges her on. Thirty-two already? Childishly, she hides a few years, but feels, more and more, that she must hurry. Go back.

---

* The French *jeu de dames* also means "game of checkers."—Tr.

PART II

The Prophets' Fire

*". . . Love humanity. This lover
will never betray you. At twenty
as at sixty, you may love it passionately."*

FLORA TRISTAN

12

A ROMANTIC'S PARIS

After a "dreadful" voyage lashed with storms, with a "cursed madman" to complicate things, Flora sees Monsieur de Goyeneche and the still tender Philippe Bertera again in Bordeaux. Then she picks up her daughter in Angoulême and returns to "the only city in the world where she cares to live."

In Paris in 1835, the bourgeois king is still better entrenched. "Paris is changing, but in its melancholy nothing has changed," Baudelaire will say. Paris is ugly with construction, an old beauty in a state of perpetual renovation. The Madeleine, the Palais-Bourbon, the Pantheon, the Collège de France are finished. In the Place de la Concorde a strange piece of equipment is getting ready to hoist an obelisk from Luxor. New bridges are being put up and animal fights are forbidden at the Barrière du Combat.

The quarrel between classicists and romantics has subsided: Victor Hugo fills the boxes at the Porte Saint-Martin Theater, on the "Boulevard du Crime," nicknamed for its melodramas, with *Lucrèce Borgia*. Alexandre Dumas is making people weep with his *Angèle*. A benefit performance signals a comeback for the "divine" Marie Dorval, George Sand's friend. But the antiromantic Casimir Delavigne can also count on his bald, middle-aged public. Scribe and Auber are winning applause at the Opera.

The young people are crowding to the Taverne, the new Latin Quarter café. On July 1 Emile de Girardin brings out his new newspaper, the *Press*. A scandal: he amortizes the cost by paid advertisements, like the English. His wife, lovely Delphine Gay, soon turns to spiritualism: typical of chronic socialites with masculine pseudonyms: Vicomte de Launay. Flora reiterates that she disapproves of these women who want to be free but don't dare assume their femininity publicly. The public is excited about Monsieur Dietz's steam engine, which takes thirty-two passengers from Paris to Versailles in an hour and a quarter. At the end of July Fieschi explodes his infernal machine, without killing the king but massacring eighteen people including a sixteen-year-old girl and General Mortier. After the attempt, a law again curtails freedom of the press and of the theater.

So on her return she finds a Paris whose people of the Glorious Three, of whom she dreamed so much in Peru, have apparently fallen into apathy.

As soon as she gets there, she establishes herself with Aline first on the Rue Chabanais, near the Palais-Royal, then on the Left Bank, on the Rue du Cherche-Midi. She goes to visit her mother, whom she has not seen since their big scene. Madame Tristan didn't know about her daughter's trip. Once—when Flora thought she was going to stay in Peru—she arranged for her mother to be offered an annual pension of two hundred pounds, which "Minette" refused.

Intermittently, Chazal remembers that after all he is a father and husband and wants to know where the children are. Madame Tristan can tell him nothing: on January 15, 1834, she assures him of "the sincere friendship that I have sworn to you for life." Uncle Laisney feels sorry for Chazal, the victim of his bluestocking of a niece. The engraver drinks more and more and works less and less.

Flora, told of her husband's efforts to find the children, shrugs: he wants to assert his rights of ownership, that's all. She goes to work, completing a pamphlet begun on the boat between two bouts of seasickness: *On the necessity for welcoming foreign women, by Madame F.T.* The publishers are wary of the unknown author; she brings out her first effort at her own expense at Delaunay's, a big bookseller in the Palais-Royal. Later she will find publishers who pay.

114

In September 1835 she corrects her proofs. It is a moral essay, very simple, in which she cautiously outlines some of her ideas. In an unknown city, young girls and women should be welcomed, aided by an association funded by public subscription. The king, who has known "the misfortune of finding himself in a strange land," can only encourage such an enterprise. The women helped will be selected according to strict rules. Fifty and a hundred years later, various Women's Houses and Clubs will be organized on very similar lines. To have women of different lands associate and live together is a first step toward that "universalism," that internationalism that Flora brings back from her travels. Isn't association also Fourier's goal?

13

THE VISIONARY

Flora brings a set of proofs to Fourier in Montmartre, at 9, rue Saint-Pierre. The apostle of association in harmonious phalansteries, of the passions and free love is sixty-three years old. He has no more than two years left to live. A crown of white hair, an aquiline nose bent toward the left, blue eyes "lit by an unswerving and abstract fire," Pellarin will say. Proudhon adds: "A certain intoxication that suffused his face gave him the look of a dilettante in ecstasy." Tight-lipped, with everything in his eyes, he is already withdrawing into himself. Weary of waiting every day at noon for one of the four thousand richest men in France whom he invited to be his patrons and not a single one of whom ever answered him, he no longer sees anyone but his disciples: sometimes Victor Considérant brings him high-strung young intellectuals, Polytechnicians or literary men, who, inevitably, are more intolerant than Fourier. They think they know better than he what should or should not be said to make the movement prosper. The more disinterested and dedicated they are, the harder the disciples try to appropriate the Master, this indispensable father. They raise a barrier between him and others, direct him, censor him, develop his thought in directions he might not have chosen. Well, a vigilant master of thought needs a faithful circle to ensure that he has not lived in vain and that his ideas will survive him. As the future narrows, he desires less the breath from outside which aerates but also may disperse his thought. In the warm inner circle he feels good: made use of, but undisputed. And it is he who bows to his disciples' tendencies. Victor Considérant pushes Fourier toward the social. Sexual freedom, "omnigyny" of multiple desires, "flighty" passions of alternation, flitting between the sexes, none of these seems to him very propitious for enlarging their cause's audience. Not long ago, Enfantin, the Saint-Simonian, in a bit of sectarian infighting, secretly borrowed from Fourier this liberation of Eros . . . and his doctrine got him sent to prison. Victor Considérant is, moreover, very much influenced by his mother-in-law, Clarisse Vigoureux, that "honest man" and mentor from Besançon. He thus deliberately emphasizes the value of association in work, the adaptation of "passions" to better living among comrades and the education of children. So much so that he will never publish *The New World of Love* in full and the complete manuscript will be discovered in the Archives only in 1967.

Flora has been told that Fourier is always at home and alone at noon sharp, awaiting the mythical patron. Her appearance produces its usual effect on the recluse, who opens his door himself. Light, slender, in that era of full-blown beauties, she doesn't look her thirty-two years and her long limbs make her look even slimmer. Her eyes sparkle either with enthusiasm or suppressed tears. Her low voice, which trembles easily, no doubt charms the old man as much as her tale of Peru, slavery, the hypocritical freedom of the ladies of Lima; all that poor copy of civilization reproduced in an Indian country interests him. Flora's story, none of which she hides from him, must have fascinated him. This energetic audacity, this noble sense of adventure and the public good, this disdain for political jobbery . . . isn't it all he's looking for? Fourier, used to brothels, doesn't understand too well the need for hostels where foreign women can find shelter. The ladies—"Sapphic" or not—that he likes to "serve" have often come to the oldest female trade in the world from having found themselves alone in a strange city.

The few hours that they spend together are decisive for Flora. She will never call herself a Fourierist; soon, she will become concerned with the division of society into classes, and the need to form a "class of the oppressed." But she will always be marked by the theory of association and the passions.

The meeting takes place in August. On September 21 the pamphlet—which will not go on sale until 1836—comes off the presses and the novice author sends it to Fourier with a letter which is a profession of faith and an offer of services. A note of tenderness vibrates in it which must have touched the old man. The sentence: "What use is it, since no one understands me?" clearly means: no one, except you.

> Monsieur,
> For a very long time I had the liveliest desire to make your acquaintance and I thank you very affectionately for the warm welcome that you were kind enough to give me. I send you one of my pamphlets. It is one of my thoughts, there are several like it in my heart, but what use is it, since no one understands me? I dare to beg you, Monsieur, to be kind enough to remember me when the time comes that you have need of a *devoted person*. I can assure you that you will find in me a strength uncommon to my sex, a *need* to do good and a deep gratitude to all those who procure for me the means to be *useful*.
> Accept, Monsieur, the assurance of my highest consideration.
> FLORA TRISTAN

At the time she is living on the Rue Chabanais, from which she moves at the end of the month. And the recluse of Montmartre comes twice, in vain, as far as the Petits-Champs quarter. The second time is on October 11. The same day, an anonymous source tells Chazal his wife's new address. Paris is the city where one believes oneself safest from indiscretions; but encounters can never be ruled out, and someone who is familiar with Chazal's ways must have seen Flora. The letter announces that the wife no longer fears the husband "because she is *rich*, she says she scorns and despises you as is her wont." The letter advises kidnapping Aline and demanding from 15,000 to 20,000 francs ransom, and specifies that his wife intends to frustrate his son for his daughter's benefit. The tone, the advice given bring out the atmosphere that Flora fled, the alcoholic bohemian's milieu in which amateur pimps, professional gamblers, and café bums at the end of their resources must not have been lacking.

118

The same day the husband receives this letter—which he will take advantage of a little later on—Flora writes to Fourier. This letter of October 11, 1835 seems like a summary, a blueprint of the two patterns according to which she will live in the following years. With spelling that is still whimsical, she explains to the prophet of the passions:

Monsieur,

I have just this instant learned that you took the trouble to come twice to see me; I am very greatful to you for this mark of friendship and feel deeply sorry that I was not at home. In the two months since I moved from the rue Chabanais I have had so many vexations, family troubles, that it has been impossible for me to find a moment to go and bring my new address. Each day I probe more deeply the sublimity of your doctrine and feel more strongly the imperative need to spend time with the people who profess it. Unfortunately, I no longer know anyone now that Monsieur Berbragger seems to want to settle deffinitively in Algiers. I want to beg you to introduce me to Monsieur Considérant who has been spoken of to me with so much praise, and to two or three ladies who share our ideas. I go little into the world, which I have never liked, and my melancholy character, disagreeable for society, makes me very poor at forming relationships. I have only one abitude, it's work, the ardent wish to be able to make myself useful, to serve the cause that we love with so much purity: use me, ah! use me! you would have my infinite gratitude for it.—I dare to beg you to come and see me, I have been obliged to come and live in this neighborhood, but I hope to be able to come close to you again before long. I am always at home all day on Wednesdays, but apart from that I go out very little and in the evening one is almost always sure of finding me.

Farewell, Monsieur, accept the expression of my deep respect and highest regard.

FLORA TRISTAN
Flora Tristan, 42 rue du Cherche-Midi
(across from the War Council).

Evidence of Flora's character and of her daily life as well, at this period when she must reaccustom herself to Europe. The "family troubles" prove that she is back in touch with her mother, her son, but not with Uncle Laisney.

Madame Tristan recovers badly from her daughter's disappearance, but she has a bad conscience: this marriage, made as an escape, turned out to be a trap. The women of the family are definitely unlucky with men. She takes her Florita's part as soon as she reappears.

Flora's only sensible friend, probably in love with her—but did he ever declare himself?—the lawyer Duclos, advises her as best he can. This being of truth and courage, struggling against laws, none of which give her any rights, moves him from the first day. The lawyer knows that legally Chazal is still master. He can do anything with his children, as long as it is not proved that he is maltreating them. Maître Duclos installs Flora with the Tanéras who run a boardinghouse on the Rue du Cherche-Midi. He finds a lady, who will become a friend, to teach Aline. What she cannot learn from her, the child will learn by taking classes at a good secular boarding school on the Rue d'Assas. Later Duclos will rent, in his own name, an apartment for the young woman on the same street. Still later on, he will advise her to put a new apartment, on the Rue du Bac, in the elder Madame Tristan's name. Didn't this madman Chazal come and threaten him in his office? Didn't he accuse him of "keeping his wife"? The hope of getting divorce legalized again is not absurd, the lawyer thinks: one day this law, never abolished, will be restored. But for the moment, Louis-Philippe needs the "priests' party."

> It may well give satisfaction to the middle class.... But, for them, legal separation is enough. It is for the wives of miserable alcoholics, for defenseless creatures in the suburbs, for the only beings that the most oppressed worker can tyrannize over, that divorce would be salutary. But these women have no powerful families, no forum in which to make themselves heard.

When Flora speaks to him, Maître Duclos has tears in his eyes. He takes her hand: "I will protect you, but by slipping through the net."

That's not what she wants. So the hunted pariah's life begins again. But Flora can work on her books from now on since Uncle Pio is sending her allowance through dear Bertera. As nothing will ever be easy for her, she must also struggle to make herself known in the rare circles where she may be understood. She begins to meet some reformers, some socialists.

120

She doesn't draw her ideas from books: to extract lessons from experience is the only way for this self-taught woman. Flora knows that the great love she still dreams of will no longer be her lot. Her need to love must be enlarged to include the whole society. In her novel *Méphis* she will say:

> If you are not accessible to glory, do good, love humanity. This lover will not betray you. At twenty as at sixty, you may love it passionately.

Is this just a last resort, then? Extreme happiness belongs to "great geniuses": "What amorous pleasure can compare with Napoleon's satisfaction in making seven kings wait in his antechamber?" A fatherless daughter, a husbandless wife, a friendless mother, Flora feels she is the epitome, the model of the worst that can happen to woman. Nothing truer than her letter to Fourier: after the endless chatter in Peruvian drawing rooms, she no longer feels like wasting her time on futilities. She dreams of having serious discussions at last with those who think, write, dream, act in the direction she wants to give to her life.

Paris has a literary set in which the principal part is played by a woman. Flora doesn't know yet that because of the dislike at first sight that she will arouse in this woman the gates of the set will remain closed to her. Curiously, fate persists in producing similar dates for parallel events in the lives of these two contemporaries.

On that week in October 1835 when Chazal is planning a new offensive, a wife determined to make a name for herself and to leave a husband she can no longer stand goes through a scene like the one Flora lived through in 1832. But with the inverse result. At Nohant, on October 19, Baron Casimir Dudevant, while quarreling with his son, turns his fury toward his wife Aurore. He shouts: "Get out or I'll slap you," then seizes a gun from the rack: "This has got to end!" In this scene, as in the one between the Chazals in 1832, it's hard to tell where acting ends and irrepressible rage begins. At Nohant, friends quickly intervene. And the domestic scene enables George Sand to obtain a legal separation in her favor, with a division of property and custody of her children. Which should make her sympathetic to women in a similar case. The two women writers, with their broken marriages, meet during the following winter. At gentle Marceline Desbordes-Valmore's house? Or Hortense Allart's? In one of the drawing rooms visited by Pierre Leroux? The old Saint-Simonian from the Rue Monsigny and *The Globe* has become a Christian Socialist. A penniless widower and father, he rules over a circle of women whom he magnetizes with his piercing little eyes, buried deep under the dome of his forehead and his bushy eyebrows. Flora sometimes comes to swell this circle. Soon George Sand will be keeping Leroux.

In any case, they meet somewhere where woman and her condition are being discussed. George slips through the net of institutions, harmoniously bemoaning their iniquity. But she takes only men seriously, and a few women who can't cross her, like her dearly beloved Marie Dorval. Flora, that evening, speaks incautiously as usual, driven by her need to assert herself. To make up for having dissembled, lied for so long, she is assuming at present her role of "Being of Truth." Perhaps she states what she thinks: George Sand is the greatest female talent after Madame de Staël. But why does Aurore Dudevant hide behind a masculine pseudonym? Why avoid the adversary instead of confronting him?

Their positions, like their characters, are irreconcilable. George Sand never stops maneuvering and playing the heroine, maternal, understanding, a victim of her child-lovers' demands. Even her looks are reassuring: dark, rather plump, with a sort of country girl's sweetness. Flora, on the other hand, slender, tense, attracts attention from the moment she comes in with her blazing eyes and supple gestures. George finds her "vain." The men's admiration, the sparkling smile with which the Andalusian welcomes their homage, has a lot to do with it. "Imperious?" But over what does she reign?

A curious encounter: there are two women with parallel lives. Flora a gentleman's illegitimate daughter, Aurore the equally illegitimate granddaughter of a marshal of France. Both, badly married, mothers of a son and a daughter, understand social hypocrisy, like travel, freedom, amorous friendship, deify love, and write books.

But George, from the time she was seventeen, had in Nohant insurance against poverty and thus a guarantee against humiliation. With a paradisical adolescence, a natural gift for expression cultivated by studies and leisure, George never had to worry about her "image," how others saw her. She constructed, with her books, the image she had decided to present. She could get rid of her husband the way you get rid of a partition that makes a room look smaller: by paying a fee. She lived to be very old, very middle-class, very judgmental, and treated the Commune as her father Maurice de Saxe would have treated a peasant revolt.

Flora, on the contrary, had an unhappy adolescence and was never free of acute material worries. Her impossible husband will persecute her to the point of trying to murder her. Her maternal love has always been threatened by the law, by her husband's craziness, by lack of money, and by the strength of her vocation. The poor missionary can't take her family with her, like George landing in the Balearics with lover, son, daughter, trunks, and maid.

Flora's passionate loves have all ended badly—if indeed they began well! George's too, with the glamor of literary controversies.

Flora fought for all that her time didn't offer: independence and work for women, the well-being of the masses. But in her books, she seems, at each stage, what she is: credulous, maladroit, contemptuous of blacks. She will often add: "I did not yet know, at that time." She doesn't hide her weaknesses—that would have been easy—and goes as far as exaggerating her cynicism. After the coup d'état in Peru, she says she is "resolved to have a career," then shows herself drawing back from the compromise and cowardice implicit in that political career. George on the other hand never appears in her books as anything but good, generous, giving without receiving, passionate, pitiful, granting poor trembling men what they could die with wanting. She hides her coquetries, her lies, her treacheries, in short the age-old proven tactics of the most classically submissive woman.

Flora, who never stops describing herself, at every moment, in her truth, with her mistakes, her lies, her weaknesses, is the honest one.

But it is George who has the talent.

When Flora is dead, George, a year younger, will refuse to "bow down before death." Flora was someone she "never liked, in spite of her courage and her convictions. There was too much vanity in her." George (who had the most chaotic relations with her daughter Solange) wonders about Aline: "Did her mother love her? What mission could make her forget and send so far away such a charming and adorable creature?" She finds Aline "as tender and good as her mother was imperious and fiery."

The future will avenge Flora: her daughter will be happy and will have a tormented but glorious son. George's daughter, on the other hand, will become an elegant lady at forty, rich and yet kept by her lovers.

"Did her mother love her?" The question will assume its full irony during these years when Flora's whole life will be determined by the fierce love she bears her daughter, by her struggle for Aline.

In any case, the literary novice can expect nothing from the glorious author of *Lélia*, and Flora quickly realizes it. Besides, the mistress of Nohant hardly likes social utopias and accepts socialists only when she falls in love with them.

Flora has begun to write her memoirs. She wants to speak for the thousands of women who run away from husbands they hate without being able to free themselves legally from them. When they have recognized themselves in this book, they will face up to their place in society. A wife who has broken with her conjugal home is a pariah. Flora's ups and downs make up the *Peregrinations of a Pariah*. And there's her title. Provocative? The whole book will be. The author weighs the consequences of this provocation: she is giving out weapons to defeat herself with. To Chazal when she speaks—albeit in modest terms—of Bertera, Chabrié, Escudero. To Uncle Pio, when she tells the truth about him, herself, and Peru.

Is it her contact with the Fourierists and socialists, with Pierre Leroux, then Robert Owen, that stiffens her at first hesitant resolve? Enough of lying; she must assert herself as a being of truth, as a pariah in revolt. The insurrection must begin with a confession.

At the end of that same month of October, Chazal, who gets excited when he drinks and drinks when he gets excited, cries that he can no longer stand this situation. His wife is in the newspapers, and no one will hire him to do any more engravings. She lives in a "superb apartment" while he lives in a Montmartre slum. He was able to get his son Ernest back by threats, but Flora has always been fairly indifferent to this sickly boy, too much like his father, easily influenced, a little sly, as weak people often are. She feels truly tied,

124

in flesh and spirit, only to her daughter, who has her eyes, her hair, her manner, who is touchingly pretty and, perhaps from having been tossed about so constantly, very precocious. It's through Aline that Chazal can get at his wife, the Chazal woman, whom everyone calls Flora Tristan, blotting out her husband from this new life of hers that is taking on some breadth. He rushes to see the public prosecutor, who shrugs his shoulders: "If you want your daughter, you have only to take her; you are the father, the law is on your side."

He puts on his national guard uniform. First, it's his only clean suit. Next, it inspires confidence. To tell the truth, he no longer has a right to this uniform, but no one pays such close attention in Montmartre. André Chazal, the drunkard, is a nice guy; he rants about revenge but doesn't do anything against the government. His creditors persecute him, his neighbors feel sorry for him, and the Widow Maury whom he courts assiduously when he's been drinking, who is playing hard to get—look, she's past fifty—keeps house for him, although he hardly pays her anything.

On October 30, Chazal, in his morning sobriety, goes to the police commissioner of his district with a touching story: his wife, who is being kept richly on the Left Bank, is perverting his daughter. She wants to make a rebel out of her. The commissioner doesn't like rebellion in adult or child. He says the father has the law on his side. "But," Chazal whines, "my wife is powerful, she has friends, she adores scandal. . . ."

"If there's any trouble, bring your daughter in the carriage to me, to the police station."

So on the 31st, Chazal, with his son Ernest in tow and provided with a couple of friends—Flora will write that they were two men calling themselves police officers, but she will only know it through hearsay—lie in ambush along the way to the school on the Rue d'Assas. A hackney carriage waits at the curb. There's the Tanéras' maid, there's Aline. The father throws himself on her, pushing Ernest in front of him. The little girl begins to scream. Her father? She has never seen him. Her brother? She has no respect for him: he doesn't keep his word, and when grown-ups question him, he yields and tells everything. Aline struggles. No doubt, whether or not Chazal gave the servant a slap, he mentions the police. The poor woman doesn't know what to do between the little girl howling that she's being abducted and these men who threaten her in the name of the law. And Flora gone for the day!

When she returns that evening, she thinks she's going to lose her mind, jumps into a carriage—it's raining cats and dogs, hang the expense—hurries to Montmartre. A closed door. The neighbors tell her: the child never stopped screaming and crying, and Chazal finally took her away. A moment of anguish: if she goes to the police, they'll laugh in her face: her husband has the right to shut even her up in his slum, it is the conjugal home. Finally a neighbor asserts that he heard mention of Versailles; good, they are with her uncle, whom Flora hasn't seen since the famous scene in 1832 when she thought she would die of fury and her uncle accused her of putting on an act. The rain falls still harder; she must find another carriage, whose driver will agree to take her to Versailles. Night and torrents of rain when she gets there.

At Uncle Laisney's, they're eating dinner: Chazal obsequious, Aline silent, with her big eyes downcast. Flora bursts in, the little girl cries out and throws herself into her arms. Flora, pretending not even to see her husband, confronts her uncle, storms that he has no right to lend himself to this abduction, that he is an unworthy being's accomplice.

"I was lacking in respect for him, it's true," she will acknowledge. The uncle, her mother's brother, the only man in her childhood, turns against her. No recourse.

"I left out of respect for the uncle, so as not to make trouble in his house," Chazal will say. In any case, Flora sees her husband come into view, with the rain coming down still harder and the carriage gone. She drags and carries the child, they run on the uneven pavements. Useless to expect any help from her uncle. He has his idol the Emperor's ideas about women—minus divorce, of course. Chazal runs too, still in uniform. He shouts: "Arrest her! Thief! It's my wife! She's robbed me!" Two soldiers appear, see this national guardsman and throw themselves on the thief with the child. Flora falls. They march her to the police station. Tears and rain drench her face. Aline sobs and the commissioner doesn't know what to do. Chazal cries: "I am the husband! I don't want her to pervert my daughter! She's a kept woman, a whore! She's my wife!"

126

Flora remembers the scene of three years before—a century—when Chazal pursued her and beat her and that the law students said: "Ah! if he's your husband, we can do nothing for you!" She shakes her head. "I don't know this man. He's crazy!"

Aline understands and cries: "A madman! He grabbed me! I'm afraid. I want to stay with Mama." The commissioner feels he can't win. Chazal runs to get Commandant Laisney, who arrives with his Legion of Honor ribbon on his civilian suit.

"He's her uncle," Chazal says.

"I don't know this man," repeats Flora in a strangled tone. (She is lying? But what weapon does she have? A pariah must lie. The struggle is to have a right to truth, without vexation.) She trembles with fever, cold, fury. The commissioner decides to put the mother and child in the hospital for the night and let Chazal sort things out the next day with the public prosecutor.

In the hospital mother and child spend the night weeping. In the morning Chazal comes back with the marriage certificate, but the Versailles prosecutor, disgusted, says he can't act: let him go and get justice in Paris. The commissioner releases Flora. Men caught between the law—their trade, and pity—their humanity. Pontius Pilate is the image of man in society.

At the assizes, Flora will recall that day: all her memories take on a tinge of nightmare: "The next day, I saw the public prosecutor, I admitted to him who I was, that Monsieur Chazal was really my husband. He advised me to return to Paris as quickly as possible. I was so tired that I was afraid of not having the strength to protect my daughter. They wanted me to get into a gondola (omnibus), but my husband was following me and could have gotten in like me. Seeing a little carriage that was empty at the head of the avenue I went over to it, I said to the driver: 'Ten francs for you if you let me get into your carriage alone with my child and if you prevent this man from getting in with me.' He did it. . . ."

"The other coachmen," Chazal will relate, "threw me on the ground and beat me, trampled me in the mud, to help their comrade earn six francs." More likely they help him up; he is not so strong.

So there they are back in the lawyer's office. Duclos sighs. There's nothing to be done but put Aline in boarding school on the Rue d'Assas. Of course, it's more expensive than day school and private lessons, but since things have gone as far as the courts, they must ask for a legal separation and stay on the right side of the law while it's pending.

During this period, Chazal meets a twenty-eight-year-old lawyer, newly come from Lyon, Maître Jules Favre, a future political figure. He is known for his subtlety in court and in procedural tactics, but also for the extreme flexibility of his principles. Maître Duclos, Flora's lawyer, knows what they say in legal circles: Jules Favre defended the Lyon rebels of April 1832. The other lawyers, and most of the accused, challenged the competence of the court of justice, demanding that they be tried before a regular court. (Political defendants in France will still be making this demand in the last third of the twentieth century.) But a political trial guarantees the lawyers long articles in the newspapers and Jules Favre, they say, "extorted" from his clients authorization to accept the court of justice. The opposition knew from then on that this sideburned siren, this sweet singer of the courts was at their service only insofar as they served his glory.

Why does Jules Favre, a liberal with secret Masonic ties, accept André Chazal's case? At the request of Antoine, the respected, honored painter who judges the Salon entries? Perhaps. Besides, nobody is more like Molière's "goodman Chrysale," an artless woman-hater, than this brilliant member of the opposition. He lives on fine speeches, but claims, when it comes to women, that one lives on good soup. Which becomes contradictory if the charming person across from you also claims to have a right to fine language. Flora, whom he has never seen, exasperates him. Pariah? Being of truth? Could one be a more intolerable bluestocking than that?

He will advise Chazal, each time, to take the most repressive attitude. And, in the "memoirs" in the courts, a sanctimonious hypocrisy and calm denial of facts when material proof cannot be produced. Jules Favre, charming drawing-room wit and seducer, has, as they say, the court's ear. He knows the average judge's state of mind. A judge, even a republican one, likes order above all, and thus a family in its proper place, with the wife attentive to housekeeping, the children, especially the husband, and wary of romantic rubbish, novels—except for pious ones—and general ideas. In short,

128

feminine. A writer-wife can't be feminine: look at George Sand with her trousers and cigar. What a scandal! This Chazal woman, born Tristan, is a sad pedant. To lay down the law on ideas or art, you must have social rank, and one isn't Madame de Rambouillet nor Madame de Lafayette nor even that awful Madame de Staël without a certain life-style and position. George Sand is still Baroness Dudevant. But Chazal's wife?

During this period, Aline, at her boarding school, refuses to go out with her father who forbids the headmistress to let her go out at all. Which Flora counters by declaring that in that case she won't pay the fees anymore. The child writes Chazal a letter that is certainly inspired, but hardly reveals the sweetness of character that will be attributed to her later on. In spite of the excellent school, her spelling leaves something to be desired; but she is only ten and a half:

> Sirs,
> I have learned that you wanted to keep me a slave in my boarding school because I did not want to go out on Sunday; but I had my reasons. But I tell you that if you act as you do right now, then don't come and tell me that you love me. I will anser that it is not trew, because if it was true you would prove it to me by not making me happy, because you make mama very unhappy and me too by tourmenting us. I offer to go out with you one Sundy a month provided you notify us, because mama will not commit herself to parties of plesure. One can't waste all one's time like that. Best wishes to my brother. Farewell,
>
> A. Chazal

Such insolence must have reinforced Jules Favre's horror of Flora. Chazal, who hardly works anymore and has no place to go but the cafés, spends his time spying on his wife or having her spied on, bribing the doorkeeper, interrogating the shopkeepers, posting his agents on the Rue du Bac. By these methods he learns that Flora is completing an important work. The title *Peregrinations of a Pariah* is revealing. It seems a publisher has been found, and will actually pay to print these calumnies. The informant says that according to Flora's maid the books tells the whole story of the marriage.

On July 28, 1836, Chazal knows that Flora has gone to Châlons, to a meeting of "hopeless dreamers." His wife's public demonstrations throw the man into a demented rage. He goes with a process-server to the boarding school on the Rue d'Assas and demands the child and her belongings: the school is too expensive and too far away for him; he has found her another. Mademoiselle Durocher, the headmistress, is afraid of this madman and of the process-server: official documents do an establishment's reputation no good. She hands over Aline, her trunk, and her bed. Chazal takes her to a school on the Rue Paradis-Poissonnière, where he puts her in "private charter," as a closely supervised boarder. He will admit it: he wants to protect the child from the influence of the dreamer, the Pariah who calls herself a "being of truth." The child is not even allowed the boarder's usual daily walk. "She was most unhappy in this house; I advised her to leave," Flora will acknowledge. For two months, the girl patiently bears her imprisonment, broken by visits from her mother in the parlor with a monitor watching them whisper, huddled close in each other's arms.

On August 31, at the hour when the day students leave, Aline dodges out into the street and jumps into a cabriolet. She goes to the Rue du Bac. Flora quickly sends her on to her grandmother at Bel-Air. Chazal calls in the police, who return his daughter to him on November 20.

Police. Process-servers. Commissioners. Public prosecutors. Society serves the lord and master, whatever he may be, and condemns the fugitive wife on principle. Maître Duclos presents a request for a legal separation.

What can Flora do while she waits? Throw herself into her work, think about society, about the welfare of all. Try to forget a reality that is driving her mad.

14

THE LEADERS OF
THE MOVEMENT

Flora has just met Victor Considérant. Always, even when he criticizes her works and ideas severely, even when he hesitates to admit her among his disciples, she will go on admiring his generous disinterest and his talents.

Victor Considérant is five years younger than Flora. Son of a revolutionary soldier, he was "born socialist" in Besançon, the home of Fourier and Proudhon. While he is still in high school, one of his teachers, Just Muiron, brings this boy, very mature and very handsome for his age, to see Clarisse Vigoureux, wife of an iron-master and a Fourierist. She has one of the finest houses in town, but good Besançon society gives it a wide berth nonetheless: Clarisse is the devil. Victor takes fire. He is handsome, eloquent, generous. He serves his apprenticeship in this circle of utopia-builders, dreaming of Fourier, his absent idol. At eighteen, admitted to the Ecole Polytechnique, he pays his first visit to the Master, who sees his most secret wish suddenly granted: to find a disciple capable of spreading the doctrine. Who would resist this boy's fire, this triumphant enthusiasm, this gift for transforming words into deeds? In the school, a whole circle forms. Later, at military technical school, in Metz, he wrests supporters from the Saint-Simonians. The battle for Polytechnic graduates, between the Saint-Simonian

School and the Fourierists, ends in victory for Fourier. They nickname Victor "Phalanstery," they come and argue in his room till morning. Around him revolves a battalion of Saint-Simonian women who forget their handsome Prosper Enfantin for handsome Victor. Désirée Véret is able to keep him for some time. But his mentor Clarisse Vigoureux is still all-powerful over his mind, and will marry him to her daughter Julie.

This twenty-eight-year-old man with his infectious laugh, his naïve and happy look, and a pugnacious beard listens attentively to Flora. He has just founded *The Phalanx*. Flora tells him: "You say that society is bad, but what are you doing, what do you suggest to change it?" She brings up all the people's thirst for basic reforms. Propose a doctrine? "The people's intelligence is too highly developed today for them to be fobbed off with words any longer. Your duty to humanity is to explain, and as fast as you can, what you can do, what we all can do to make a reality of the Eden that, on Fourier's word, you have conjured up for us."

She is sitting across from him, in an armchair, the way Jules Janin will later see her: "Admirably pretty. . . . Just seeing her, with her brilliant eyes, curled up in her armchair like a grass snake in the sun, you would have guessed that she had her roots in far-off places, that she was the daughter of sunbeams and shadows." Flora isn't too proud to play the exotic and bring up Peru so often that no one realizes she was born at Vaugirard and grew up on the Place Maubert. Her intimates call her Florita the Andalusian.

Considérant, sensitive to beauty when it quivers with intelligence, says: "Write all that for us. We'll publish it."

On September 1, 1836 the letter appears in *The Phalanx*, with the reply. Nothing could be more relevant today in the last third of the twentieth century than this reply centered around desire, harmony, the relations of man to man, in short, antirepression. It expresses the essence of the basic utopia, the aspiration of man oppressed by an industrial society:

> We want an organization that allows man, in satisfying all the demands of his nature . . . to find happiness. . . . It is thus by the exercise of his powers, his passions, and not by their repression, that we claim to bring harmony to humanity.

Readers agree with Flora: theories aren't enough without organization. Through this letter she comes into contact with men and women of all trades: cabinetmakers, weavers, and painters as well as philosophers, writers, lawyers.

Her first circle of friends is formed. She meets Marceline Desbordes-Valmore, growing old indulgently. A poet respected by the literate and even recited by the barely literate, this woman knows everything about life's hardships, the complexity of love relationships, and the bond between mother and daughter. She has tremendous admiration for her husband, an untalented actor but a tender man. The public hisses? It's because Valmore is too intense, too real. People's taste is warped by "phonies." The critics jeer? It's because they can't stand originality. He can't find any work but obscure road tours? What a mission, to bring art to the masses! Flora admires Henri de Latouche's abandoned lover for showing such faithful conjugal tenderness. Marceline admires the Pariah's courage: she knows that road.

At about the same time, Robert Owen, who has been fighting for reform in England for forty years, arrives in Paris. She invites him to the Rue du Bac; he is taken there. This man, already old, represent everything she admires. He has fought, he has spoken: he was self-taught, a self-made man. A rich manufacturer. They listened to him. Then when he rejected God, society rejected him. He went to America to try out his phalanstery: New Harmony. He came back to New Lanarck in England.

There he is at sixty-five, his vigor unchanged, his eyes deepset, unblinking, with his beautiful white hair, severe features, fine sideburns following the line of his cheekbones. Flora receives him with several other change-seekers. She, huddled in her armchair as usual like a grass snake or a cat, tells him, of course: "I am a pariah," and he smiles. A man of austere habits, he is fighting for the reform of marriage and the family but hardly hopes for it any more for this generation: it's education that counts. A strong, tranquil goodness emanates from him; he speaks English, the others reply in French, a fledgling International. At that moment Flora knows Fourier was wrong to treat Owen and Saint-Simon as charlatans; socialist groups, so few in number, use each other as targets instead of uniting. How ridiculous! The trouble with Owen is that he isn't proposing any concrete organization, any more than Considérant's Phalanx. That day Flora must already be thinking what she will

133

write: "I am neither a Saint-Simonian nor a Fourierist nor an Owenist." And yet these three men, at the same time, without realizing it, become certain "that work through association is the only way to ensure men against oppression and famine."

Sitting across from Owen, she listens to him so intently, assimilating each thought, that she gives the impression of speaking with her eyes. Soon the young woman's lips are forming the words the Englishman is pronouncing; she becomes the speaker, relies on him, identifies with him. It is her strength. She is not an Owenist when, later, she rethinks these ideas, criticizes them, and sees that he is not a theoretician. But for the moment she is Owen, instinctively using what a century and a half later will be called "identification" and used in "psychodrama." Except when she wants to convince an audience and gathers all her forces together within herself, Flora practices "empathy." Symbiosis precedes criticism.

They speak of the "infant school" to which Owen is dedicated at the time and which she has visited: the Englishman explains:

"Children's intelligence revolts against the suffering that is inflicted on them, against all harsh and severe treatment."

"Then they don't give any punishment or reward in your school?"

"No. That system provokes envy, jealousies, vanity. It warps judgment. Kindness and love exert unlimited power over children. The others' expression of joy contents the author of good. A naughty child is a neglected child."

"You think that kindness alone is enough?"

"The natural consequences of good and evil are enough to draw the line. Everyone's intervention is enough to check the use of force. I have forty years of experience in this field. Believe me. The child's curiosity, well used, makes him acquire truthful habits. Truth has great power over everyone."

"But right now in England, every school from the most miserable to the most aristocratic, Eton and Harrow, uses corporal punishment."

"Formal education is antisocial. Reading and writing are simply tools with which we can communicate knowledge, good or bad, and which have no value for children unless we show them how to use them suitably. What they should be taught is to reason and judge. Otherwise, they can learn to read and write and at the same time acquire the most vicious habits. The best teaching method, if it is not applied to the best subject, remains bad."

"Your system is much criticized: you take children into school at two but don't teach them to read until they're seven or eight."

"Our method is to teach the child nothing that isn't the direct consequence of what he already knows, and knows well. His instinct and intuition must first be exercised on the objects before his eyes, which are subject to his senses. Teaching must begin with learning about the material world. The child should know how to draw before knowing the names of the things he draws."

"You are often accused of having left the ranks of Christians."

"I will rejoin them when Christianity frees itself from the mistakes with which each one encumbers it in his way. It's with a view to happiness in this world that God advises men to love each other and be united."

That evening Flora writes down the whole interview in her diary; later she will turn it into a chapter in her *Walks in London.* Her diary is the patient storehouse in which the impatient woman keeps the daily fare that will feed her books.

15

THE INCEST TABOO

Flora devotes herself to work. She has not seen Aline again: lawyer Duclos has presented the request for legal separation and feels it is better not to get into any conflict. On January 4 the little girl writes her a serene letter.

Just a few days after the interview with Owen, Flora receives a letter mailed in Montmartre. It is from Aline: her father does "things," makes "gestures"; he frightens her. They all sleep in the same bed. She is afraid. He comes home very excited. She is afraid.

Horrified, the mother runs to see Duclos who advises sending a friend whom Aline knows well, to try to speak to her. Monsieur Kervan, a landlord—thus a voter, thus honorable—will later depose at the trial: "Madame Chazal didn't understand anything in this letter . . . I went to Montmartre . . . I met young Aline in the street. She was so changed that I didn't recognize her. She told me about the attempts that her father had made on her."

So pale with rings under her immense Oriental eyes and that look of a little hunted animal . . . She repeats: "I'm afraid of him." Her replies are specific: one bed for three, with the father in the middle. He comes home late, he has often been drinking. And then: "I don't like anyone to touch me like that."

The friend wants to take Aline away, but she refuses. No: her brother is sick, she is going to get medicine, she must bring it back first. The friend slips her some money.

That evening, it is raining. Flora is receiving visitors when suddenly the servant, opening at a ring of the bell, sees Aline, dirty, wet, trembling with fever, who rushes to her mother. Maître Duclos is there: he advises putting the child to bed with something to calm her and calling in a police official in the morning to take down what the child says and file a complaint.

In the morning, Duclos and the devoted friend are there waiting for the police. At that moment someone rings the bell. The door is hardly open when Chazal rushes in, grimacing, haggard, twitching with tics, making senseless gestures: "My daughter. I've come to get her. I demand. I have the right." Flora throws herself against the door. "In a state of fury impossible to describe, she forms a barrier between her daughter and the man who had dishonored her," Duclos will write.

Flora is shaking too, she screams out everything she has been keeping bottled up inside her. The memory of that day when Chazal tried to rape her in the attic on the Rue du Fouarre. The revulsion she has always felt for him. Her horror of the man who condemned her for so long to run away from all men. He is an abject criminal.

"You're going to be arrested. Orders have been given. It's not for me to save you. Get out . . ."

She throws herself on him, she tries to push him down the stairs. Chazal trembles, splutters: "I won't leave without my daughter. I want her back. I want to see her and speak to her."

"He wanted to get the child's silence by threats or caresses," the petition will comment.

At that moment the police commissioner shows up: "If you want your daughter, you can take your case to court. I'm here to question this child. You'd better go."

Chazal will write: "In spite of my violent indignation, I showed only a cold contempt. They wanted me to run away. A fugitive, I was assumed guilty." He is also indignant that the "law official," the commissioner, distorted the child's vocabulary: "It was important to them to style her."

The police officer questions Aline who answers in detail. He puts it into his language, which is not that of the child. "She complains of touchings of the sexual parts, at the same time as with her own hands she served as an instrument of pollution. Aside from that nothing appears to establish that violence was specifically used nor that a more infamous attempt was made on her."

Chazal will be put in jail for seventy-six days at Saint-Pélagie. During this time, the suit he had brought against the headmistresses of Aline's last boarding school for letting his daughter run away comes before the court. Maître Favre, since his client is in prison, represents the plaintiff alone. Duclos, since the husband is accusing him of keeping his wife (but he also wants to have "the elderly man who was on the Rue du Bac" investigated: "is it he who's keeping her?") has asked another attorney to represent Flora. Chazal's case is dismissed and he is ordered to pay costs.

But Jules Favre encourages him to write in prison a whining memoir, a fine document, a sort of manual of sexism, as we would say today, in which he accuses his wife—without ever bringing any other proof than extracts from the *Peregrinations of a Pariah*. An odd sequence of events: the book has not yet appeared in the bookstores: so Jules Favre obviously got a manuscript or a set of proofs. The lawyer's style is so visible that Flora attacks him.

The lawyer defends himself disdainfully: what does he have to do with these squabbles? *The Court Gazette* gives an account of the trial and this crazy bluestocking thinks she's been libeled? So let her pick a quarrel with the newspaper: he and his client defended themselves normally. Chazal, having written a memoir in jail, has thirty-five copies printed and passes them out among his friends. Flora says that "the vileness of the language vies with the cynicism of the thought"? That is the opinion of a literary lady no doubt less annoyed by the insinuations aimed at her habits than by the sentence: "Her glory is not yet up to the Staëls', Cotins', and even lags behind George Sand's." She is indignant at being accused of intrigue, vagrancy, adultery? But all that is drawn from her own book, these *Peregrinations* that she presents as an autobiography; where she says "I." Besides, how she exaggerates! Maître Favre jeers. Neither this memoir nor the *Gazette* represents an "accusing voice that caused a stir in the salons, throughout Paris, France, the two worlds."

16

ENCOUNTER IN A MIRROR

The year 1837 also marks an encounter. In her novel *Méphis* she disguises the facts but lets her fantasies come through. We can reconstruct the state of the author's soul from this dialogue:

> "And why do you suffer?"
> "I suffer because I would like to be loved and nobody loves me. Life without love is arid, it is cold, empty, and I would rather die than stay long in this tomb."
> "Poor child! So you believe that in this world people with great and generous ideas are loved? Imbeciles who can be dominated, nincompoops who would swear to the superiority of shameless rascals . . . that's who gets loved."

The desperate and always unsatisfied quest for absolute love (what the surrealists will call "mad love") is a romantic convention. But, as with her social ideas, Flora's romantic writings are just a way to bring order into her emotions. Her profession of faith contains, each time, a confession.

These men about her: lawyer Duclos, Doctor Evrat, a socialist and doctor for the poor, Philippe Bertera with his long letters, don't really love her. They are charmed by the bruised grace of a victim who is never beaten, by courage combined with good looks, by a rebel with a gracious silhouette. That's not "mad love." She feels emptiness in her heart.

Her faithful admirers clamor for a portrait of her. Newspapers and bookstores would like one too. A painting would be costly; an engraving perhaps? Painting and painters have always fascinated her. Even during her marriage, in her brother-in-law Antoine's studio, she thought about art. But it is a work's meaning, its message, that matters to her; her aesthetic remains social: "The work's concept reflects the era, the individual's 'doing,' " she will write. For her, painting and sculpture are primarily a message, just like music, and were that long before printing was invented. "Picturesque language" is made up of allusions, symbols. In spite of these principles, however, she is sensitive to novelty of form but doesn't know it, and thinks she admires *The Raft of the Medusa* for its despair.

In choosing an artist to do her picture, she looks for resemblance, grace, what she calls "poetry." A portrait of George Sand pleases her. This disdainful woman, happy with her lovers, has rejected her in vain; she remains a model. The portrait is entitled *Lélia* and the artist is named Jules Laure. He is from Grenoble, is five years younger than Flora, and lives in Paris with his mother. The young woman asks him for an appointment.

The studio smells of turpentine, acid, heated steel and varnish. For her, the illusions and disappointment of her matrimonial adventure are still linked with this "artist smell." The pupil who looked admiringly at André Chazal's skill awakes in her to breathe it in.

Impossible to feel indifferent, serene, composed as a lady who wants to commission her portrait should be. The artist comes to meet her in a gray smock covered with stains and holes. Slim, muscular, robust. Aquiline nose, full lower lip. A touch of Marie-Antoinette, she thinks. Fine, clear skin, with black mustache and whiskers, while his hair is almost blond. "These two colors threw his handsome features into relief." The "proletarian," the adventurer she describes in her novel will look like this, slightly idealized: Flora rarely departs from reality. His forehead? she will call it "superb": it is high. His eyes are blue but they have a dark glint.

140

"My socialist friends have spoken a lot about you, Madame." Antique or oriental clothing is spread out on armchairs and couches: since Delacroix, every painter surrounds himself with shimmering fabrics. Jules Laure is drawing a Hamlet: it is Frederick Lemaître. He looks into her eyes and she breathes more heavily. His eyes remain on her and Flora feels as if she is floating. Objects take on fantastic, gigantic shapes. Suddenly the painter bursts out laughing.

"But you are a very good subject, by God! Do you know that until now only Madame de Girardin has proved as good a subject for hypnosis?"

"You are a hypnotist?"

"There is a set of facts there whose theory has yet to be discovered but which are incontestable. . . . Certain beings fascinate."

From the first words, there they are, deep in human profundities. Forward, great subjects. God? He doesn't believe in one; even his mother is a materialist: he wasn't raised in a religious tradition. Humanity? Injustice outrages him, but every society is unjust. So he has made a marginal life for himself: when he goes "into society" he compromises, he approves. As soon as he is alone with his pencils, his brushes, his chisel he is happy. Fight for the poor? He doesn't feel he has the strength.

Jules Laure holds Flora's hand, and she doesn't pull it away; he has not kissed her fingers. He looks at her. She speaks.

"I believe in a new law, a law of love and union. But I am afraid that like Christ's it will only triumph through martyrs' blood."

"And you feel ready for martyrdom?"

"I am a pariah, I have nothing to lose. My daughter will be strong and brave, having learned to be. I can only aspire to spread the ideas of the future. I want to live as a being of truth."

He doesn't mock her, he doesn't pat her hand and assure her she is too generous.

He takes her seriously, answers: "The artist is forced to be truthful. A painter cannot make his brushes lie. He can, for a fee, put personages on a canvas, but if he doesn't feel them . . ."

This meeting will be the first of many. Jules Laure is married to a woman whom he doesn't love; he loves only his mother . . . and love. He will love Flora. At the Salon of 1837 he will exhibit a Portrait of

Madame Flora Tristan, then, two years later, two Portraits of Madame F.T.

Always, Flora's lot will be harder than others'. Marie d'Agoult, the countess abducted by Liszt in 1835, can bear the composer's children and still entertain in Paris, where her legitimate husband lives. In this same year, 1837, she is expecting her second child.

The same with George Sand. Her husband also kidnaps their daughter; she goes to the subprefect and the police, and Baron Dudevant "very politely" restores Solange to her mother. It is because she got custody of the children along with the legal separation. And yet she lives with her lovers so publicly that another woman of letters, Girardin's wife, will write: "The story of her affections is all there in the catalog of her works." But Countess d'Agoult and Baroness Dudevant are rich, accepted by the world of letters and good society. Flora will always be on the fringe. A pariah.

Fourier's death causes this pariah great sorrow, and she avidly finds out the details: he was really a prophet according to her dream. For months she had no longer seen him. He refused to open his door even to Victor Considérant, even to a nurse. He was found on October 11 in his long coat, kneeling at the foot of his bed. He didn't want to die lying down. He had watered his house plants up to the last moment. This ending hollows one more abyss in Flora: this prophet already apart from the world, already enclosed in his inner world was still welcoming to her, recognized in her a sister in battle. She will call herself a non-Fourierist, but will never forget this celestial forehead and this look of the great beyond.

Finally, in February 1838, she gets her legal separation. An indubitably "sexist" decision: the man is accused of attempted rape on his daughter, but he gets custody of his son and Aline must be put out "in apprenticeship" since he cannot afford to pay her board. In fact, Madame Tristan senior takes both children home with her and forbids her son-in-law to approach them without a witness.

17

THE SIREN

Eighteen thirty-eight, year of the second turning point. At thirty, she went out to meet another world, slavery and near-luxury, coup d'état and mad love. At thirty-five, she enters the world of letters and ideas—and public notice. *The Peregrinations of a Pariah* finally appears in the bookstores. She writes a novel, *Méphis or the Proletarian,* where we find bits of transposed biography, but also, for the first time, fantasies, examination of which yields a secret Flora. Newspapers ask her for articles. She begins to emerge as a militant, and plans her last trip to England.

It is a terrible winter, with young people breaking their legs skating on the frozen Seine. An influenza epidemic—Flora has a mild attack—kills 1,640 in Paris in the first two weeks of February. Flora recovers her health, and her will to live, in a wool muslin dress, a velvet burnoose trimmed with white rabbit fur, a quilted hat, an imitation cashmere shawl. She goes again to see *Hernani,* in which Marie Dorval is finding new glory; at Pleyel's on the Rue Cadet she hears a pianist more moving than Liszt, a dark angel in a halo of Polish unhappiness. George Sand can't tear her eyes from this Frederic Chopin.

Hardly recovered in time for Mardi Gras, Flora is suddenly seized with a desire to relive Arequipan amusements on a Parisian scale. A crazy resolution: to go alone and masked to the ball at the Opera. No one goes there unescorted except women looking for brief encounters. Who will know? She gets out the *saya* and *manto* that served for the Liman women's intrigues, throws over it a domino sewn by her maid, and, in a rented cabriolet, goes to see this ball where Balzac, five years later, will set the first chapter of *Splendors and Miseries of Courtesans.*

Flora too is writing a novel, and wants to immerse herself in the setting where she will show her hero, Méphis—short for Mephisto, the spirit of misfortune and not of evil—meeting a noble girl who loved him, who was separated from him by slanderers, and who, on finding him again, goes crazy.

A conscientious novelist, more talented at describing reality than at pure invention, Flora has even been to visit an asylum. Madness is one of her obsessions.

We shall see her, in London, moved by an asylum prophet and later believing that to go mad for an idea is a sign of election—when it is her own idea. For the romantics, raving is the word of God. In the same way, starting with the surrealists, certain radicals will consider mental illness a sign of unconscious rebellion against social pressure.

But on this Mardi Gras night in 1838, Flora feels joyous, ardent, prey to that taste for festival that those who are deprived of it carry within them. Seldom going out, leading the most frugal existence, she allows herself this childish satisfaction of being "someone else," refusing all responsibility, she whom daily life overwhelms with responsibilities. In Arequipa, at carnival time, the highest born ladies carry baskets of imitation eggs filled with multicolored inks, which they throw from their windows onto the passersby; this vulgar amusement permits refined revenge. She has always dreamed of a theater where the spectators will be actors at the same time: this gilded hall, emptied of its seats, gives her one this evening. In fact, she tells herself, this show exists permanently in this narrow little circle that grandiloquently calls itself "the world" or "society"; the actors all think they are playing illustrious leading roles, when most of them, like the actor Valmore, Marceline's husband, get more boos than bravos.

At the Opera almost all the women, but very few men, are

masked. Only the jealous ones hide their faces, from those they are jealous of or from strangers. Groups form and dissolve, flow and ebb. A man tries to embrace the Liman woman: "Lovely mask, I know you." She imitates a Spanish accent: "I don't think so, señor, I'm only passing through." "I'm a student: if you knew how students make love . . ." "I am a nun, señor, I don't know earthly love . . ." As she goes by, she seizes a handful of confetti from a basket and throws it. A masked man whom she hits comes and grabs her. He is an Englishman; discovering that she knows his language, he won't let go. She finally gets frightened, assures him that a jealous lover is waiting for her, and says he may write to her, general delivery, giving him her maid Alexandrine's name. Less than a year later, this innocent intrigue will be brought up in the court of assizes by her husband's lawyer, to show her "dissolute habits."

Now the *Peregrinations* have come out, the press has to mention them. Victor Considérant's *Phalanx*, on announcing the book's appearance, expressed the hope that it would contain social ideas and thus come into the newspaper's domain. Does Considérant find that the story lacks ideology? He doesn't mention it again.

On January 1, the *Women's Gazette* publishes a quite unsatisfactory article. Flora knows the director, Herbinot de Mauchamps, a strange man, more ready to extol her beauty than to discuss her ideas seriously. This time again—as with Flora's first pamphlet—he praises the author's grace, her imagination, her passion, but regrets that the Pariah did not accept the peaceful retreat offered by Chabrié. As for the cause she is advocating, he fobs off responsibility for it onto "Fourierists, republicans or others."

On February 13, the *Journal of Debates* speaks disdainfully of these "lady authors" who think they are social prophets. Attack marriage? Legalize divorce? France is a Christian country and the Church must protect the family. The freedom of the ladies of Lima? If it is so enviable, why did Madame Tristan come back to Paris? *The Artist*, in which Flora has published, praises the author's talent and passion, and admits that superior women ought not to be subject to the common lot. Not a word about the ideas advocated. In short, Flora sees to what extent even social militants are unconcerned with women's cause.

On the other hand, the dreaded consequences are upon her very quickly. Uncle Pio sends word through Bertera that he is withdrawing her allowance, that she has deceived him, that she libels him and slanders Peru, her father's country. An incredible medieval touch: Don Pio de Tristan has Flora's autographed book burned in the public square in Arequipa, before the people, Dominicans, magistrates and notables. In her father's country, Flora is a witch and a soul forever damned. In Paris, she has lost 2500 francs a year, her only regular income, and is now once more an "Andalusian Pariah" (she still clings to her origins), a penniless wanderer.

Undaunted, she completes her novel. Does she write it to imitate George Sand, because novels are fashionable? Or because she needs, after writing her memoirs, to tell her deepest dreams, her fantasies, and can only do so by dressing them up as fiction?

About confessions, she says:

> The person depicted lives in us, and without sharing his opinions or his tastes, we are tormented by his anxieties, enjoy his rights, and suffer his sorrows.

But how to express that she feels herself at once a tragic man, promised to every adventure, and a woman who believes in the untrammeled rights of passion? In a novel, she can give herself two mouthpieces. *Méphis or the Proletarian, a Philosophical and Social Novel*, as she will later describe it, is at once a succession of melodramatic adventures in the style of Eugène Sue, and a declaration of intentions. "Proletarian" is a synonym for damned (as in "the damned of the earth"). You may become a millionaire; if you are a pariah, you remain a proletarian. Méphis can be a doctor or a banker, it hardly matters: born at the bottom of the social scale, he remains "socially damned," forever "proletarian." The woman, Maréquita the Andalusian, a singer, is the illegitimate daughter of a famous soprano and a great lord. The man expresses Flora's ideas, the woman her adolescent loves—romanticized—her insatiable need to love and be loved. Two volumes, 755 pages, a good document on the era's preoccupations: magnetism; the rising power of bankers and their struggle against the prejudices of the hereditary nobility; the fight between old and new rich, between the rich and the oppressed. A document, too, for psychoanalytic criticism, and a declaration of rights for the "social novel." Flora's aim is to denounce:

> So many stories are dismissed as romantic: if they were accepted as true, it would be necessary to get busy redressing the ills they point out.

Conclusion: humanity must be brought a new law,

> the law of love and union summoned to make all struggle between men cease, but like Christ's, of which it is the consequence, it will achieve its triumphs only through martyrs' blood.

Maréquita's and Méphis' daughter will become the Woman-Messiah. In reality, Flora attributes this mission to herself more and more, and slowly arouses in herself an acceptance of martyrdom. But not before elaborating her doctrine, and finding her apostles.

Méphis is unnoticed by the press, but finds a public. Strangers write to Flora.

The spring and summer of 1838, in spite of Uncle Pio's defection, are happy months. New friends come to her and so do new ideas. Nothing could be more stimulating than the gatherings on the Rue du Bac. They drink orgeat: Flora's existence is becoming more and more frugal. Almost all her companions are men. Marceline Desbordes-Valmore hardly ever comes: one goes to her. A few young actresses, a few Saint-Simonian or socialist women sometimes appear. But Flora's relations with men have always been easier. Strange relations: the "victorious struggle against the need for caresses" seems to have stabilized almost all of them at the stage of amorous friendship. Did Jules Laure go further? Probably, but from 1839 on, their relationship seems less close: Flora commissions a portrait from another artist, Tapiès.

Frigidity, inhibitions compensated for by verbal ardors, romantic declarations, deeds of unfulfilled passion. In short, green fruit; puppy love . . . at thirty-five. Or voluntary sublimation? The exaltation of sentiment, of community of action, contradicted by a possessive temperament?

To understand her, on the eve of a time when all of France, avid for gossip, is going to criticize and judge her, let us cite the strange tale of a platonic lover. Two years after his idol's death, he addresses to her what we would call an elegy to castrating or "phallic" woman:

> Flora Tristan is the superb personification of the most complete and implacable pride. She believes in Gods: do not strike out the s. Gods, according to her, is Father, Mother and Embryo. . . . Too superb to be vain, Madame Tristan asserts herself by abjuring her personality. . . . Everything belongs to her: your ideas, your work, your person, and she doesn't even value its ownership. You are nothing; neither is she. She is simple and gentle enough to throw you into fits of hydrophobia and you get out of her caressing friendships with I don't know what yen to bite someone . . . or something, especially if you've been fasting. . . .

In short, aroused, unsatisfied, and the more starved because Flora's frugality goes badly with the customs of rather gluttonous times, the lover is stuck with all his hungers. Irritated, cursing, swearing not to come back . . . and coming back the more often. The narcissistic game is extended to the intellectual domain. Humility, abolition of the individual before the common cause are aroused in private and public life at once. Abbé Constant's confession illuminates the strangeness of Flora's relationship with socialists and especially socialist workers. In their eyes, this single woman, who preaches against the indissolubility of marriage, promises free love . . . and doesn't keep her promises.

The portrait goes on:

> For pity's sake, don't try to resist her in anything. Love her, on the great and unique condition that she will not love you. Those who love Madame Tristan, she kills. She is a siren who doesn't sing, but devours. She is cruel kindly, she tortures you smiling.

This hymn to the praying mantis is published after the Siren's death by a man who has never stopped loving her . . . and gets his revenge.

Alphonse-Louis Constant, who is called "Abbé" although he was never ordained a priest, is seventeen years younger than she. Workers' son, a gifted painter, a mystic, deeply religious, he leaves the Church when he has scarcely become a deacon. A hypnotist and theosophist, he dedicates himself to Flora and will become her intellectual executor. It all begins with a portrait he does of her.

148

(Flora admits to commissioning a score of them.) After his exhausting inspiration's death, he will publish *The Emancipation of Woman or the Pariah's Testament, a posthumous work by Madame Flora Tristan completed according to her texts and published by Alphonse Constant.*

One has to know this portrait of an adorer to gauge the inanity of the accusations made by Chazal and his lawyer. The debilitated, abandoned husband, drowning in alcohol and disorder, can bear it less and less for the runaway to rule over others. He was able to force Flora—but she was only seventeen—beyond the stage of platonic effusions. How could he understand that he gave her a horror, a fear of being pawed?

So there is Flora, in 1838, in all her complexity. Less fearful about the children, whom her mother is taking care of. Yet with the constant threat of a fresh attack by Chazal ever present. She has put a *Petition for the Reestablishment of Divorce* into the hands of deputies with a liberal reputation, on December 20, 1837. She has published the *Peregrinations* and is correcting the proofs of *Méphis.* She knows she is poor again, the family allowance withdrawn. Eats little, wears dresses made by her single maid. Gets around on foot. Entertains with orgeat. Doesn't indulge in any luxury. Lives on the ground floor of 100 bis, Rue du Bac, which will become too expensive for her—around 1840 she will find more modest lodgings in the attic of number 89 on the same street. Mixes with her literary ambitions the great idea, more and more elaborate, of her vocation. She is vowed to a nonviolent social mission which still may lead to martyrdom. Ready to accept incomprehension, if she can rely on a group of friends, with, already, a tendency to make disciples out of them. Convinced—still lacking experience—that the workers will welcome her ideas with enthusiasm. In her heart she still has her need for tenderness, "expansion, caresses, love." But she has renounced passionate love. In those days, a woman of thirty-five could say that nature decreed it was time for such a renunciation: the age for a "displacement of the senses," for their giving way to intellectual activity, had come. In fact, Flora does not experience this lulling of the senses, but her withdrawal from the carnal act is the more striking for that. Escudero, in the overheated atmosphere of a civil war, liberated her for a moment. In Paris her secret fear, heightened by Chazal's persecutions, makes this ardent woman prefer to "master" herself.

MURDER

On May 20, André Chazal draws a tombstone on which he writes: *The Pariah. It is justice that you flee, that will not escape you. Rest in peace as an example to those who go astray enough to follow your immoral precepts. Ought one fear death to punish someone wicked? Doesn't one save his victims?*

On June 11, he buys two pistols, fifty bullets, two molds for casting bullets. On July 1, he confides to one of his friends that he is determined to kill his wife—"in under a week or so." The next day Antoine Chazal, the brother, the prize-winning painter, comes to his house with another friend and tries to take the pistols away from him or at least make him promise to give up his plan. Without success. They warn the mayor of Montmartre, they write to Madame Tristan, senior. To keep the engraver from plunging deeper into his madness, they ask her to send him Ernest, whom she is keeping near her. The young man—he is sixteen—comes to his father's and is frightened by his overexcited state. He warns Flora, but not until September 2. The father, upon coming in, gets out and handles his pistols. When the son questions him, his answers are confused. The boy thinks Chazal wants to find fault with Aline. But Chazal has seen his daughter twice and nothing happened. Flora understands what is agitating this man, that her books and the reviews of the *Peregrinations* that have appeared have overexcited him to the raving point. On Sunday, Chazal practices target shooting. He writes to Flora and asks for a meeting. Lawyer Duclos is worried. Flora hardly goes out anymore during the day, and alone as little as possible.

On August 8, Chazal writes a letter to the public prosecutor. This document, which should have alerted the authorities and brought about an alienist's intervention, will be read at the hearing.

Chazal demands:

> . . . protection against the influence that my wife always exerted on my daughter's education . . . isolated, without family, she is being

raised in the school of the courtesan *Pariah* . . . it is disturbing to think
. . . that the social contract being broken, abandoning me to myself,
may reduce me to suicide to rid me of the persecution of the
wicked. . . . Social justice being powerless, it is from my courage that I
must draw the protection necessary for my children's future.—Monsieur, I believe I must add this memorandum to the numerous and
useless protests with which I have burdened you. . . . Before the law,
man was his protector and his children's, it was the law of nature. I ask,
without hoping for anything, that my daughter be put, during the
course of my instruction, out of reach of all influence, until, the law
taking its course once more, she may be entrusted to a tutor who will
return her to society, to her family, to her brother. . . .

The trial, like this letter and like the preliminary examination,
shows that Chazal has sunk, not only into complete destitution, but
into a mental confusion from which he emerges only fitfully. He
contradicts himself at the assizes—as he has been doing for months—
in the same sentence.

Questioned about his reason for buying the pistols, he is evasive:

Chazal: "My reason is obvious, I bought the pistols to defend
myself . . . in case of aggression instigated by my wife."

The President: "Were you not on the contrary obliged to make
use of them to murder your wife?"

Chazal: "Yes, it's true, I wanted to use them against my wife . . .
or rather against another person. Hate and vengeance do not enter
my heart. I did not want to strike my wife . . . I wanted to spare her
and strike lawyer Duclos, her accomplice, the artisan of all the
infernal machinations that have reduced me to despair. I also
wanted to make another individual perish."

The latter's name will never be pronounced. No doubt because
Chazal never succeeded in identifying this mythical lover among
the men who visit Flora. Little by little the obsession harries him
night and day. His "wife has many friends, she is listened to favorably, relied on, recommended . . . Lawyer Duclos is *the law*. . . ."

Twice Flora finds her husband on her track. The first time on the
Rue du Bac: he has nothing in his hands, she says. The second time
on the Rue de la Planche as she gets out of a cabriolet. "I saw that he
had both hands in his pockets, in which his pistols were visibly

outlined." He asks for a meeting. She is so obviously afraid that the driver makes her get back into the carriage. Chazal will claim that she took offense "because he addressed her familiarly as *tu*."

Flora will add that her brother-in-law, the renowned painter, could, by intervening during this month of August, have "saved both families from the dishonor that is striking them." A food and wine merchant on the Rue du Bac relates that between August and September Chazal came to his place seven times in three weeks. He noticed his attitude. He stationed himself near the door, observing the street for two hours, or reading "with great tranquility." Chazal completes the story: "It was a geometry book."

The President: "So, at the moment when you were preparing to carry out your thought of murder, you were calmly reading a geometry book?"

Chazal: "Yes, Monsieur, it's very simple. You try to give your ideas another direction. You have to read something, after all."

The Montmartre woman who kept house for him certainly played a sentimental and tender part in Chazal's life: for fifteen months he hadn't given her the ten francs wages he promised, but, she says at the trial: "I have been paid since I claim nothing." She will bear affectionate witness in his favor and prove very reticent on the subject of Aline. He writes to her, at the end of August:

> My dear mama Mori,
>   Weary with my long domestic troubles, weary of laying my sorrows on all around me and on my children, I am resigning myself to emancipating them by putting them under a tutor's protection. If prejudices did not stifle in you the interest that you have always shown in me, I would press your kindness into service. I beg you not to desert the house. I highly recommend Ernest to you. Keep me informed of all that happens. I commend myself to my brother. If the prejudice that dominates everything inspires him with repugnance, go to Monsieur Roublon, the printer-lithographer, to have Ernest taught lithography. He seems to be getting a taste for it. If consent is necessary and a signature is required, let me know. Whoever is good enough to keep my place at my children's side will have eternal rights to my gratitude. I hope that my confidence, so many times betrayed, will not be misplaced this time. When it's all over, forget me, that is my last wish.

So he has no intention of killing himself: "Let me know." Besides he will say he "is not cowardly enough" to kill himself. On the other hand he knows he will be cut off from society: the "prejudice that dominates everything" is the one that censures murder, or did his brother turn away from him after the business of Aline?

He also writes to Madame Tristan senior.

On September 4 he dictates to a public scribe a letter that he signs Pommier, the name of the secretary of an association of literary people, summoning Flora to a meeting at his house at eleven at night. On Maître Duclos' advice, the young woman goes to Pommier's at nine and learns that the letter was a fake, meant to lure her into the street when there were no more passersby around. So Flora is on the alert.

On September 9, Chazal takes his pistols and leaves his slum on the Place de l'Abbaye. Ernest questions him, he answers: "If I am pushed to the limit I will strike quite a blow."

On September 10 he leaves at nine in the morning and at eleven arrives at the food and wine merchant's where he installs himself with his geometry book.

He will say at the hearing: "Before putting my plan into execution, how many battles I had to go through with myself!"

When he met Flora at twenty-three, the man was already boastful, spineless, vain, and demanding, but was desperately seeking tenderness and above all social recognition. The failure of the marriage, the stir created by his wife, the picture of him given by the *Peregrinations* completed a mental degeneration that had already begun before the young wife's flight. What was sick and bitter in Chazal crystallized into rancor against the woman he could neither make happy nor vanquish. Here the times were important only in that it was impossible to get a divorce. But the divorce trials and murders of passion of our time are just what reveal the permanence of this type of vengeance.

In the shop, Chazal hardly eats and doesn't drink: "I didn't want anyone to think I needed to get myself worked up by drinking wine," he will say at the interrogation.

At two thirty in the afternoon, Flora is still not there. He goes out onto the sidewalk. An hour later, Flora, who is on her way home, sees him coming to meet her, his hands in his pockets; she discerns the shape of the pistols.

Here, the murderer's and the victim's versions diverge a little.

> *Flora:* "I was coming home. I was about forty steps from the house when I saw him coming toward me. I knew at once from his expression that he was going to kill me. I could have escaped him by running into a shop. But I had suffered for too long. I was resigned to my fate. He came within five or six paces of me without making the slightest move, then went a little past me. I followed him with my eyes, turning my head. The moment I lost sight of him, he fired. I fell on my side. I saw that he had another pistol. Fear gave me strength. I got up again, I flung myself into a shop that happened to be open."
>
> *Chazal* (when, at the beginning of the trial, they summarize for him his wife's deposition at the preliminary hearing, he amends it with, *The Court Gazette* says, "an incredible self-control and calmness"): "The thing is quite simple. When I saw her, I went up to her, not nicely, not badly, without even an atrocious air. I did not pass her, but when I reached her side, I fired my pistol shot. It's very simple, I don't see why the fact has to be embellished with a lot of details."

The shoemaker Marteau, into whose shop Flora comes and collapses, hears her murmur: "Arrest that man. He's the one who's murdered me. He's my husband." Chazal will say that he let himself be arrested without any resistance. Marteau, other people in the neighborhood, passersby, come up and disarm him. They ask him if he intended to kill himself with the second pistol. He answers, "No, I am not cowardly enough for that. They wouldn't give me justice. Well, I gave myself justice. Justice slept, she will awaken. I am content now. I am happy. I had had a weight on my chest for several days. I am comforted. Take me to the police." And he gives the address of the police station. The shoemaker Marteau comments, "I have never seen such sang-froid. This calm, this impassivity—I can only attribute it to madness."

Chazal tells the people around him that he is a victim. That they've gone as far as sending his children to murder him.

The President: "What do you mean by that?"

Chazal: "I was talking about moral murder. They wanted my children to murder me morally. It's much more painful than physical murder. You die a thousand deaths instead of dying once."

He will still say, on learning that Flora is wounded and not dead,

154

that he is "very angry" about it. During this time the crowd is guarding him in a concierge's lodging. The police come to take him. He offers no resistance.

Flora is carried home: it's on the ground floor, no stairs to climb. Doctors Lisfranc and Récamier quickly rush in. The bullet is lodged "under the left breast"; they can't get it out. The rumor runs from the street to the cafés, from the police to the papers. A woman of letters murdered by her husband right out on the street. Is it George Sand? But that very evening she comes to the Opera with Liszt and Madame d'Agoult: they are giving *Benvenuto Cellini* by Berlioz, an unknown genius whom Liszt is helping. So it isn't George. Then who? Flora Tristan? What has she written? The next day's papers mention *The Peregrinations of a Pariah*. An autobiography? Curiosity sends them to the Palais-Royal bookstalls. The books disappear. Soon a new edition will have to be brought out.

Little known on September 10, Flora Tristan is famous on the 12th. Sympathetic neighbors have spread a thick layer of straw under her windows to muffle the noise of horses and wheels. Elegant carriages jam the quiet Rue du Bac: everyone who knows Flora comes at the news.

On September 15 *The Thief* tells the whole story, summarizing as usual the other papers' articles. It concludes: "Today, Madame Chazal's condition is alarming in spite of the care of the doctors who have ascertained that considerable damage was done in the region of the heart by the bullet which they have been unable to extract."

On September 20 they amend: "Madame Flora Tristan's condition, which we had announced as very serious—according to the other newspapers—is on the contrary quite satisfactory."

On the 30th: "The news of Madame Flora Tristan's health is quite reassuring. The doctors have permitted this lady to go out in the garden, and even to go out driving. Before long, she will be able to go back to work."

On October 10: "Madame Flora Tristan is well enough to have taken up her literary tasks again. The last issue of the journal *The Artist* contains a remarkably erudite work by her, entitled *On Art Since the Renaissance*." (In fact, this work was finished at the time of the attempted murder.)

In the beginning of December, the newspapers rise up against the

155

severity of the courts of assizes: in all of France, there have been forty death sentences in three months of which three were pronounced in two sessions in Paris, plus many sentences of hard labor.

When the preliminary examination is over, Chazal is sent before the court of assizes: attempted homicide with premeditation upon the person of his wife.

Lawyer Duclos and all the men of law are explicit: the "vile being," the man to whom Flora is "riveted by the chain of legal slavery," may lose his head.

Then Flora, barely allowed to go outside, gets up and goes to bring the liberal deputies—the ones to whom she presented her *Petition for the Reestablishment of Divorce*—a *Petition Leading to the Abolition of the Death Penalty.*

This move creates a sensation. *The Law*—a judiciary journal—like *The Court Gazette* with which it will merge—announces the act on December 19. Flora has had her text printed up along with the covering letter: she will send it to every member of Parliament. The press comments on the nobility of the victim who is trying to save her would-be executioner.

From their previous dealings, Flora knows Jules Favre well enough to know that he will turn the business around, try to make her into a defendant, turning the murderer into a victim. The *Peregrinations* will be his arsenal. Let us note that Flora herself wrote Uncle Pio the truth about her parents' marriage. In the same way she delivered to her enemies, with her *Memoirs,* everything in her life that didn't conform to the laws, the customary prejudices, the hypocrisy that the jurors at the court of assizes certainly share.

18

THE TRIAL

The courtroom in which President Deglos is sitting with his jurors on January 31 and February 1, 1839 is full by nine in the morning.

Perfumed ladies showing off this winter's hooded pelisses and velvet hats invade the room as far as the counsel's benches an hour in advance. They smile at Jules Favre: he is under thirty, he has just "come up" from Lyon, but he is already a darling of the drawing rooms.

Yet sympathy goes to the victim, and curiosity too. Many of the women and men present have read the *Peregrinations*. The boldness of this amazon running alone about France and on the seas, refusing to play a leading role in Peru after having been a chambermaid in England, seduces the romantic spirits. Some titled persons recall that "illegitimates" of good family held high rank under the Old Regime. A bemedaled man speaks of Bolívar: in *The Artist* on July 31 Flora Tristan published the letters to her mother and the story of the friendship between the Libertador and Don Mariano de Tristan, her father.

The jurors are in their places. The accused is called.

The Law describes him: "He is a small man. He wears a long coat of a pale yellow." *The Court Gazette* calls it a "man of property's coat," finds the defendant's face quite insignificant and notes that he calmly arranges his numerous papers. "No emotion whatever and he seems to note with satisfaction the curiosity he is arousing."

Chazal constantly presents himself as a victim who is denied justice and even the right to keep his children. His aim, he says, was to prevent his daughter from suffering the influence of "the being of truth," "the courtesan Pariah."

In his vocabulary, as in Flora's, the word "proletarian" is used for the poor, the victims, as opposed to those in power. For him, "society" is the mass of contemporaries: the people. Which leads to: "I needed to justify myself before society as a whole, for we poor proletarians live much more with society than with judges."

Lawyer Duclos, for him, is the devil. Didn't he go so far as to seize Chazal's furniture, so he could be declared destitute before the process-servers and have his son taken away from him?

"I was told: your wife has many friends, she has influence, so she won her case. I would have needed process-servers to get the judgment that gave me custody of my son enforced. But you can't approach these gentlemen without money." There is laughter in the courtroom. The president gets his revenge: "So you shot your wife to avoid legal fees?"

Asked, "Do you have precise facts of immorality to bring against your wife?" Chazal is evasive: "No. I'm not one of these husbands who go and wait behind doors to catch his wife in the act. No."

"So, you haven't any facts?"

"They refused to make an investigation for me."

He has nothing against his wife but her writings. It's from them that Jules Favre expects to draw his best points. The *Peregrinations* are there, on top of his brief, with many pages marked.

The public is waiting for Flora. The court is adjourned: she fell ill on the way to the Palais.

When the session reconvenes, that slender, lithe little figure has trouble pushing her way through toward the witness stand, the crowd is so tightly packed. A long whisper follows her: "The Pariah," "Flora." She comes slowly forward. Not for an instant does she look at the accused on his bench; he, on the contrary, flushes, goes pale, mutters, fidgets, doesn't take his eyes off her.

158

"She is elegantly dressed, her green velvet hat adorned with a black veil graciously frames a face remarkable for the delicacy and regularity of the features. A pretty Grecian nose, lovely black hair, expressive eyes, a Spanish complexion pleasantly attract one's attention," says *The Law*. And the *Gazette:* "She is short . . . eyes of the purest beauty give a very characteristic expression to her face whose tanned complexion reveals her origin ever so slightly."

She has scarcely arrived when she feels faint. She is given a seat. Several times, a guard brings her a glass of water. Her voice is almost inaudible. When asked, she gives her age as thirty-two—she is thirty-six: Flora has been taking four years off her age for a long time and will go on doing so, even during her mission, until the end.

Her whole life will be reviewed; it is as if she had to relive everything. Sometimes she gets her dates mixed up. Sometimes she is outraged. But, it is obvious, she has vowed not to crush Chazal.

"You married the accused in 1821. Before that weren't you at his place as a colorist?"

"No, Monsieur. I worked for him, but I was at my mother's. I only went to his house to take some lessons."

Her whole life. They talk about the scene in 1832. Uncle Laisney, the "old soldier," is called to the stand. He repeats that in his opinion the scene was staged.

Flora protests: "He doesn't understand how the sight of Monsieur Chazal irritated me. A look, a gesture from him was enough to exasperate me. . . . We were talking about the children, the discussion became heated like all those I had with my husband. . . . He made as if to take a chair, to beat me, that's when I took a plate and threw it. It didn't hit him. My uncle has always believed it was an act."

Yes, her whole life is unveiled, described in detail, dissected, before these lovely ladies on the lookout, these sarcastic men, and Jules Favre who is trying every moment to make her out a criminal: the story of her flight from home; and what did she live on from 1825 to 1829, when her uncle started sending her money? and does she have documents from the Englishwomen who employed her? Can she at least give their name? . . . She refuses to answer. That past is dead.

Jules Favre begins to read, from the *Peregrinations*, the part that

can most outrage the jurors. Chabrié's love. The scene where, with
the sailor's head pressed against her, Flora tells herself that if she
married him in California she would love him more. . . . Then the
lawyer, with ringing voice and arms flung out, declaims before this
comfortably settled bourgeoisie:

> I hear people comfortably established in their homes, where they
> live happy and honored, cry out against the consequences of bigamy
> and cry shame and contempt upon the individual who is guilty of it.
> But what makes it a crime if not the absurd law that establishes the
> indissolubility of marriage? . . .

Flora interrupts:
"I have never spoken in praise of bigamy. That's in bad faith."
Jules Favre: "Mr. President, I demand that the robe I wear be
respected."
Flora: "Mr. President, I am here as the victim of an attempted
murder and Monsieur Chazal's lawyer is trying to make a defendant
out of me. I have never spoken in praise of bigamy. In my despair, I
wrote a few lines against the indissolubility of marriage. I have
expressed my views on divorce in a petition that I presented to the
Chamber."
Flora thinks she will never get to the end of these hearings.
The President: "What are your current resources, Madame?"
Flora: "My uncle makes me an allowance of 2500 francs." (It is
already no longer true, but no one knows.)
The President: "Your writing must bring you something?"
Flora: "Very little, monsieur. I have been writing for only fifteen
months."

A new emotion: they call her son Ernest, who, distressed and
upset, contradicts himself and recants.
The next day, she has to hear Jules Favre describe the marriage
like a true-romance story:
"In his studio was a poor young girl, very poor, without even
wood to keep herself warm, but beautiful too, very beautiful, with
an ardent imagination, a burning heart. They found each other.
They loved each other." Flora interrupts the defense counsel's

speech—an unprecedented act: "No! no! I never loved Chazal and he knew it." Jules Favre gets even by reading the story of her affair with Escudero.

The attorney general waives the indictment. He contents himself with saying that the facts brought up by the defense were not all true. That it is impossible to acquit the defendant of attempted premeditated murder. But that he asks for a verdict of extenuating circumstances.

The court condemns Chazal to twenty years of hard labor (which will be commuted to imprisonment). Before she dies, Flora will summarize this experience: "I was shot because I protested against infamy, and society branded me while condemning my murderer reluctantly."

The marriage, for this reason, is over. A month later Flora and the children are given permission to use the name Tristan only, since Chazal's has been infamously disgraced.

She has nearly died. She has paid the highest possible price for what she will now—for five years—possess: freedom.

19

A PASSION FOR SOULS

Restored to life! She really thought she would die, and now this death has given her freedom. The children in her name. The *Peregrinations* reprinted, selling and making *Méphis* sell. Other projects. Newspapers asking for articles, publishers ready to advance her money on future books (the publisher of the *Peregrinations*, however, has not kept his promises and she has to sue him). Since Uncle Pio's defection, money has again become the adversary that must be defeated each month, so that soon Aline will decide to be a milliner and ask to become an apprentice.

Cousin Goyeneche in Bordeaux is also outraged by the *Peregrinations*: he has been duped, he is described as a narrow-minded, dry-hearted bigot; he no longer answers letters. When Flora tries to see him in 1843, he turns her from his door.

Money is hard to find for a lady-who-writes without a man to support her. Flora knows now that in Paris you have to be someone, a "character," to get anywhere. It's the legal scandal that has made her known as a writer. At a period when "advertising" has scarcely begun to take hold—through Girardin's paper—in the press—she foresees the power of publicity.

It is a year for worldliness. Jules Janin, a brilliant journalist, a man

162

of versatile opinions but easily moved by feminine grace, describes her as "admirably pretty" and prints this opinion. He invites her to his parties. Maybe he hopes to make an impression on her? Their relations, it seems, remain purely social.

After the trial, the Pariah suddenly finds herself "in fashion." A dashing young Parisian "must have danced with her at one of Jules Janin's routs," a publicist says. The ex-Abbé Constant, very young and already in love, draws a pleasant portrait of her, which is published at the end of 1839 in flattering company, in *The Beautiful Women of Paris and the Provinces Accompanied by Letters to Beautiful Women*, an anthology of great names, from Balzac to Victor Hugo, from Théophile Gautier to Gérard de Nerval. The letter to Flora Tristan is not signed, but could be by Jules Janin. He will describe her later with her "long black hair that could serve as a cloak," with her "ardent flaming cheek, fine white teeth, regular and provocative." Desire is manifest here: "Grace in her bearing, firmness in her step, austerity in her dress." But he either knows her well or understands her with the intuition of frustrated desire: "young as she is, *one understood at once that she no longer worried about pleasing or being found beautiful;* for her that was a forgotten or *despised* feeling. . . ."

So she loves only "souls." But a good number of them, it seems, and in every walk of life.

Thus there will be the false Abbé Constant, whose bitter canticle explains many enthusiasms, and many aversions too.

At the same period, Jules Laure's portraits of Flora are a success at the Salon. The engraving that her future adherents will buy will be taken from one of these pictures. Her relations with the painter —who everyone assumes is her lover—will last, but on what level?

Her diary and letters contain more social facts than intimate confidences. Flora only makes her private life public cautiously, since the too direct confessions in the *Peregrinations* deprived her of her comfort. The hero of *Méphis* will look like Jules Laure and have his interest in magnetism, but everything will be disguised, transposed. Nowhere will Flora speak of the lawyer Duclos, or of Doctor Evrat, although she sees them constantly. We shall soon see the mystery that surrounds the writer of the preface to *Walks in London*. It is often necessary, therefore, to read between the lines.

Her correspondence reveals the whole gamut of toughness, humor, charmer's graces, and insolent irony of which this multiple being is capable.

The "souls" that she loves with all the intensity of a castrating—she calls it "ennobling"—censure of the will are, in contrast, numerous. We can see in her sudden uncontrolled rages, her fits of discouragement, and even in her certainty that she is chosen for a mission, for an apostleship, the price she pays for her rejection of sexuality. In a few years, her overexcited nerves will lead her to the threshold of ecstasy.

Among these tyrannized "souls" is—already—a prophet. The sculptor Ganneau with his bumpy forehead is in the process of inventing Evadism, a religion of an Adam-and-Eve couple of equal redeemers.

A friend takes Flora to the Ile Saint-Louis where, in the back of a courtyard, a shed serves as a studio for the artist and a temple for the religion. He is carving in stone a symbolic androgyne, and is beginning to sign himself "Mapa (mater-pater) who was once Ganneau," preaching that everyone should call himself by the linked first syllables of his mother-and-father. For Flora that would be Théma. He comes to see her to convince her to become the Mater, the Eve of the founding couple. Flora knows how equality of the sexes is twisted, whether it's Saint-Simon or Fourier who proclaims it. She saw Enfantin, the father of a future Couple, ruling over a harem of unequal women in the name of a future equality. Even Fourier grants women every moral and mystical superiority, but not equal rights in the city, in society. And Saint-Simon's former secretary, Auguste Comte, gets rid of equality by taking off his hat to it through the cult of the Virgin-Mother Clotilde de Vaux, his platonic mistress. So she wants to defeat Ganneau in his very doctrine. To convert him to a real equality. Like any dogmatic, he resists.

Later Ganneau, a bearded magus, will have disciples: the editor Hetzel, the reformer Félix Pyat. The archbishop, worried about this talk of a new religion, will file a complaint. Then—but Flora will no longer be there—the great wind of '48 will blow away this mystique, and Ganneau will be left alone in his studio-temple, his "apostolic pallet."

Flora speaks of Ganneau in revealing terms to Traviès, a painter she also wants to commission a portrait from:

> I have already told you that I loved this man's soul in a very special way. My soul has never rested so softly in another soul as in his. Since the day I saw Ganneau, I have not left him for a second; he walks by my side like a brilliant star on which my sight rests with love.

The adventure with Ganneau—brief and entirely spiritual—is repeated exactly with Constant: tyranny, the requirement that you "love her provided she doesn't love you." Taking possession of one's mind and work, one's whole being, although—says the unhappy lover—she doesn't even "value" this possession, and the sudden coldness, the abrupt cruelty. Here, she admits it and—let the future psychoanalyst rejoice—gives the motive:

> However, according to my opinion that one must *destroy the individual without pity,* on the eve of my departure I hurt Ganneau in the cruelest, the most barbarous way! I will tell you some day how many inner tears each one of the drops of sweat I saw running down his forehead cost me. But, by Christ, it will not be said that I yield now to the weakness of the group. I wanted to *crush*—so as to assure myself I was really strong—alas, I'm not as strong as I thought. I think continually of the pain I caused him and his pain breaks my heart.

A fine analysis of sadomasochism? The point where a clear mind meets an unconscious whose disturbing repressions erupt now and then? All the psychoanalytic clichés of "phallic, virile woman" and "virile demand" can be applied to Flora.

Another letter to Traviès comes back to her feelings for Ganneau, but also shows us how she sees herself and especially how she wants to be seen:

> London, this 16th of July '39.
> Dear brother,
>   I received your good little letter of June 27. It is just what I expected, I am rarely wrong. I too would like to see you again. As soon as I get to Paris, we'll have to talk for many hours on many subjects so that you can take possession of my physiognomy. Start thinking now about what you will have me wear, in what attitude I'll be posed.

Think, my dear brother, that this portrait will be of the *Pariah*, a woman born Andalusian and condemned by society to spend her youth in tears and without love! This poor woman murdered, and dragged before judges not as a *victim* but as a *culprit!* This woman whose heart, whose brain, whose lips are still boiling with youth and whose hair is white! Traviès, one of my dearest wishes is to have my *portrait very like.* That's why I had it done more than *twenty times,* twenty times a failure! They pester me to pose here. Ridiculous! *Me!* Pose for an Englishman!

You haven't spoken to me about Ganneau! You haven't *sent me his portrait!* We don't know each other, you don't know how I love that man. I have begged one of my friends, very good and very devoted, to go and see you. Receive him with friendship, his heart is worthy of yours. He must explain to you how I want you to frame G.'s portrait with a wide band of black velvet. Have it ready for my arrival which will be in the first two weeks of August. I still have many things to say to you and I feel that we will become very good friends. But I have no more room. Farewell, I shake your hand and kiss your forehead as a sign of union and brotherhood.

Flora.

Traviès de Villers is fashionable. Since he helped found the *Charivari* and the *Caricature,* he sketches, draws, and paints the heroes of "Literary Life" as well as Balzac's imaginary heroes or the simple participants at dinners in town.

But a new shutter is opened on Flora's mysteries with another letter that she will write in London, on August 1, 1839, as she watches the English rain come down. This letter was published by André Breton in *Surrealism Itself;* he makes no comment on it. Neither he nor we have been able to discover who this mysterious Olympe was, nor how long this feeling lasted. But we already see the quasi-visionary trance, the mystique of feeling that will possess Flora for the five years she has left, taking shape. When in the last months of her life she shows us her disciple, Eléonore Blanc, the little laundress, crying: "I love you!" we are dealing with the same total sublimation.

LETTER TO OLYMPE

You know very well, strange woman, that your letter made me shiver with pleasure. You say that you love me—that I hypnotize you, that I put you in ecstasy. You're making fun of me, perhaps? But watch out—I have long wanted to make a woman love me passionately—oh! how I'd like to be a man so as to be loved by a *woman*. I feel, dear Olympe, that I have reached the point where no man's love could satisfy me—a woman's, perhaps? . . . Woman has so much power in her heart, in her imagination, so many resources in her spirit. But will you tell me that, *since attraction of the senses cannot exist between two people of the same sex,** this love, this passionate exalted song that you dream of, cannot be achieved from woman to woman? Yes and no. One reaches an age when the senses change place, that is when the brain embraces everything. But all that I am writing is going to seem madness to you! Alas! You don't understand God, woman, man, nature as I do. This winter I absolutely must give *a course* for *you* and two or three others who are the most sympathetic. I am now living an immense—and complete—life, I must make you believe in my life, dear Sister. My soul, you might say, has come out of its envelope: I live with souls. I identify so much with souls, especially when they are nearly in unison with mine, that I take possession of them, so to speak. I have possessed you for a long time—yes, Olympe, I breathe through your chest and through all the pulsations of your heart. One day, and it is going to horrify you, I must tell you all that you regret, all that you desire—and from what ill you suffer. The power of *second sight* is the most natural thing—that's all. Simply a soul that has the power to read what is happening in other souls—hypnotism is nothing but the superiority of one individual's fluids over the other's fluids. You see, darling, that for me love, I say *real love*, can only exist from soul to soul. Now, it is very easy to conceive love, two women can love each other, two men *idem*. All this is to tell you that, at this moment, I feel an ardent thirst for being loved. But I am so ambitious, so demanding, so greedy or so fastidious at the same time that everything I'm given doesn't satisfy me at all. My heart is comparable to Englishmen's mouths—it's a pit in which everything that goes into it is crunched, is crushed and disappears. . . .

"Since attraction of the senses cannot exist between two people of the same sex . . ." An astonishing sentence for a woman of thirty-six who has known Paris working-class districts, asylums, prisons, houses of correction for prostitutes in London, the lazy feminine communities of Lima, Peruvian convents, in short all the places where lesbianism has developed at all times. Can Flora, the explorer, the observer, the "great reporter" of a Latin-American civil war and of English life, the theoretician of society, still be so

---

* Author's italics.

naïve? And if not, does she say this as reassurance or provocation?

Did Flora ever "go on to the act"? Was she a lesbian? It's very unlikely, just as she could never have made love with men, except with the "beloved souls" of exalted disciples. This cerebral woman desires—Constant admits it as well as the letter on Ganneau—the tyrannical possession of spirits: the body is important to her because it is indissolubly tied to the soul. At once a spiritualist and a materialist, she makes herself a Gods (she clings stubbornly to the "s") to suit herself, "Father, Mother, and Embryo," and surely doesn't believe in body-soul duality.

IDEAS AND MEN

The uplifted language, the invocation of the divine in acts of social propaganda, the interest in global systems also represent currents of the time. Neurotic—but less so than Fourier sinking into his final paranoia, less so than Wilhelm Reich the Freudian a hundred years later—Flora never loses the sense of the possible. We shall see to what extent her system—which foreshadows Marx's on so many points—is established with scrupulous realism. Moreover, this hypersensitive, hypertense woman has known all her life how to confront the most concrete obstacles.

She has known society, its justice, its police, she will know them until the end, through the brilliance of drawing rooms or the charm of friendships as well as through constant, petty vexations and the most sordid repression.

Flora's last years are spent in social and psychic exploration of a rare intensity. Neither Fourier nor Saint-Simon had as deep, as personal experience of all walks of life, and especially the poorest.

Her London friends see her as Doctor Fée, a professor at the Strasbourg Medical School, will see her a few years later. This representative of the comfortably established intellectual middle class finds in her

> a strange air which one quite quickly became used to. Her mobile features, always animated by benevolence, were pleasing at first sight. She had a soft voice and easy speech; she could tell a story well and in a lively manner, giving proof of education and shrewdness. Sensitive to excess, she often had tears in her voice when she spoke of devotion,

charity, friendship, and especially the sufferings that she could not alleviate. Good-natured and loving, she remained a primitive; the excitement of her life, her misfortunes, her travels, her literary ambitions, the disappointments of vanity, the flight of youth were unable to affect this excellent nature.

These characteristics are those of the times; let us detach from them the personality which is now asserting itself: precise observer and future Woman-Messiah.

Turgid style? In this period both poets and revolutionaries were constantly using the strongest word. A century later poets will look, on the contrary, for the rare and virgin term, but Marxists of all persuasions will keep up the habit of overstating, outbidding. Verbal violence becomes an accompaniment or substitute for physical violence.

Let us not be surprised by the constant sublimation, the aspiration to ecstasy. Nor by the attraction toward "magnetism" or hypnotism that Jules Laure communicated to Flora. The need to "live ahead of oneself" (as Louise Michel the *Communarde* will say in the following generation) embraces everything: change in social institutions, but also the need to communicate above and beyond the rational. At the end of the century the upholders of "scientific" socialism will exclude the cult vowed to exaltation, to the call of the soul, to replace it with the secret culture of group excitement, then with what in the long run they will christen "personality cult." Meditation, contemplation, fasting, drugs, everything that neo-Hinduism, Eastern, and Far Eastern trends will give the opponents of overindustrialization is already found in romantic socialism. Enfantin went to Egypt to look for the Mother, lived as an Egyptian, and ended up undertaking the construction of the Suez Canal. Considérant will go to Texas to set up a phalanstery in the wide open spaces—and come back to become a deputy. Flora is keenly interested in workers' salaries and the ways and means of various groups, but she also feels it is vitally, urgently necessary to reaffirm her courage, to find new strength in communal ecstasy.

This pioneer—inevitably—fully reflects her era: those who read the socialists: Saint-Simon, Fourier, Considérant, Owen, Cabet also and especially read the romantics. Anglomania already reigned in intellectual circles through the writers: Sir Walter Scott, Byron,

Shelley, whose work was the mother's milk of romanticism. Now it is beginning to reign over socialist thought through England's economists and her Chartists, opponents who call for a new social contract. Every twentieth-century Marxist knows by heart his "Marx's three sources: the German philosophers, the English economists, the French socialists." Born fifteen years before him, Flora Tristan still draws from the same sources, especially the first two. Germany was brought to her in Peru by a man who wasn't in any sense an intellectual: her cousin Althaus. She devoured Goethe rather than Hegel whose work is known to her more through hearsay. On the other hand, she knows her England. And above all, she adores Ireland and the patriot O'Connell. In France his fire, his fury have dethroned even the prestige of the Polish martyrs.

Ireland becomes the subject of the students' elegies and social novels. When in some serial a young person falls for a modern Hernani, he is nearly always Irish. O'Connell's popularity annoys an Englishwoman, Mrs. Trollope, who publishes a *Paris and the Parisians,* a nice little travelogue about the lower- and middle-middle class, students, and bohemians. Mrs. Trollope is astonished and irritated to hear Lamennais claim that the Irishman O'Connell is an idol of British youth. Mrs. Trollope is a Tory: for her the Irish patriots remain low-level agitators, common-law criminals improperly disguised as heroes. For Flora, O'Connell stands for Méphis, the victorious pariah, the proletarian, in other words, the triumphant outlaw. It may be while meditating on O'Connell that the Pariah recognizes the necessity of defending a class: the oppressed, in a happy country. She will apply to workers and women, word for word, what O'Connell threw at the Irish: "Bury your old hatreds in a common grave. The moment has come to unite and recognize your strength." For a long time, for her, women have been the most oppressed group. But through her experience of poor districts (the Place Maubert in childhood, the lodgings that followed), her observations in Peru, and her current reading, she knows that every rich country contains a "nation" of the miserable and oppressed.

Then she gets the idea of taking one of these countries, showing how two classes form absolutely distinct communities within it, opposed in everything, and how even a common language and history fail to unite them: the oppressors are full of culture and apparent artistic refinement and lead an attractive and pleasant existence. The oppressed fail at restoring their strength—as the blessing says—the better to serve, not God, but the rich. They die of it before their time.

So Flora decides to explore England, or rather London, in all its social classes, to show the French the state of society.

When did she meet the man who, in the first editions, signs a long preface "A.Z."? These are not initials, but a symbol: everything from A to Z. He is an economist. He obviously approves of the Charter proposed by the Working Men's Association in 1838. In Flora's circles, this "People's Charter" is much debated. Many of its proposals could be applied in France: universal suffrage; secret ballot; abolition of poll taxes; parliamentary indemnity (which would allow men without fortunes to become deputies). The Working Men's Association (matrix of the First International), moreover, has a sort of fascination for "workerist" French socialists, among whose ranks Flora can be counted. This association composed solely of workers prefigures her Workers' Union.

As to the writer of the preface, Flora calls him "a friend of mine who has had ties with the English government for thirty years." But she has a way, at this period, of sliding lightly over, somehow misrepresenting acquaintances and personal friends. The contents of the preface: the emphasis on political economy, education, the colonial system in India, all suggest someone, a Frenchman, she met before she left: Joseph Rey.

At a sale of "romantic documents" in Paris in the late 1950s, I was able to read a letter in Flora Tristan's handwriting. Simply signed Flora, it spoke to her correspondent about "marvelous cooperation" in her work, and in "a cause equally sacred for both" and about the "affectionate veneration" that "the best educated and most remarkable workers in England" feel for the correspondent. She alludes to "mutual experiences in places abandoned by God." Dated 1840, the letter was addressed to "Monsieur Joseph Rey, counselor to the Court of Grenoble." Which makes him the possible, even probable, author of this introduction.

Joseph Rey, a Grenoble magistrate, born in 1779, was then sixty. A republican, he was condemned to death in absentia for contempt

171

of court in 1820. He went to England, where he lived in Owen's circle. In 1826 he gave the London Owenists twenty lessons on "General Principles of Legislation Based on Moral Philosophy and Political Economy." Included in the amnesty, back in France, he translates Owen, makes his principles known, is the first to introduce the word "cooperation" in French. He shows the necessity of giving "the greatest political influence to the class of the needy by misfortunes or to that of individuals who have only the barest necessities." He soon turns toward Fourierism, spends time in Paris with Filippo Buonarrotti and Etienne Cabet, but also with Michel Chevalier. In 1835 he publishes *Letters to My Wife on Early Childhood Schools Known as Halls of Asylum.* Now Flora, in London, has high praise for these schools and proposes establishing them in her "Workers' Union Center" according to the same principles.

In his memoir and explanations, Chazal spoke of his wife's "relations" in the judiciary world which made its judicial processes illusory. Was he alluding to Joseph Rey (as well as lawyer Duclos)?

Rey, with his many experiences and disinterested courage, must have been charmed by the young woman. And Flora, before leaving for England, must have looked for contacts and introductions to the Owenites and Chartists.

During one of his frequent trips to Paris he may have come to the Rue du Bac and she will have explained her plan to him: To go to London, which she knows well, look at every walk of life afresh, present a true and living picture of them. A document. A report. Through the example of England, most industrialized, richest, most technically advanced country and the one where the proletariat is the most important, she can show the French the necessity for change. One can see better from farther away.

20

LONDON: SOOT AND RAIN

In London, Flora boards with a lady her friends have found. She knows England well—it is her fourth trip—she has seen it slip from the opulence that triumphed over Napoleon to the pauperism of the ravenous factories. It is summer: everywhere the sky is "composed of sun, stars, blue cloth." Here "for six days the weather has been fierce as a pirate, as Chabrié would say. It hasn't stopped raining for an hour." The sky is a "nest of gray feathers" which sometimes fall in swirling clouds. The storm prevents the mail from arriving. Her hostess's dinners are pitiful. Invitations in town cost too much "in dress, in carriages, in shillings for the servants, and finally in boredom." Flora swears this country is for the ducks. "As for the men condemned to wallow in mud and the unfortunate *cats* which haven't even the innocent pleasure of walking on the gutters, their existence is profoundly miserable." The Englishwoman gives Flora tea, which she detests, or gin which she can no more drink than whiskey or porter. Disappointed by "the sacred conjugal Name," the good landlady is resigned to a fate "which is that of the majority of Englishwomen—and to console herself for it, she is courageously devoted to drink." But she helps Flora by accompanying her on her explorations among women. When she goes into the slums, two friends, Chartists, or "Owenites," serve as her bodyguards, armed with stout canes.

On her arrival, Flora is received in smart houses. She sees the French exiles surrounding "His Imperial Highness Prince Napoleon-Louis Bonaparte, direct pretender through his mother to the throne of the French." She devotes a scathing chapter to these schemers and speculators and particularly to the French in England.

From the first invitations in town, no doubt to ward off boredom, she has been talking about equal rights for men and women. A Tory paper, its attention thus alerted, devotes a paragraph to her. From then on she is revolutionary, radical, bloodthirsty. In short, the Tory press wins her the sympathies, not of the French republicans of London who intrigue around Bonaparte, but of the English reformers.

Moreover, she knows the customs of the rich the best way: from backstairs, from the hidden seamy side.

England seems less prosperous to her than in 1826 or 1829. The workers' misery catches her heart. Was she less virulent ten years ago? Or did the lady's maid, though so close then in position to the most exploited, not perceive it? You only find what you look for: the reluctant servant, a Pariah who had not yet fully assumed that role, tried to see these very poor people as little as possible. They were the ones she wanted to stay away from, as in Paris on the Place Maubert. They served as a yardstick for her. "I haven't sunk as low as that: I'm washed, clothed, shod, warm. I mustn't fall so low." Unhappiness is being low: look at hell in paintings: down below. You have to find the shortest way up, the path toward the paradise of the rich. All through adolescence, her youth, she might have fallen "so low" at any moment.

The distance between her and those who are "low" has grown. Now they touch her heart, move her to tears instead of being a nightmare to her; now they appear to her in their true stature. They are many but don't know it. United, they could counterbalance the power of the middle class. She looks intensely. And sees. Extreme misery leads to inhumanity. As an adolescent she believed that wicked and stupid people become poor. Now she knows: it's the opposite. In Peru she saw this "sidelong glance, which makes these cold faces look stupefied, wild, horribly wicked." She thought it was peculiar to slaves. But no: the East End offers her, in white, in yellowish puffiness like saltpeter on the walls, all the hate she saw in the blacks and Indians of Peru, the night they thought their masters were defeated. It is the pariah's look. She is a pariah. A soul deprived of liberty has no weapon but hate.

> This look is found everywhere, in everyone who is dependent, subordinate. It is the characteristic feature of twenty million proletarians. There are nonetheless exceptions and these are almost always met with *among women.*

Her first plunge into the hell of London. The first flash of an idea that she will soon bring to light. The workers in this very industrial country and all over Europe can form a "class." In fact, they do form one, but they don't know it. The bourgeoisie has made itself into a class: the third estate. It began its revolution in 1789 and is still carrying it on. But this revolution succeeded with the help of the people, whom it did not benefit. On the contrary. With the abolition of guilds by the Le Chapelier law, the people find themselves even more isolated, disarmed, abandoned. And if they form a "fourth estate" which unites with the third estate, which one is the winner thanks to them? The proletarian estate would carry on its struggle against the class in power. The novelty of the times is this class struggle. What this struggle needs to succeed is not violence: it's union. In France, the proletariat is just getting over a long period of ambiguity. Since 1789 it has been said: "the people, the nation" made the revolution. But the middle class alone monopolizes power and makes use of radical ideas. As factories multiply, so does the proletariat, yet it fails to acquire a conception of itself as a distinct class. The artisans, who are less crushed by misery, are still not free of Jacobinism, yet it is among them that the intellectual vanguard will find militants for the two mainstreams of the workers' movement: anarchy and socialism. At the moment, Flora sees them fighting for association and cooperation.

In England the situation is different, lacking a revolution to unite the classes in the people's name. Two strata of society are recognized, symbolized by the two Houses of Parliament: the Lords, an aristocracy that is still effectively powerful, and the Commons, the already powerful middle class. The proletariat feels completely out of it.

Since 1825, small local trade unions have been trying to expand. The Reform Bill of 1832, which aroused great hopes, gave freedoms only to the lower-middle class. The workers, bitterly disappointed, turned to antiestablishment organizations. Up until 1834, Robert Owen and his friends tried to form a cooperative, an association of all the construction workers: this Grand National Guild fails, but will serve as an example. The London Working Men's Association will propose its Charter on May 8, 1838, and form the Chartist movement on August 8. Flora knows, before the trip, that the W.M.A. was founded in 1837 by a worker, William Lovett, and that the association sends "missionaries" throughout the country. Upon her arrival, she makes contact with these men, artisans who have already crossed the border of misery and want to rescue those who are sinking into what is called "pauperism." An 1834 law on aid to the indigent makes the recipient's situation more odious than misery; the workers are ready to listen to those who speak of rebellion. The most eloquent speaker, Henry Vincent, who preaches in the West of England and in Scotland, others who "evangelize" the northern moors in secret meetings by torchlight, are soon being persecuted. On February 4, 1839, they present a petition with 1,280,000 signatures to the House of Commons: on July 12, Commons rejects their demands.

Flora wants to attend sessions of both Houses of Parliament. Women are not admitted? Never mind. She hasn't lost her taste for disguise. What a pleasure to be someone else, and even more, a man, one of the oppressors but also one of the sex with whom she is most comfortable. To the English, any foreigner is so odd that his sex doesn't matter: male and female exotics are equally incomprehensible; an Oriental may very well be small. So she dresses as a "Turk": turban, false beard, baggy trousers. A diplomat takes her; she doesn't lack contacts among the "exploiters," even if her friend the republican Marrast pays court to the future Napoleon III. Having tried both, she still prefers the haughty urbanity of lords to the arrogant vulgarity of the middle-class rich.

Yet it's in the House of Commons that she experiences a crucial moment. This "coachman in his Sunday best" mounting the rostrum, ruddy-faced and stocky, is O'Connell, the Irishman. What a being "of verve and poetry . . . I know of nothing so miraculous as this man!" After him, she wants to meet the revolutionary leaders.

A friend she doesn't name—perhaps Joseph Rey, perhaps an Englishman—takes her into the back room of a nightclub, in a narrow alley off Fleet Street. It is the National Convention—secret—of the Chartists. William Lovett exactly represents her ideal: a conscientious worker; from then on she understands that the workers' emancipation can only be the work "of the workers themselves."

She thinks she is back in the glorious revolutionary past and evokes the great figures of the French Convention. The brilliant George O'Connor, an Irish gentleman, long overshadowed by O'Connell, here takes the bit between his teeth. She doesn't know that in the course of this same Convention, men of "moral strength" like Lovett or Brontern O'Brien—who talks to her about the need for the working class to obtain the help of the lower-middle class—will be secretly opposed by an armed organization that will end up, in November, with an insurrection at Newport and a repression with dead, wounded, and harsh sentences. But she will remember O'Connor's exhortations. Later, the National Charter Association will present a second petition to Parliament, this time with nearly three and a half million signatures, which Parliament will again reject.

She feels that these men are her brothers, that she is one of them. Their words burn her. How can she hesitate? It's up to her to spread the same demands in France. Moreover, their program leaves an essential gap, always the same, that of women's rights, while Englishwomen "play absolutely no role in society." Flora understands still better, here, that women must struggle, even with the most aware revolutionaries, to have their right to equality specified from the beginning of the struggle.

Her book will speak of other English hells, such as Glasgow, and Manchester from which the young Engels, son of a textile manufacturer, will soon draw his experience of the workers and resolve to undermine society.

Flora still knows very little about French workers' lives. They thus seem to her less totally unhappy than here: "For the English proletarian, even bread is a luxury"; he eats only potatoes. The moment he earns a few pence, he drinks in order to forget, and she sees in him once again the malignant degradation of the Peruvian slaves.

177

The harshness of organized industrial labor shocks her: in her childhood the manual laborers in the Place Maubert still led almost an artisan's existence in the little workshops; she is not used to factory-barracks. To tell the truth she doesn't realize that France too is changing rapidly; but she soon will.

> In English factories you don't hear, as in ours, singing, chatting, and laughter. The master doesn't want a memory of outside existence to distract the workers from their task for one minute: he requires silence, and a deathlike silence reigns, the worker's hunger gives such power to the master's word.

Never a conversation with the master, who never even returns the worker's greeting. Even a slave is sure of his bread, whereas this proletarian can be dismissed at any moment.

> The hospital? It's a favor to be admitted. If he's getting old, if he is disabled in an accident, he is dismissed, and he begs furtively for fear of being arrested.

They are strict in the mills, "they measure grudgingly the space in which the worker must move around." Neither cleanliness nor healthiness, except for the machines.

What she observes in England recalls the amazement of the European in the United States around the middle of the twentieth century. In the nineteenth, isn't England imperialism triumphant? (That's what the preface signed A.Z. says in so many words.)

Flora discovers heavy industry:

> The machines' power, their application to everything, astonishes and strikes the imagination with amazement? Human knowledge, incorporated in thousands of forms, replaces the functions of intelligence; *with machines and division of labor, only motors are needed: reasoning, reflection are useless.*

England presents to Flora the embryo of the society against which rebellion will become generalized in the 1970s. France in 1839 is still a land of craftsmanship, and the factories of Alsace are "clean, neat, and well-kept workshops." As Europe will be Americanized in the second half of the twentieth century, so France is

Anglicized a century earlier: Anglomania is already beginning in Paris. Flora's conclusions are still valid after a century and a quarter of disappointment:

> If at first I felt humiliation at seeing man annihilated, no longer functioning except like a machine, I soon saw the immense improvement that would one day come out of these discoveries of science: brute force wiped out, physical work executed in less time, and more leisure left to man for cultivating his intelligence; but that, to achieve these great benefits, a social revolution is necessary.

Flora visits the gas works because "beer and gas are, in London, two great branches of consumption." So she asks for a "ticket of admission" to see a gas works in Horse Ferry Road, Westminster.

THE GAS WORKS

We entered the great *boiler room:* the two rows of furnaces on each side were lit; this furnace is quite reminiscent of the descriptions that the poets of antiquity have given us of Vulcan's forge, with the difference that a divine activity and intelligence informed the cyclopses, whereas the black servants of the English furnaces are cheerless, silent, and exhausted. There were a score of men there carrying out their tasks with precision, but slowly. Those who were not busy remained motionless, their eyes cast down, they hadn't even enough energy to wipe off the sweat that ran from their bodies. Three or four looked at me blankly; the others did not turn their heads. The foreman told me that they chose the stokers from among the strongest men, that nevertheless they all became consumptive after seven or eight years' work and died of phthisis. That explains for me the sadness, the apathy imprinted on the faces and in all the movements of these unfortunate people.

Labor that human strength cannot sustain is required of them. They are naked, except for little linen drawers; when they go out, they throw a coat over their shoulders.

I was choking, I was in a hurry to flee from this stinking furnace when the foreman said to me:

"Stay a moment more, you will see something interesting; the stokers are going to take the coke out of the ovens."

I went back to my perch on the balcony: from there I saw one of the most appalling sights I have ever looked upon.

The boiler room is on the first floor, below it is the cellar destined to receive the coke; the stokers, armed with long iron pokers, opened the ovens and took out the flaming coke, which fell in torrents into this cellar. Nothing more terrible, more majestic, than those mouths vomiting flames! Nothing more magical than that cellar suddenly lit up by live coals which tumbled, like the waters of a cataract from the highest rocks, and like them are engulfed in the abyss! Nothing more frightening than the sight of the stokers, who are streaming just as if they were coming out of the water, and are lit up before and behind by these horrible braziers, from which tongues of fire seem to shoot out at them as if to devour them.

I awaited the end of the operation, wanting to know what would become of these poor stokers. I was astonished not to see a single woman arrive. "My God!" I thought, "haven't these workers any mothers, any sisters, then? Have they neither wife nor daughter awaiting them at the door, as they come from the burning furnace, to wash them in warm water, to wrap them in flannel shirts, to give them a nourishing, strengthening drink, then to say a few words of friendship, of love to them which may comfort, encourage, and help the man bear the cruelest miseries?" I was very distressed: not one woman appeared. I asked the foreman where these men, bathed in sweat, went to rest.

"They go and throw themselves on a bed which is under this shed," he answered coldly, "and after a couple of hours they will begin stoking again."

This shed, open to every wind, assured them of nothing but rain; it was ice cold there. A kind of mattress that is utterly indistinguishable from the coal that surrounds it is placed in one corner; I saw the stokers stretch out on this mattress, which was hard as stone. They were covered with a very dirty overcoat so permeated with sweat and coal dust that you couldn't guess what color it was.

"There," the foreman said to me, "you see how these men become consumptive: it's from going so carelessly from heat to cold."

As far as I know, not a single head of a factory like those I have just described had the humanity to provide a room that would be moderately heated, would contain tubs of warm water, mattresses, woolen blankets, where the stokers could come, upon coming out of their furnace, to wash, rest, well wrapped up, in an atmosphere related to the one they are leaving. It is really shameful, infamous for a country that things should happen as I have just related.

In England, when horses arrive at their destination, people hurry to throw a blanket over their backs, to wipe off their sweat, to wash their feet; then, they take them into a well-enclosed stable, furnished with good dry litter.

Some years ago the inns were put closer together when it was realized that the distances between them were so long they shortened the horses' lives; yes, but a horse costs a millowner forty to fifty pounds sterling, whereas the country provides him with men *for nothing!* . . .

After admiring O'Connell, the traveler wants to get to know the Irish in London: an English gentleman, she says, journeys throughout Europe "to take his boredom traveling" but never sets foot in "the classic horrors of St. Giles." She describes:

THE IRISH

Irish misery is represented in the midst of one of the richest districts in London. It is there that one must go to know, in all its horror, the misery that occurs in a rich and fertile country, when it is governed by the aristocracy and for the aristocracy's benefit.

Long and beautiful *Oxford* Street, used by a crowd of carriages, this street with its wide sidewalks and rich shops, forms where it begins an almost right angle with *Tottenham Court Road*; at the head of this last street, across from Oxford Street, is a little alley that is almost always obstructed by an enormous cart loaded with coal, which hardly leaves any room for a person to go by squeezing close to the wall. This little alley, called *Bainbridge*, leads to what is called the *Irish quarter*.

Before I left Paris, a Spaniard recommended three London districts that were important for me to see what I could learn from them: the *Irish* quarter, the *Jewish* quarter, and the place where they sell *stolen scarves*.

In England, patriotism is only a spirit of rivalry; it consists not of love for one's neighbor but of claiming to be better than every other nation.

In St. Giles, one feels asphyxiated by emanations; there isn't enough air to breathe or daylight to make one's way by. These miserable people wash their own rags and hang them out to dry across the narrow streets, so that atmospheric air and sunlight are completely intercepted. The mire beneath your steps exhales its miasmas, and on your head the trappings of misery drip their stains. A delirious imagination's dreams do not begin to equal the horror of this dreadful reality! When I got to the end of the street, which was not very long, I felt my resolution weaken; my physical strength is far from matching my courage; my heart sank and a fierce headache pounded my temples.

I hesitated, wondering whether to go on into the Irish quarter, when suddenly I remembered that I was indeed among *human beings*, among my brothers, my brothers who had been suffering for centuries, and in silence, the agony that was overwhelming my weakness, although I had only been experiencing it for ten minutes! I mastered my suffering; my soul's inspirations came to my aid, and I felt an energy that was up to the task I had set myself, to examine all these miseries one by one. Oh! then a compassion that I cannot describe swelled my heart, and at the same time a bleak terror enveloped it.

Picture men, women, children, trampling barefoot the infected mire of this sewer; some leaning against the wall for lack of a place to sit down, others squatting on the ground; children recumbent in the mud like pigs. No, unless one has *seen* it, it is impossible to imagine such hideous misery! such profound debasement! more complete degradation of the human being! There, *I saw* children entirely *naked,* young girls, nursing mothers *barefoot,* with nothing but a shift falling to pieces so that their bodies, almost completely naked, showed through. Old men huddled in a little straw become a dung-heap, young men covered with rags. The insides and outsides of the old hovels are in keeping with the tatters of the people who live in them. In most of these dwellings, neither windows nor doors close; they rarely have paved floors; they enclose an old oak table crudely made, a stool, a wooden bench, a few tin bowls, a *kennel,* where father, mother, sons, daughters, and friends sleep pell-mell; such is the *comfort* of the *Irish quarter.* All that is horrible to see! and how can one reconcile this enslavement of millions of Irish and millions of workers in England and Scotland, receiving only a very insufficient salary for their needs as compensation for work which exceeds their strength and shortens their lives; how, I say, can one reconcile this horrible oppression with the abolition of the slave trade and the feeling of the Negroes?

So you think that they emancipated their Negroes as Christian nations freed their serfs, establishing them on the land? Oh! no. The Negroes in Jamaica are, without any doubt, less unhappy than the worker in English factories or the Irish peasant, because the fruit of their labor has more value, but they are not *freer;* they are made *entirely into English proletarians;* they are not allowed to own any land; they are bound to pay a high rent for the hut they live in, to maintain the roads by labor or taxes; and the theft of a banana is punished by white parish officers as justices of the peace in England punish the theft of a few potatoes: by whipping. You may rely on the British imagination to create *duties* and *taxes* which force the Negro to work no less than his master made him before emancipation. It is unquestionably an improvement of the slave's lot that the capriciousness is removed from punishment; but this improvement, which will encourage development of the population, is of course in the proprietors' interests.

It is clear that emancipation done in this way is one of these apparent generosities that turn out to benefit their authors; but the government devoted the sum of six or seven hundred million to this measure.

Oh! this is another secret. The ministers, in presenting this method of emancipation, were assured of the support of English commerce, because the residents of the colonies, who were in debt to the merchants of the metropolis, could only free themselves with the indemnity given for emancipation. The ministers could not have gotten them to adopt the much more economical system of gradually buying out the Negroes, through the work of successively freed Negroes, although this system would have offered the signal advantage of ensuring the moral education and apprenticeship of the emancipated, whereas simultaneous emancipation could guarantee nothing but the payment of English creditors.

Thus, the great act of *humanity,* that has been extolled to us for thirty years, is nothing but a well-thought-out, well-planned *commercial calculation,* and the whole continent has been fooled for thirty years! The charlatanism of the honorable gentlemen who make up the British Parliament made us believe in the philanthropy and disinterestedness of a society of *merchants!* In the presence of such a deception, one would be tempted to suppose that Europe, that the whole human race has, like individuals, moments of apathy, drowsiness, and folly. However, this varnish of hypocrisy with which they adorn their acts is not only to impress foreigners; they also want these proletarian masses whom they fleece to the bone, whom they bleed white, whose very bread they weigh out, they want—cruel irony! —these slaves, who bend under the burden, to *believe they are free* ...

---

* The reader must not forget that I was in London in 1839, and that I wrote these reflections in the first months of 1840. Since then, public misery in England has increased immensely. The masses are starved by the aristocracy; each day the proletarians, the workers die of hunger by the thousands, and the British Parliament's philanthropy no longer fools anyone. After the session of last June 16, what individual in Europe would be simple-minded enough to believe that it is out of Christian charity that Sir Robert Peel, Lord Stanley, Brougham, the party leaders, and the majority of both Houses pursue the emancipation of the Negroes so ardently? What torture inflicted on the slave by a cruel master's anger ever equaled the torments of hunger! And in order to get a few shillings more out of their lands these honorable gentlemen make "thousands of their compatriots" perish in horrible agonies! Listen, you who are still fooled by English hypocrisy, listen to the egoistic reason that the minister alleges for having Mr. Ferrent's motion rejected; see how imperturbable, how devoid of all remorse this monstrous assembly is while VOTING FOR THE DEATH OF ENGLISH PROLETARIANS!

Mr. Ferrent asks the House, on July 1, to form a committee to present a petition to the queen. This petition would solicit the immediate use of a sum not exceeding one million sterling (25 million francs), to relieve temporarily the distress and misery of the working classes in manufacturing districts. "Twenty million sterling," the honorable member says, "were voted for the emancipation of the slaves in the West Indies. Could one refuse so paltry a sum to the people who are suffering?"

These sights of the people's "freedom" have made Flora want to see repression. So she visits two prisons, Newgate and Cold Bath Fields, one ordinary, the other reformed.

At Newgate, the attitudes of the jailers, officers, and wardresses strike her by their humanity. But in the women's section she discovers, among the dazed and indifferent, dirty and hostile, a beautiful young mute: a mother in misery who stole to feed her children. A theme from the novels of the period, a female Jean Valjean, an even more touching figure—Flora feels overwhelmed.

> While the wardress went on speaking to the governor, I was looking at the imprisoned mother, hoping she would at last turn her head toward me: she remained calm and still. I wept, and a sigh escaped me that the unfortunate woman heard. With an abrupt movement she turned her head, looked at me, and our eyes met. Oh! how could I portray all the tenderness and pride I saw in her eyes! All I read in them! . . . Poor victim of our social condition! Her head seemed to me to be surrounded by a halo! Her looks veiled by tears, the twitching of her muscles, the trembling of her lips were all so eloquent that I heard her say to me: "Oh! You are a mother too! You understand my agonies! Like me you would have stolen; your children's hunger would have given you the courage for it too! You feel what strength I needed to brave everything. Thank you! Thank you! woman, you understand me! . . ."
>
> Oh! that woman carved the memory of Newgate in my mind forever!!!
>
> The part of the prison reserved for men is much bigger, but perhaps also more bleak than the women's: all the faces I saw there were atrocious.
>
> The children are divided into two categories: those imprisoned for a first offense, and the recidivists; they all display such extreme effrontery that, to conceive it, one must oneself be convinced of the extreme

---

Sir Robert Peel: "I would not have taken the floor, if I did not fear to appear indifferent to the people's misery. The motion before the House seems dangerous to me. *It is a precedent which will not fail to be invoked later, and which will infallibly lead to an enormous increase in taxes.* The government works quietly, but efficaciously too, to come to the aid of popular distress."

Mr. Duncombe supports the motion: "I shall never cite enough examples to demonstrate the intensity of the distress. For my part, I would be quite disposed to vote five million sterling rather than one, but the House, incredulous to the end, will never believe in the people's distress until it sees four or five hundred thousand men dying of hunger bring the hideous spectacle of their misery into London."

The House puts it to a vote: Mr. Ferrent's motion is rejected by a majority of 106 to 6.

ease with which childhood gets used to facing anything, fearing nothing, suffering everything. The average number of children who arrive in this prison each month is *forty*: they are taught to read, write, and count.*

The other prison, at Cold Bath Fields, seems to Flora to deserve its name of "model establishment." Yet she feels what all repression takes away from human beings: the right to be recognized, and thus to communicate:

Mr. Chesterton was eager to accompany me and show me over the house in the greatest detail. One sees that it has become his "thing," and that he considers these unhappy prisoners his family; he knows nearly all of them by name. With such a governor (he has been there for ten years), one may wonder what the officers must be like. If, remembering what most of our jailers in France are like, I was amazed by the good bearing of the Newgate wardens, I was full of admiration on seeing those of Cold Bath Fields! These men, almost all chosen by the governor, have gentle expressions which harmonize perfectly with their tone of voice and their considerate politeness. What a salutary effect habitual association with such guardians must produce on the prisoners! For one cannot doubt the influence of gentle and humane manners, in reconciling with society men whose hearts are embittered against it.

At Cold Bath, Mr. Chesterton has brought the division of prisoners to its farthest limit. The recidivists form five categories; those condemned a sixth time are sent to the Millbank penitentiary or to Botany Bay; the other prisoners are classified according to the nature of their crimes.

The governor makes sure that the regulations of the prison confided to his care are executed with a scrupulous firmness. These rules, I must say, seemed to me very harsh! They imposed permanent silence and idleness, and solitary confinement for the slightest infraction.

The prisoner must not speak to his companions on any pretext, nor address a request to the officers. If visitors ask him a question, he must not answer; only, if he feels ill, he may ask to see the doctor. Taken immediately to the infirmary, he is examined; they put him in a good bed, and all the attentions his condition requires are lavished on him with an affectionate charity.

---

* One may be a *felon* at seven, consequently one can be hanged at that age. Blackstone reports that, in his time, the jury condemned eight-year-old children to death who were executed; I have seen some of that age condemned to deportation! . . .

(Moreau-Christophe)

The prisoner who breaks silence is severely punished.*

Prostitution seems to the traveler the very symbol of social vice. For Flora, for whom the carnal act is difficult, this humiliation symbolizes female slavery. Here she finds again a key theme of romanticism, which Tolstoi and Dostoievski will take up again and on which Hugo rang all the changes, from the high-class courtesan Marion Delorme to honest Fantine.

Flora understands the soldier who risks his life for a penny a day, the sailor, the highwayman: "All three of them find in their *trade* a bleak and terrible poetry! But I could not understand the prostitute." For Flora, a woman of passion who deifies love, "prostitution [is] a dreadful madness, or it is so sublime that my *human being* cannot be aware of it. Facing death is nothing."

Her analysis reveals that her key idea is already formulated: social attitude is a function of freedom of choice.

CHILD PROSTITUTION

Virtue or vice supposes the freedom to do good or ill; but what can be the morality of a woman who doesn't belong to herself, who has nothing of her own and who, all her life, has been trained to escape despotism by scheming and constraint by seduction? . . . It is thus, then, that this monstrousness may be attributed to your social condition, and woman may be absolved! . . .

In London no one commiserates with the victims of vice; the streetwalker's lot inspires no more pity than the Irishman's, the Jew's, the proletarian's, or the beggar's. The Romans were not more insensitive to the fate of the gladiators who perished in the ring. Men, when they are not drunk, kick prostitutes away, they would even beat them if they weren't afraid of scandal, which would result from a battle with the pimps or police intervention.†

---

* It is difficult to believe that they succeed in making the prisoners observe this silence; yet they do, very rigorously. It is so irksome that several prisoners say they would prefer death.

(Villermé)

---

† While I was in London, a city merchant, suffering from an evil disease, thought he could attribute his illness to a prostitute he knew; he had her brought to a house of assignation: there, he pulled her skirts up over her head, tied her up that way with a rope, wrapping the top of her body as in a sack; then he whipped

186

Honest women have a harsh, dry and cruel contempt for these unfortunates, and the Anglican priest does not comfort every unfortunate like the Catholic priest. The Anglican priest has no mercy on the prostitute; he will be glad to give an emphatic speech from the pulpit on Jesus's charity and affection for Magdalene the prostitute, but for the thousands of Magdalenes who die each day in the horrors of misery and neglect, he has not one tear! What do these creatures matter to him! His duty is to deliver an accomplished speech in the temple at a fixed day and time, that's all. In London the prostitute has a right to nothing but the hospital. . . .

Independently of the houses of ill repute that are found on every London street, where the prostitutes take the men they solicit in the streets and where several of them live, there exist in certain districts lodging houses kept by receivers of stolen goods, to which all sorts of thieves resort; several of these houses contain fifty beds, occupied by persons of both sexes. In some of these houses, only young boys are admitted, so that they may not be maltreated by those who are stronger. These children having no less address, presence of mind, knowledge of their trade than any thief, the lodging house keeper wants to benefit as much as possible from all their thefts, and doesn't want to let in men by whom the children would be robbed; but women are not kept out, or, to speak more precisely, *girls of ten to fifteen,* for it is rare that the thief's companion is a grown woman; these little girls are accepted as the *mistresses of the young boys* who bring them there. The scenes of depravity that are enacted in these dens, Doctor Ryan says, are indescribable . . . and would be *unbelievable* if one described them!

Almost all the twelve- to fifteen-year-old boys sent to prison have had relations with prostitutes and are visited daily by their mistresses

---

her with a switch, and, when he was weary of beating her, threw her out into the street in that state. This unfortunate woman, deprived of air, was suffocating; she struggled, screamed, floundered in the mud. No one came to her aid. In London, one never interferes with what is happening in the street: *That's not my business,* the Englishman answers you without stopping, and he is already ten paces away when these words come ringing in your ear. The unfortunate woman, lying on the pavement, no longer moved; she was going to perish, when a policeman came by, went up to her, cut the rope which bound her clothing. Her face was purple, she was no longer breathing, she was asphyxiated. She was taken to the hospital where prompt aid saved her life.

The author of this atrocious attack was called before the magistrate and condemned, *for committing a public nuisance, to six shillings fine.*

Among a people of *ridiculous prudishness,* you can see it doesn't take much to *outrage public modesty.* . . . And what is most astounding is that the magistrate saw nothing in this action but *a minor infraction to punish.* Yes, in this land of so-called freedom, the law is for the strong, and the weak cannot invoke its protection.

who call themselves their sisters. Mr. Talbot estimates that there are in London thirteen to fourteen thousand young prostitutes *from ten to thirteen,* who are endlessly renewed. He says that Guy's Hospital has had within eight years 2,700 cases of venereal disease between the ages of ten and fifteen, and that a much greater number of children of that age were *refused for lack of space.* "I have seen," he adds, "as many as thirty in one day sent away from a hospital, although they were in such dreadful condition they were hardly able to walk." Doctor Ryan also says that a great number of requests are addressed daily to the Metropolitan Free Hospital by twelve- to sixteen-year-old girls with syphilis. "I have often been shocked," the doctor continues, "in workhouses and other places of public charity that I attended as a doctor, by the great number of children who come for treatment of venereal diseases."

There are five institutions in London to help prostitutes who wish to leave their dreadful career; but these societies' efforts are, in general, too ill directed, and their means too limited to be able to do much good. The total number of prostitutes to which the five asylums offer a refuge annually does not exceed 500. Five societies help and get work for only 500 of these unfortunates! The only one that attacks depravity at its source is the society to prevent child prostitution; this society makes active use of existing laws; but, with all its zeal, it can only feebly hinder crime both by the insufficiency of the help it receives and by the insufficiency of the legislation. Thus the keeper of a house of ill repute, who may have captured and abducted children of ten to fifteen to sell them into depravity, will, if the charge against him is not dismissed, get off with *eight to ten days imprisonment;* whereas a woman of the people, or whatever other individual, arrested selling fruit or whatever it might be on the sidewalk will be punished by thirty days imprisonment! . . .

A police magistrate, after much research, estimates the number of prostitutes in London at 50,000; but this is only an estimate, for even now that the police are better organized, they have no way of achieving accuracy in this respect. Since 1793 the population of London has doubled, so one can suppose that vice has increased more than proportionately, considering that inequality in the division of wealth has remained at the same level, employment has not increased at the same rate as the population, salaries have become smaller as a result, and no real improvement in the proletariat's lot has yet been effected by the government.

However, Doctor Ryan estimates, according to information that he has gathered from police officials, there are from 80 to 100,000 prostitutes in London, of whom half, others assert two-thirds, are under twenty years old.

One can only estimate their approximate life span; for until 1838 there was no law in England requiring registration of deaths. Mr. Clarke, the last chamberlain of the City of London, estimates the prostitute's life at four years, others put it at seven years, while the "Society for the Prevention of Child Prostitution" estimates that the annual mortality rate of London prostitutes is 8,000. Mr. Talbot thinks, according to the results of his research, that there exist in London 5,000 *houses of ill repute*: this is as many as the number of shops that sell gin. Dr. Ryan reckons that in London there are 5,000 individuals, men or women, engaged in providing the houses with girls, and 400 or 500, whom he calls *trapanners*, occupied in setting traps for girls of ten to twelve in order to lure them by *will* or by *force* into these appalling dens. He estimates that 400,000 persons profit directly or indirectly from prostitution, and that 8,000,000 pounds sterling (400,000,000 francs) are spent annually in London on this vice.

The Society for the Prevention of Child Prostitution was established in May 1835. In its address to the public, it exposes the state of depravity of the lower classes in London; it asserts that there are schools where young people of both sexes are trained in swindling and every act of immorality; that prostitution and theft are *openly encouraged* by those who profit from them; that crime, in short, is regularly organized, and it calls the citizens' attention to the most atrocious attacks that are committed with impunity in broad daylight on the streets of London to nourish the most infamous of traffics. There exist, it says, a great number of men and women whose business consists of *selling little girls of ten to fifteen whom they have trapped*. The children, lured on plausible pretexts into halfway houses or houses of debauchery, held in strict confinement for two weeks, are forever lost to their parents.

In May 1836, the Society's committee in its progress report remarks that "whatever pain every moral man must feel at sight of the scenes of vice displayed undisguised in the metropolis, nonetheless the most revolting spectacle is offered by the hideous increase of child prostitution. Under cover of night, and even in broad daylight, unhappy children roam the streets, diverted from the paths of virtue, from their parents' protection, by miscreants who have achieved their destruction for gain and who yet remain unpunished."

Among the seduced girls the committee helped during its first year of existence, I notice the case of a child of thirteen or fourteen; the slave merchant who had led her astray and in whose house she was detained was acquitted! For the rest, in the Society's reports for the years 1837 and 1838, several facts of the same kind are related, and the traffickers in human flesh got off with *a few months in prison*.

After telling about some of the means of enticement used on the children it has helped, the committee adds: "The numerous artifices used to lure inexperienced children (of both sexes) into the maelstrom of misery are so complicated, so varied, that it would be impossible to describe them in detail; that is why we shall speak only of the treatment these unfortunate creatures receive once they have fallen into the trap. As soon as the young child enters one of these dens, she is stripped of her clothing, which the master or mistress of the establishment takes possession of; they dress her up in a dazzling costume, made for rich women, and acquired second hand. The regular customers are notified, and when she attracts no more people into the house, her master sends her to walk the streets, where he has her watched in such a way that it is impossible for her to escape; if she tries, the spy, male or female, who is following her, accuses her of stealing the clothing she is wearing from the master of the house; then the policeman arrests her, sometimes he takes her to his station, but more usually he returns the fugitive slave to her master from whom he receives a reward. Back in her infamous lodging, the unfortunate girl is cruelly treated; stripped of all clothing, she is left all day *completely naked,* so that she cannot escape, often she is even *denied food.* When night comes, they give her back her clothes and send her out again to walk the streets, still watched by a spy; she is severely punished if, in her nocturnal courses, she does not bring back to the house a certain number of men, and she may not keep for herself one penny of the money she receives."

Houses of prostitution are forbidden in England, but the proof of their existence is difficult to furnish; those who frequent them, held back by shame, cannot bear witness against them before the law; and the police, unable to get into these houses unless disorders occur there, are unable to establish a felony. The neighbors can get them suppressed by the officers of the parish, only by deposing that they are disturbing the peace of the neighborhood.

For the rest, the law's prohibition is absurd; for since prostitution is an inevitable result of the organization of European societies, what governments should be doing is diminishing the intensity of the causes that breed it and regulate its practice.

In the reports of 1837 and 1838, the Society's committee reports the steps it has taken against keepers of houses of ill repute and individuals who were debauching children; but the penalties incurred for keeping these houses, for leading astray and debauching children of ten to fifteen, do not exceed *one year's imprisonment,* and most often one to six months. It even happens that the charges against the accused are dismissed, considering that these children of *both sexes, from ten to fifteen,* found in their houses, *consented either to go there or to remain there.* Such is the legislation that protects the proletarian's family. As for the children of the rich, constantly watched over and supervised, they are seldom exposed to these seductions.

Depravity is so widespread and the price they get for children so high, that they resort to all kinds of tricks to procure them. In 1838, the Society's committee called the attention of patriotism, virtue, religion, and humanity "to the shameful efforts that are continually being made to feed debauchery with new victims. One can hardly go down the street without encountering some way station of this infamous commerce. Numerous agents are employed to capture, to trap in a thousand ways innocent, inexperienced children, and the suburbs, the bazaars, the *parks*, the theaters, provide them endlessly with new prey. Your committee has, furthermore, proofs, it adds, that permit it to affirm that the keepers of houses of ill repute and their agents *are also in the habit of going to the workhouses and penitentiaries, and that they frequently get young girls from them.*

Despite the mask of hypocrisy that upper-class people continue to wear in order to keep up the people's zeal, they hardly show themselves disposed to second the efforts of the Society for the Prevention of Child Prostitution; while in the thirty-seven years of existence of the Society for the Suppression of Vice, which aims solely at pursuing people who *do not observe the Sabbath, or vendors of obscene publications and fortunetellers*, it is noteworthy that this society has constantly met with aid and support everywhere, because one can sleep very well, on Sunday, to the reverends' sermons, renounce Aretino's writings and keep his vices; moreover, by subscribing to a society which claims *to work for the suppression of vice*, one acquires a reputation for being *virtuous*, a reputation which English *Robert-Macairism* * sets great store by.

The committee of the Society for the Prevention of Child Prostitution said in May 1838: "While the members of the committee were pursuing the execution of operations begun, they had to struggle against obstacles of an extraordinary nature; these obstacles arise out of almost universal apathy and indifference to the Society's aims. The members of your committee have been met in their courses by the mockery and contempt of a profane and immoral world, by the censure and disapproval of those who believe that libertinism *is necessary* to society's welfare, by disdainful inattention and neglect from religious men: they have not found aid and encouragement anywhere; but amid the impious rebuffs of this mob, the jibes and laughter of all, they have had the courage to persevere, sustained by awareness of the importance of the goals whose achievement they pursued, and by the affectionate care and sympathy of their subscribers."

English depravity begets nothing more odious than those monsters of both sexes who travel through England and continental Europe setting traps for children, then return to London to sell them.

---

* Robert Macaire is a character from nineteenth-century French drama, symbolizing the con man, especially in business.—Translator.

The aristocracy and middle class are not spared. Flora describes the "finishes" * and the poor girl they get drunk so they can torment her, the receptions—which she knew too well—and the men's life in the clubs, the most English, the "élitist" of institutions. There one reads all the newspapers; for a moderate price one eats a French chef's cooking with sauterne and champagne. "Such are the great material advantages obtained by the club; now let us examine the intellectual results." There are none, for "no one feels bound to the others, nor obliged even to greet them."

> This society always intends, by association, to attain a material advantage; do not ask it to unite in its thought, its feelings, its moral being, for it will not understand you. . . . There is something frightening about this social materialism.

We find a comic side in the "puff," that is to say, in the English bluff.

Once again, the picture recalls the modern European's image of the average American: the Englishman, constantly preoccupied with the idea of seeming richer than he really is, converses only in "puffs" with a stranger; this is also why he often spends ten times more than he can afford. Flora tells of cruel hoaxes: a help wanted ad sends twenty unfortunates to ring the bell of someone who wants nothing, to annoy him. She is outraged by this "profound indifference to the poor man's lot." Too intimately informed about what a search for employment requires in time and "expenditure on dress," she characterizes these puffs as "odious crimes" revealing "a great depth of cruelty in the heart."

But Flora has too much sense of humor not to be amused by the puff for the *splashinghouses,* where a " 'fashionable' who has neither land nor hounds, but who has credit at his tailor's," can get himself splashed with mud for three shillings. This is because when one is fashionable one must go hunting, and show oneself afterward at the club covered with the mud of a certain county: the splashinghouses have at their disposal all the muds of England and Scotland.

---

* *Slang.* A house of entertainment where the night is finished. *(OED)*

The servant who acts as a groom asks with the greatest seriousness if Monsieur wishes to *come back* from Buckinghamshire, Staffordshire, Derbyshire, Kent, etc. When the "fashionable" has made his choice, he mounts the four-legged automaton (a jointed wooden horse); the ingenious mechanism lifts its front and hind legs, stamps, trots, and sends it rider as much mud, and with the same irregularity, as could a real horse running through the fields. The operation over, the elegant gentleman, a hunting-crop in his hand, goes to show himself in Bond Street, Regent Street, Piccadilly, Pall Mall, etc., so that all may believe he has taken part in a superb hunt.

Sociological, barbed, moved, indignant, and sometimes funny, the book shows how Flora's resolution is maturing, how her vocation is hardening. One scene foreshadows the mysticism of the end. When she visits the insane asylum of Bedlam, which is clean and whose poor inmates are well fed although they are not dressed, she meets a compatriot. When she hears his name she feels faint: Chabrié. A doctor tells her: "His madness is rare: he thinks he is God." The poor soul throws himself on his knees before her. At the first meeting he seems in his right mind; when Flora sees him again upon leaving, he trembles. He tells her she is sent, not to save him—it is too late—but to "save the idea that I come to bring the world. . . ."

> "I come to make all bondage end, to free woman from man's slavery, the poor from the rich, and the soul from the bondage of sin." This language, it seems to me, did not denote madness: Jesus, Saint-Simon, Fourier had spoken thus.

She leaves, deeply disturbed.

Thus, with very few statistics, and many exclamation points, but with a pitiless acuity in describing social relations, Flora Tristan unquestionably anticipated Friedrich Engels's *The Situation of the Working Classes in England*. Arriving in Manchester in 1842, he will publish his analysis in 1845. Can he and his friend Marx, "omnivorous readers," be unaware of *Walks in London* on sale at Jeefs's in Piccadilly? Engels will speak very highly of Flora Tristan in general, but does not cite her book among his sources. To denounce society one must seem serious: would it be serious to refer to a woman? Engels's sexism remained quite unconscious: he will feel, in his old age, an indulgent sympathy for an especially ardent young person whom the "internationals" fear, a certain Rosa Luxemburg. If Dickens had read the *Walks*, he would have recognized many of the scenes and characters he was later to portray.

The book comes like a verdict against those who reduce their own people to such misery. Observing the apathy of despair among the oppressed, one can only imagine a better future guided by the Owenites and Chartists.

Another strange and amusing observation, which only a Catholic—even a lapsed one—could formulate: young girls, raised in unbelievable prudishness, who are not permitted to pronounce "thigh" or "breeches," read the Bible all day long, a book abounding in murders, incest, violence, and perversions. Moreover, in the prisons, it is from among the recidivists that the greatest readers of the Holy Book are recruited.

21

THE PROPHETS' PARIS

These years leading up to the tidal wave of 1848 are propitious for prophets. The Saint-Simonians split up, unite with the Fourierists who in turn split into factions, newspapers multiply, the religious turmoil goes well beyond Lamennais or Pierre Leroux. The social organism is looking for a new matrix, but doesn't manage to shake off this king accepted by surprise. The middle class rules, but no longer likes to be reminded of Saint-Louis or the Sun King, and has had enough of having to blush for the Terror or the regicide. And something else, below the middle class: the mob, the people, are solidifying: mutual aid societies, guilds, freemasonry. None of them are legal unless authorized, but all or almost all manage to get organized. Then the police notice the offense, break up the society, ban the newspaper. And it starts all over again.

Advanced circles, based on progress, made up of intellectuals, artists, craftsmen, workers, quite distinct from one another but with parallel ideas, are avid for reading matter.

Walks in London interests these publications: *The Review of Progress, Fraternity, The New World* (result of a Fourierist schism); they review the work, publish chapters from it. Flora no longer has to beg to place articles, nor to fear her words are falling on deaf ears. For the first time she no longer thinks she is "sowing on stony ground."

Literature becomes involved. It moves out of romantic gothicism into social criticism. Victor Hugo has taken a stand against royalty and George Sand goes into her populist phase. Saint-Simonians come to ask her to be the Mother of the supreme Couple: is she not the friend of Lamennais and Pierre Leroux? Marie d'Agoult becomes Daniel Stern, writes art criticism in *The Press*, but above all begins to take an interest in politics: before he left her, Liszt showed her the importance of the masses. Hortense Allart de Méritens hears Béranger boasting about "the little paper, *The Workshop*, which brave workers bring out every month and edit themselves." A Saint-Simonian songwriter, Vinçard, an old friend of Prosper Enfantin, writes a detailed eulogy of the *Walks* in *The Popular Hive*: "This great and worthy work must and will bring its author sympathy, glory, and love." Flora, beside herself with joy, finds out all about Jules Vinçard. He is seven years older than she, a woodworker and songwriter. Best known for a Saint-Simonian song: *Look out: You alone are king,/ Awake,/—Producer, impose your law,/ Show by doing/ —To the scribbler's century/ The peaceful future/ That is opening for the worker.*

His biography is rich: self-taught, learning to read from an almost illiterate mother ("I taught him what I didn't know myself"), he was converted to Saint-Simonism in the Master's lifetime. Enfantin, his philosophical mentor at the start, soon annoys him with his infallibility. But when the Father comes out of prison and leaves for Egypt, Jules Vinçard gets the survivors of Ménilmontant back together. Little by little, his disciples leave him for other, more revolutionary reformers. Vinçard becomes more sensitive about it every day, more jealous of his influence.

He will write Flora that he wishes no title other than "Saint-Simonian worker" and that he refuses to see himself named among the "illustrious socialists" . . . but this is only from fear of mockery. The sympathy that the Woman-Messiah arouses soon renders her suspect to him.

Flora already thinks she has one unknown friend, an admirer. Another admirer, but one she meets: a dissident Fourierist, Jean Czynski. He sees her while visiting a Mademoiselle Ch—, who,

Flora says in a letter, "never stops making all the prominent Poles in Paris admire my hair." This "woman with the little black dog" "pursues [her] in a strange way." At least she introduces her to Czynski, at once bucolic and worldly, enthusiastic and conciliatory, who has his differences with Considérant: "Phalanstery" definitely goes too far toward socialism, republicanism.

Czynski, dripping with Slavic charm and kissing Flora's hand every other sentence, shows her his letter to Arago. The deputy muddles everyone together in his antisocialist ire: Cabet the communist, violent men like this Proudhon, a barefoot provincial who has just thrown a firebrand: *What is property?* and answers: "Property is theft." Well, Arago is mixing this terrorist up with the prophet of harmony. Czynski writes a *letter addressed to Monsieur Arago: Fourier has nothing in common with Babeuf and Saint-Simon.* Strangely, the Fourierists find it quite natural that people should confuse Cabetists with Babouvians, Saint-Simonians and Proudhon, as long as they set Fourier apart, since he protected property, Czynski assures, and even gave paying back the phalanstery's capital priority over paying for talent, if not for work.

Flora is equally amused by the hand-kissing and the inaccuracies. She knows that Considérant has also replied: *Against Monsieur Arago. Protest addressed to the Chamber of Deputies by the Editors of the Pamphlet "The Phalanx."* They follow up their defense of the necessary value of socialism with a long theory of property rights. Flora thinks Considérant is right: Fourier was a socialist. But Czynski brings her brochures full of goodwill: *The Workers' Future, Women's Future,* and another, a newer one: *Colonization of Algiers According to Charles Fourier's Theory.*

Why, in a society where the partisans of association, of new relationships among humans, are so rare, is it necessary to divide even Fourierism into rival branches? Flora thinks how great a uniting of all the reformers would be: Saint-Simonians, Fourierists, all of them. How can they not understand that it is for them a question of life or death? Flora remembers that July 29, 1830, when the whole street and every street seemed stretched out toward the same goal. But by August 1. . . . And yet, she believes in the progress of history. Union *must* be possible. These too middle-class intellectuals pay it lip service. Now the workers, *they* have common interests. They could—they must unite. But who tells them so, then? Each one is the head of a sect?

She charms Czynski. How can you be anything but agreeable to a man who—between two kisses of the hand—overwhelms you with *written* compliments? "You will be forced, sooner or later, to join us." He has written: "Madame Tristan has done the English people a great service by unveiling the misery and all the social evils that prey on the capital of Great Britain." He hopes that an English-woman will write some *Walks in Paris*, unaware of Mrs. Trollope. He publishes the chapter on Parliament.

To tell the truth, Flora doesn't believe in these overly middle-class Fourierists; they can make her book known, but she can't become one of them. Her confidence goes to Victor Considérant, but *The Phalanx* hardly takes notice of the *Walks*. Besides, Czynski gathers around him authentic workers who found a strictly cooper-ative "trustworthy bakery" at Ménilmontant (shades of Enfantin's phalanstery). It is trying its wings (in 1841 it will close, after three years though it was planned for nine). Flora, in spite of her money troubles, buys a share and takes responsibility for organizing the consumers. Thus she meets the cabinetmaker Androh. Czynski and his group leave for Texas the following year. So she will lose a circle in which she felt at home.

The *Walks* are selling: they go through two editions in a few months. It is decided to publish a third, this time a popular edition, for 2 francs instead of 7,50, as well as an extract: *The Monstrous City*. Except for the first edition, none include the introduction signed "A.Z." Did Flora quarrel with Rey, if indeed he was the author of it? Or did she decide it was unnecessary for someone else to present a work which already had its public? The following editions incorporate a careful analysis of new publications. For example, Villermé's basic and very official work: *Report to the Academy of Moral and Political Sciences on the Physical and Moral State of Workers Employed in Silk, Cotton, and Wool Factories*. Or Buret's book, *On the Misery of the Laboring Classes in France and England* (1840). Engels must have gotten something out of this last one too . . . to the point of borrowing the title.

The popular edition of the *Walks* includes a dedication that is at the same time a manifesto. Officially, it is Flora Tristan's turning-point.

This life—like every life—unfolds piece by piece and the woman who wants more and more to be the Woman-Messiah, that is, a propagandist and, if possible, head of a socialist school, has little relation to the young secret rebel, who didn't dare admit her unhappy marriage or even her children and went away to Peru. The trip to Peru, with Chabrié's love, restores her self-confidence, and the Peruvian adventure, bathed in luxury, bathed in inequality, bathed in prejudices too, forces her to know herself better. On her return, she knows her dual nature: having a taste for elegance but rejecting it as a failing. To sum up, the sense of error that the wife felt in breaking up her marriage is transformed into a consciousness of social privilege and a rejection of these inequities. But the attraction toward the aristocracy persists, constantly struggled against, not without some rages and violence, which show up as discord, misunderstandings, and conflicts. In the *Peregrinations*, she speaks of her "nervous system": fatigue reduces her to tears. She is subject to mirages, visions, a sliding of familiar objects toward the fantastic that she will describe—rather flatly—in *Méphis*. She faints easily, but sometimes shows unexpected resistance as in her fight for Aline, and imperishable endurance, as in Peru.

First Flora deified love, looked for the absolute man, the sister soul. Then she wanted to assert herself through ambition. Political in Peru, with Escudero this need to fulfill herself was transformed into a need to speak out, to write, to communicate via the printed word. The writer, the romantic tells herself, is the only one who can make a real mark on her times without leaving behind the memory of a tyrant or a corrupt politician. But writing does not mean real communication: one must act, one must make one's ideas triumph through organization, one must arouse others to acts that will be the implementing response to one's ideas. Flora, with her self-critical lucidity, must have known she was not much of an artist. She proves it by writing no more novels after *Méphis*, which fails as a book. On the other hand she knows her gift of sympathy, the "almost magnetic fascination" that she exerts on many beings. Little by little, despairing of love and glory, she believes herself, knows herself a prophet. Aren't even the insane touched by this radiance, like the madman in Bedlam? The romantics have a primitive faith in speech that surges from the unconscious when the obstacle of the conscious yields: in the speech ·of what are called madmen.

We aren't claiming that the French of before the 1848 Revolution had the same impulses, the same fetishes as citizens of the nuclear, post-Marxist, post-Freudian and partly postindustrial era. Flora's consciousness cannot be that of a militant of female emancipation today. But strong parallels can be drawn. For the rationalist, scientific trend of industrialists and their theoreticians (limited by superannuated religion, badly adapted to social changes) was substituted then, among certain people, this trend called "romantic" or "utopian" that took into account deep impulses, passions, desire. Fourier evoked what Freud explained. At this time, from 1840 on, Flora is launching ideas, words of order, attempts at organization that Marx will gather up into a system. Saint-Simon remains the ancestor whose posterity—the producers—partly fulfill the prophecy but deviate from the goal, which was knowing in order to love one another, communicating in order to unite.

Flora Tristan is entering her social years, which she will experience as a *guru*, a prophet. Every messenger has this mixture of organizational common sense and mysticism. It is heightened in the self-educated, because they need to call on inspiration to impress themselves on the outside world. Anyone who has overcome lack of formal education is at once proud and insecure. Today we debate the value of formal education: Flora, on the other hand, lives in a time when a diploma, a title are beginning to replace birth and family, and since they guarantee a good career, take on the same power as money. With a secret in her family origin—but a justifiable claim to aristocracy—with a lack of elementary learning that, in this woman of international culture, leaves its mark in whimsical spelling and peculiar punctuation, with a lack of money that nothing can compensate for, Flora can count on nothing but the vibrations—as we would say—that emanate from her, her aura, what her contemporaries call charm or magnetism, fascination. Perfect elements for making up a prophet, an Eastern-style guru, like Enfantin or Considérant (but they were at the Polytechnique), like Leroux (but he gets help from Christianity), like Fourier (but he was a man).

A woman, self-educated and poor, Flora is pushed by the force of things toward bare-armed men, the oppressed: proletarians. *They* cannot count on others: in England as in France "the laws passed have changed nothing about the state of things." They cannot count on anyone but themselves. Some of them know it. These aware workers become intellectuals by an effort that she understands perfectly, since she has had to make it herself, are the ones Flora is looking for. And so we have the *Dedication to the Working Classes* in the popular edition of the *Walks:*

> Workers, it is to all of you that I dedicate this book; it is to instruct you on your position that I wrote it, so it belongs to you.

Generosity and arrogance: Flora's impetus and limitations are contained within these few lines: she is instructing the workers.

Flora is still a supplicant with regard to the writers of the period, and women who count. George Sand still doesn't like her—and even less so after the quarrel between Flora and Agricol Perdiguier, George's idea of a worker, on whom she modeled her novelistic hero. Hortense Allart de Méritens, a lady of letters who has no talent but a lot of friends, writes to Sainte-Beuve—who could have launched the book with a few lines:

> Madame Tristan has sent me here her *Walks in London,* in a new revised edition. It is a cry of pity and indignation for the English people. As these sentiments lack taste and delicacy, you won't want to read it. Tell me if she has sent some copies to Marie (d'Agoult) because she is trying to get women to dispose of them.

In a few words what misogynists will always call female perfidy shows through. Flora sees in these underhanded tricks the answer, elaborated over the centuries, of the woman who has been "trained to evade capriciousness by seduction"; she writes that with reference to prostitution; it is also true for these diplomatic insinuations—which so many men habitually employ.

Kept on the fringe by the literary successes, male and female, a poor relation of success, Flora gets inspiration from reading the workers. Three especially: Jean Gosset, a freemason; Pierre Moreau, called "the Tourangeau," Agricol Perdiguier, whose nickname is "Virtue-from-Avignon." All three want, by reforming the old guild, to found unions encompassing all the workers in one profession and creating bonds between these unions: in short, they have the idea for the trade unions of the future.

Around the same time, Flora meets two women who are going to become her friends. Marceline Desbordes-Valmore, much older than she, responds with interest and even enthusiasm to being sent the *Peregrinations*. Flora goes to see her. At fifty-four, after much suffering, the elegiac, the purest of poets, is still charming. She has poor lodgings, incessant material worries, an actor husband without recognition and often without a job, but Marceline still has a seductive face and the sweetness of her verse. Flora brings her Aline, who recites "Dear little pillow, soft and warm at my head," which of course delights the author. Flora knows whole poems by heart:

> *Do not write, I am sad and I want to die away.*
> *Fine summers without you are love without a torch.*
> *I have only known how to love and to suffer.*
> *My poor lyre is my soul.*

Besides, they have had experiences in common. Daughter of a painter of coats of arms, Marceline knows Antoine Chazal well: she met him in his teacher Girodet's studio. Flora has read this aging woman's very autobiographical novel, *A Painter's Studio*. Even their lives . . . and Marceline confides in this literary newcomer, poor, long persecuted, often discouraged. She knows about poverty in childhood: her father lost his money in the Revolution. She knows about difficult family situations: her mother took her to her native Guadeloupe, which they found in the midst of revolution and where, when her mother died, she found herself a friendless orphan at an age when other children are learning to read. On her return, in early adolescence, her pretty voice promised her success for a moment. In Rouen, where she sang, the glorious Grétry noticed her and got her a job at the Opéra-Comique. Then love, the "divine breath," swept her away. Mad love for Henri de Latouche, who loved her for so short a time. Her lover's leaving her frays her nerves to such a point that she loses her voice, never to regain it. It is then that she marries François Lanchantin, who uses the stage name of Valmore, and that the life of wandering and poverty, with their little daughter, begins. Right now she is living on the little her writing brings in, the little that Valmore earns on tour where he is so often booed, and finally on an allowance from the Duke de Montmorency. When the duke was elected to the Academy, he wanted to give her his salary: another prince did it for Béranger. But Marceline refused the charity. Yet she takes a small income. Flora's peregrinations, the attempted murder, the trial deeply moved this forever vibrating lyre-soul. The two women will always be united by a real tenderness.

After *Walks in London* appeared, an admirer wrote to Flora. The name, Pauline Roland, was unknown to her. But her correspondent, a disciple of the Saint-Simonians, then of Pierre Leroux, invites her to an evening at the *Independent Review* where George Sand plays the leading role. Pauline Roland is Flora's size: 5 feet 2 inches, a bright, pleasant face with brown eyes, and if her nose is too long and her mouth too wide, she is no less attractive and lively. Flora, seized with a fine chauvinistic impulse, contrasted the English workers' misery with the "workshops" of Alsace which seemed pleasant to her. Pauline shows her Villermé's study. Flora has to take it into account in the last edition of the *Walks*. In Alsace, the investigator saw workers working fifteen and a half hours a day, plus walking a league or more to get to the factory. He describes "pale, thin women walking barefoot through the mud; dirty, emaciated children covered with rags, greasy with the oil of their trades and carrying in their hand the piece of bread that must satisfy their hunger." Industry definitely produces the same effects in every country. Moreover, Pauline has published a *History of England*. Flora meets Pauline's friend, Jean Arcard, with whom she lives openly and very poorly on the Rue Jacob, raising their son. Pauline, while Flora was going to Peru and meeting Escudero, also went through two mad loves, of which this was one, for which she gave up everything. Their friendship is founded on solid bases. No exaltation here, but a great community of thought. Pauline has abandoned "any idea of personal messianism." She admires and accepts Flora's plan.

Thanks to Pauline Roland, the "Workers' Union" will continue to serve as an example during the revolution of 1848 and afterwards, in the trade unions. Pauline will introduce Flora to Jeanne Deroin, future founder of *Women's Opinion.* Pauline will take care of Aline. This friendship will last beyond death. In 1842 she will quote *Walks in London* at length in a study on women's work.

Pauline Roland and Jeanne Deroin are among the few women who come to the Rue du Bac. Flora has moved to No. 89 on that street, where she has found a wainscoted lodging, high up, on the fifth and last floor. Her visitors are foreign intellectuals abroad, young socialists, self-educated workers, artist-prophets. They talk about work through association and a religion of humanity. Young Alphonse Constant—who isn't yet calling himself Eliphas Lévi—and the sculptor Ganneau, with his bumpy skull and his emotional sweats, develop their theories there. Jeanne Deroin, in no way a romantic, finds them all a little high-strung; Pauline, on the other hand, finds enthusiasm to match her own.

The idea of the Workers' Union takes shape from month to month: by the third edition of the *Walks* and its dedication to the workers, everything is in place.

It is 1842, Flora is thirty-nine and almost penniless. She will later write: "I made workers out of my children." Indeed, Ernest is learning mechanics and will join the navy; Aline wants to become apprenticed to a milliner: material conditions motivate them more than ideology. The domestic accounts of the ex-Pariah in the process of becoming a missionary reveal that she is still feeding herself on "flowers of the air": 4 sous worth of bread, 5 of butter, 3 of salad, 2 for an egg, 1 franc 42 for sugar, 10 sous worth of coal bought as it is needed. Everything, moreover, is bought in small quantities: thus she is not tempted to use more. Letters seem to be a big expense: 6 sous and—this must have been a manuscript—12 sous. She has an intermittent servant—an accessible luxury in those days. Her clothing becomes more and more "austere."

In good faith, she feels she is a proletarian, a mother of apprentices, a woman of the people. The middle class no longer gives her anything.

Even her reading changes: few novels, many works on economics and books, articles, pamphlets written by workers. The workers must free themselves, unite internationally, form a class. The middle class did it, with the third estate. It *imposed* itself. It was the head of this seizure of power of which the people were the arm, this power taken thanks to the people. Look how it made a new revolution in 1830, still thanks to the people. But, without asking the nation's opinion, it chose itself another king. It established a parliament, not "to protect its interests, for no one is threatening them, but to *impose* its conditions on twenty-five million proletarians, its subordinates." To form a class the proletariat must unite, and in every country: *an international workers' union is essential.*

This idea has never before been developed so systematically. In France there are no Chartists or Working Men's Association: there is the guild where the initiates and old hands jockey for position and bully the young, and there are associational socialists, phalansteries. But neither Saint-Simon, with his single class of "producers," nor Fourier, who doesn't want any class divisions, but a vertical association in a state of harmony, nor even Considérant, a socialist but also more concerned with politics, envisaged this uniquely workers' union. The communist Cabet, curious offspring of Babeuf and Fourier, is now thinking about a model society. Flora has read *Voyage to Icaria*: but why a little model republic, when it is urgent to reform society everywhere? And what does universal suffrage matter? The middle class will only twist it to its own advantage unless the workers present a united front.

Let us note that in this time of struggle for parliamentary democracy, when women are demanding the right to vote, Flora never joins in this too strictly political fight. Elections, parliament would only interest her if the oppressed, workers and women, were united.

In 1841 she reads a pamphlet written by a typographer, Adolphe Boyer: *On the workers' condition and its improvement through the organization of labor.* She is thinking about getting in touch with the author when she learns of his suicide in October through *The Workshop*, which he worked on, *The Phalanx*, and *Fraternity*. She, who has felt this total disgust, this temptation to non-being, several times—especially in Peru—feels a mysterious affinity with the desperate worker. She will retain the main idea: "The workers' happiness and future depend upon the organization of labor, *and it is practicable even today.*" The last part of the sentence counts for Flora: forming the workers into a class is not a projection into the distant future, but an immediate goal.

Adolphe Boyer proposed simple reforms—which, in fact, have only come about in France very recently. Thus, each district would have an employment office and would transport workers to areas where they could find work as they transport soldiers joining their regiment.

Flora will put a word in memory of this brother in despair into the *Workers' Union.*

Another book strikes her: *Plan Tending Toward Reviving the Guild,* published in 1842 by the Father of Blacksmiths, the lodge-keeper-workman of the Rue Beaubourg, Gosset the freemason. He calls on young blacksmiths to refuse to be divided into rival guilds. The others—led by the great Perdiguier—blame him for divulging secrets, denouncing the way the Mother lodgekeeper, by giving credit, demoralizes, and how the "sendoffs" for those who leave bankrupt and the various baptisms and festivals can corrupt the workmen. He calls for the union of all workmen. Soon, the initiates forbid the blacksmiths to stay with him, and bloody brawls break out. He holds firm, advocating a "general association of all regenerated French workers."

22

A "LADY" AMONG
THE WORKERS

Flora follows his fight enthusiastically. On February 4, 1843, she will meet the man, powerful, bearded, rather solemn, muscular and virile. Gosset is four years younger than she. They like each other, and she asks him to present her ideas, to read the outline of her book to his "Committee for the Workers' Union."

So there she is on the Rue Beaubourg, at the Lodge, in a very simple room where several blacksmiths are seated, with clean clothes and fingernails. Gosset's wife opens the door: what does she think of the beautiful stranger with her elaborate simplicity?

The summary says:
I. How the workers must proceed to form the Workers' Union.
II. How the Workers' Union must operate from a material point of view.
III. From an intellectual point of view.
IV. The use of funds.
V. Construction of hostels.
VI. Conditions of admission to the hostels for old people, the handicapped, and children.
VII. Organization of labor in the hostels.
VIII. Moral, intellectual and professional education for children.
IX. The necessary results of this education.

Flora borrows from her observations in England and at the same time from Saint-Simon, Owen, Fourier, Cabet. But the ideas have been rethought.

She also sums up the goals:

1. To form a working class by means of a compact and indissoluble Union.

2. To have the working class represented before the nation by a defender chosen and paid by the Union, so that it is understood that this class has its right to exist, and the other classes accept it.

3. To protest, in the name of the law, against infringements and privileges.

4. *To have the legitimacy of ownership of their own labor recognized* (in France, twenty-five million proletarians own *nothing but their own physical strength*).

5. To have the legitimacy of the right to work recognized for every man and woman.

6. To examine the possibility of organizing labor in the present social state.

7. To build Workers' Union hostels in each region where children of the working class will be taught intellectually and professionally, and which will shelter working men and women injured while working, and the old or infirm.

8. To recognize the urgent need to give women of the people a moral, intellectual, and professional education, so that they may become moralizing agents for the men of the people.

9. To recognize in theory the equality in law of man and woman as being the only way to achieve human unity.

What do these workers, rebels and proud of it, think of paragraphs 8 and 9, and what can Madame Gosset think of them? Flora

208

will soon learn that she has hardly been convincing: the principle is good, but hopelessly idealistic, Madame Gosset will say. What does this lovely lady know about the lives of blacksmiths' and other workers' wives? Does she know that work is scarce and if the women start competing for it too, the men with families to support will be still more unhappy? Madame Gosset must have seen a cartoon on the Saint-Simonians, ten years before, showing a "blacksmithess," short-skirted but wearing a hat. A joke and no more. Become man's moralizing agent? Of course, when you come to see them, all decked out, smelling good, they smirk and strike poses, but for the women who empty their chamber pots. . . .

Flora thinks she has sowed on good ground, and puts her mind to continuing the work everywhere. Vinçard lets her know that the workers have at least fifty meetings for "pleasure" in Paris, and points out some lively ones: such as the Songwriters' Contest, where he won his poet's laurels. Béranger himself went. So Flora goes to one held at a lemonade-seller's back room at 23 Faubourg Saint-Denis. Sitting on long benches, the guests drink wine and listen to singers improvising, they tap their glasses on the table to disapprove or else they applaud. No one gets up when she comes in; a few bantering looks, that's all. Faithful Doctor Evrat and a new admirer, Rosenfeld, a talkative Jewish typographer, ironic and feverish, are with her. No one seems to be concerned about the Woman-Messiah, even after she has shyly said a few words about her plan: to write a book, a sort of little catechism explaining the lines of the "Workers' Union" with a song, a kind of worker's Marseillaise, that she would like to throw open to competition. Some applause, murmurs of "why not," then the session continues, and the lady's presence provokes or, on the contrary, inhibits the bawdy choruses, according to the singer. At any rate, they look at her.

The Hive finally answers her appeal: Vinçard tells her that the worker's newspaper has decided to print it. The secret ballot gave her fourteen white balls out of fifteen: the only black one belonged to the most garrulous. Five ladies—unusually—attended the session; they are not allowed to vote, not being on the editorial staff, but they warmly approved.

Joy at last, the goal at last! She is recognized, accepted, by her own kind, by her peers. Ah! the working class is quite another thing from the bourgeoisie! Her whole life will not be enough to give to these disadvantaged people what no one gives them: her time, her love, the gifts of her imagination and her pen . . . to be their guide. . . . Soon she asks to see them, to be heard. Rosenfeld tells her about the meeting with his corrosive irony: these gentlemen take themselves as seriously as a middle-class administrative council. They would have to receive the lady-author in a special meeting: when should it be, and should they accept this departure? Then Vinçard got up and gave them a reason that convinced them all: it's a lady who asks this favor of us.

"You should know that you've been made a concession not at all as an author, but because you are a lady, a woman, or if you prefer, *woman*."

Enthusiastic approval, then this hesitation—Flora doesn't understand: she must "find the why."

Today, we understand both much better and worse. The constant conflict between the classes is, at the end of the twentieth century, much more visible, and more expressed in constant strikes, union struggles in every country, an explicit ideology of class struggle constantly invoked by parties backed by millions of voters. There is nothing like that under Louis-Philippe: only the boldest dare to point out that neither mutual aid societies (still hard to get authorization for) nor guilds are enough. The phrase, working class, sounds new. When Flora explains that the union of all working men and women will allow them to form a class, thus to demand participation in government on the model of the middle class forming the third estate, the idea is revolutionary. Liberals', social Christians', even republicans' goal is to quell "hate between different classes." They are all trying to keep this "fourth estate" from becoming self-aware. Neither Saint-Simon, nor Fourier, nor Considérant, nor even Cabet has gone so far. As always, most of the oppressed class finds the comprehensive plan for its liberation "utopian." Some years after Flora Tristan, Marx and Engels will declare that they alone are scientific socialists, but others will accuse them of daydreaming and being utopian. Soon we shall see both the workers and the communist Cabet call Flora's plan utopian. Today the classes, although fully recognized as such and officially at odds, are much less immediately recognizable. No doubt the gap between dollar millionaires and immigrant workers from poor countries is as great or greater than the one between the Duke of Buckingham and the stokers in the London gasworks. But on the surface, the Parisian worker's life-style and the banker's are less differentiated; ready-made clothing makes outside appearances uniform; everyone has his own vehicle and electric and electronic machines.

Intellectually, too, the media and the fascination of television multiply the common subjects of conversation. Even the rites and cults of gadgets, idols, cars, and certain films spread out vertically among the population and no longer horizontally within one class. So *external* relations have necessarily changed. The middle-class type who need to say "boy" or "my good man" no longer exists, and even slang is becoming more a question of generation than of money or education. Furthermore, the essential revolution, the reading revolution, is over.

So we understand better the attitude of the most advanced workers, the ones from *The Hive* or *The Workshop*, who want to withdraw, organize, write their own claims and doctrine, and don't care for this middle-class woman coming to bring "salvation," this aristocratic messiah who reminds them every second how "devoted" she is to the people. The Russian *narodniki* (leaders), shortly afterward, also "went to the people" and experienced the disappointments toward which Flora Tristan is heading. Let us not forget that in 1968 the political vanguard of French students, immersed in Maoist Marxism, convinced that truth is found in the masses, also went for "the masses' ear." They would have laughed at Flora's vocabulary: one isn't a Woman-Messiah anymore, but a proletarian militant, a revolutionary, who must "feel among the masses like a fish in water." Yet these girls and boys, with a very different mode of speech and the opposite ideology, lived through the same experience. They came, not to "bring salvation," but to organize, to help, to put their time and—they thought—their knowledge of theory at the people's service. Today the masses think they have "workers' parties," whose theory and practice, they think, are of working-class origin. In fact, the authors of the theory and model of these parties are Marx, Lenin, Mao Tse Tung: intellectuals. The organizer of the Italian Communist party, the most important of the western Communist parties, was the intellectual Palmiro Togliatti. To get around the difficulty, these are christened "new style intellectuals" and accepted. Those, on the other hand, who preach reform, a profound recasting of revolutionary practice, are rejected as "petty bourgeois" intellectuals.

So, feeling deeply imbued with her mission, Flora enters the "fairly clean room" on an alley near the Rue Saint-Martin where twenty editors of *The Hive* are waiting for her, on February 13, 1843. She is flanked by Doctor Evrat and the ironic Rosenfeld. She comes in; no one rises, no one comes up to her. Vinçard the Saint-Simonian, Vinçard from the Ménilmontant phalanstery, has written her: "Your plan, my dear lady, is magnificent"; he mentions the luminous simplicity of her scheme and her heart. She invited him to her house, but he didn't come. This evening, he shows no sign that he values her. How discouraging, in the badly lit room! On some faces she discerns indifference, on others vanity. More likely each of them must have been secretly observing the "outsider" and trying to look as self-confident as possible.

Flora is staking her life. The agony of failure is only masked by a new passion. The need for ecstasy is the best sublimation of the death instinct. To be recognized as a messiah makes you sure you're alive, justifies you.

Doctor Evrat reads a chapter; toward him, she has the irritations of intimacies, spiritual or carnal. He reads badly, he puts no fire in it, none of the warmth she would have put. What is the point of exposing herself? She is afraid. Her feet and hands are icy and her throat is dry. Evrat is finished. They put it to a vote by secret ballot and she is afraid she may faint any moment. There: it's over fast: only one black ball. One look at the closed face convinces her that her enemy is Vinçard.

Now Evrat is reading the chapter on women; the most shocking for them; and not one woman has been invited to this meeting. How can they accept, not so much equality as the idea of woman as the worker's "moralizing agent"? Vinçard gets up this time: "Why say that the worker goes to taverns and drinks? The middle class says it enough. Why give them arguments?" And a carpenter, Roly cries: "I don't deny that they go to taverns. But you have to hide this vice from the middle class, not proclaim it."

So there is Flora confronted by the eternal dilemma of the "positive hero" and of "varnished, polished, lacquered truth," in short the dilemma of "socialist realism" which will dominate Communist parties in the West from about 1925 to 1956 and, much later, in the countries of "popular democracy." You have to show a worker, a militant, without vices or, even better, show him correcting his vices by becoming aware, joining the struggle. You have no right to "bring grist to the enemy's mill." There is a corollary to this cliché of Communist discussions: "do not demobilize the working class"; in Paris they say: "do not demobilize Billancourt," because for a long time the Renault factories at Billancourt symbolized the fief of the conscious, that is to say, the Communist, working class.

Now Flora's great principle is in the sentence she will write a month later on the back of a letter of Agricol Perdiguier's: "Workers, remember that to flatter the great is base, but to flatter the people is a crime." The core of her doctrine is precisely to abolish the distinction between manual and intellectual labor and consequently the contempt in which the worker's labor is held:

> From the moment when there is no longer any dishonor in working with one's hands, when work is even an honorable fact, all, rich and poor, will work.

And contempt for the worker will thus become incomprehensible.

> From the day when working-class children are raised with care and people apply themselves to developing their intelligence, their faculties . . . from the moment when there is no longer any difference in education, talent, good manners between the children of the people and the children of the rich, I ask, what will be left for inequality to consist of?

To which they will reply that it consists precisely of the inequality between rich and poor, if wealth is not acquired by skill, but inherited. But, like Fourier and Considérant, she doesn't dare tackle the abolition of inheritance (and a half century after the first Marxist revolution inheritance is gradually reestablished in the U.S.S.R.).

At 11:30 at night she leaves, exhausted, trying to tell herself that Vinçard is jealous and Roly vain, that they're just hopeless. But she knows, deep down, that she is blocking the real reason.

On March 2, at another meeting, she loses her temper with Vinçard, tells him "her" truths which are not very pretty, and as always when she lets anger master her, subsides into doubt and denigration of herself and others. She feels like a misunderstood messiah, arrives at absurd conclusions, which she had better reject if she wants to act: "I see that it's madness to try and discuss their interests with them; they must be presented with the law that will save them ready made."

With other prophets, those she considers her peers, relations are no easier. On February 12, she asked Enfantin for his book on the *Colonization of Algeria* in exchange for *The Workers' Union*, which she thinks will soon be out. Prosper undoubtedly remembers the lovely woman whom he honored with his attentions one evening and who did not fall under his spell. He replies that he is too poor. Flora must have cried: is this the man who lived on bread and milk? But he is too precious an ally. Back from Egypt and in spite of all his disappointments, he still has influence. She answers, mentioning her own poverty, and asks him at least to lend her the book. But Enfantin definitely has no use for the Woman-Messiah, who saw him when he was the Master and who is going to talk about it—and say what? The supreme Father of the phalanstery is no more patient or tolerant than the priestess of the Workers' Union:

> *You have examined me upon my past* and you want to find in my current work proofs of the influence of your judgment. I did not ask you for this *public* judgment; whatever it may be, it seems to me *that you therefore should find it natural to remain* personally a stranger to me.

However, Considérant publishes an excerpt from the *Union* and reviews it in *The Phalanx* of March 20 and 31.

On the other hand, the workers are still distrustful and even hostile. The same people who stimulated Flora and gave her the idea for her plan are rejecting her. Flora's incomprehension of this attitude is oddly naïve for a woman who has seen so much vanity, rivalry, and intrigue caused by pride. After having written so much about these personality conflicts in Peru and Paris, she doesn't want to see them when they involve her.

She had great hopes of Agricol Perdiguier, nicknamed Virtue-from-Avignon, two years younger than she, a carpenter, poet and writer. This man with the eloquent, ruddy, joyous face participated in the June 1832 revolt. He admired Cabet in his pre-"Icaria" phase and two years later published some books on the Devoir de Liberté society's tour of France. In 1839 his *Guild Book*, which Pagnerre will publish in a second edition, arouses enthusiasm. Social questions are the order of the day. George Sand gets involved, writes *The Worker Touring France*, and starts one of those maternal friendships she is so fond of with Virtue-from-Avignon. The Saint-Simonians applaud, the public is curious about guild rites. All the Carbonari and freemasons see in this evidence that the workers are capable of creating their own organization. In 1841 Agricol Perdiguier tours France again in a steamboat, at George Sand's expense, welcomed everywhere by happy disciples, arousing much envy and, among other guild reformers, like Gosset, a dejected distrust. Flora sends him her plan and the first pages of *The Workers' Union*. On March 25, his reply chills her. What, she claims to have "invented" the Workers' Union? And what about him? And Gosset, and Pierre Moreau? So she thinks the workers are incapable of insight into their own condition?

He accuses her of decking herself in others' laurels, of claiming to be an innovator when the Saint-Simonians of Ménilmontant, the Owenites, the Fourierists *"acted* in every sense of the word." In particular he shows, quoting at length the review in the *Two-Worlds Review,* that his own book already tended to "invest the working class with legislative power" and that "civil war is at the heart of my theory." Flora replies with a vehement sincerity, on March 30: "Although I have already had quite enough disappointments, your letter is the most poignant I have experienced, the most deeply painful. . . ." So in this whole plan aimed at revolutionizing the world, he notices only the fact that he is not sufficiently praised in it?

Perdiguier, do you know what you're missing? It's flattery. Well, Brother, I won't flatter you one bit. I want to *serve you* and not *use you,* so I will tell you the truth frankly, simply and *rudely.*

215

He replies in five points; she judges him insolent, vain, thinking he's infallible, and comments: "When you get to this point, it's really crazy!"

So Virtue-from-Avignon and the Woman-Messiah temporarily break off all relations.

The whole month of March is punctuated by failures. While she is battling Perdiguier and Vinçard, she goes to see Béranger to ask him for a song to illustrate—and launch—her book.

He lives in Passy, very simply in spite of his fame. At eleven o'clock, he is having lunch with some worker-poets, including Savinien Lapointe, the shoemaker. She presents her request.

"Singing produces an extraordinary effect, almost hypnotic, on workers gathered together. If you could give me a song whose chorus goes: 'Brothers, let us unite, Sisters, let us unite,' my Workers' Union would go to everyone's heart."

Savinien Lapointe discourses on the worker's soul, which he claims to know, because he is one. The good Béranger says very simply: "Your title is good. But I don't write songs when and where I like. I must wait for inspiration, and I'm getting old. But if this song comes to me. . . ."

> I wanted to insist [Flora remembers], it was even stupid of me, I knew it afterwards. "Listen," he said, "if some good inspiration comes to me on it, I'll be glad to do it, but I'm not promising anything. I must tell you: for a long time I haven't had many happy inspirations."
>
> And when he said these words with a really touching simplicity, a touch of sadness passed over the poet's features, I was moved to tears by it. It is very hard to be old.

This refusal is on March 29 and Flora leaves Passy as serene as if Béranger had accepted. Two days later, the mail brings a rejection which, on the contrary, plunges her into despair, tears, an agony close to torture: Pagnerre, Agricol Perdiguier's and many other socialists' publisher, refuses to publish *The Workers' Union*.

CONTRIBUTIONS

Standing at her attic window, she looks out at the roofs before her and suddenly the towers of Saint-Sulpice release in her "a very

216

special effect." Inspiration. A priest built this church by begging for funds, penny by penny. . . . All right, she will publish *The Workers' Union* on contributions. . . . She will go and knock on doors.

> This plan came into my mind so suddenly that it felt as if an outside force commanded me to act. To take a big sheet of paper, to write at the top: *Appeal to all persons of intelligence and devotion; we ask for their help in printing the* Workers' Union *book;* to sign my name to the paper; to get my daughter, my maid, my water carrier to sign; to run and see my friends . . . all that was done within twenty-four hours. . . .

A consistent character trait of hers: ideas come to her through struggle. No effort is too great for her to show what she is worth.

> To find three people, I sometimes have to go out twenty times on foot, that's hard; but love is so great in me that none of all these tiresome chores disgust me; what I find tiresome is meeting indifference, especially among those I serve.

Refusals are not lacking. The glorious Rachel out of miserliness, Delacroix and David d'Angers out of dislike of socialists, the banker Lafitte and several other ex-Saint-Simonians out of disillusionment with the working class. But, in spite of their break, Agricol Perdiguier gives three francs, a half-day's pay, as does Rosenfeld the lithographer. In spite of her persistent dislike of this apostle who is too much like herself, George Sand gives 40 francs, and ostentatious Eugène Sue, 100; the actor Bocage gives 20 and so does Princess Christine del Belgiojoso, the muse of the Carbonari; Doctor Evrat gives 100, a merchant, Ch—, 200, and L—, a landowner, 300. The list of modest donors includes Béranger, Adolphe Blanqui, the revolutionary's brother, several women of letters, from Madame Ancelot to Louise Colet, from Hortense Allart to gentle Marceline Desbordes-Valmore, Pauline Roland and Marie Dorval. We find the Firmin-Didots, printers and freemason-workers, Victor Considérant and milliners, carpenters, mechanics, singing teachers, masons, lawyers, deputies too, and high officials. The populist Paul de Kock distinguishes himself by giving one franc, while the mason-poet Charles Poncy gives 3 francs and workers succeed in getting together considerable sums. In two months of work, Flora, exhausted but happy, has collected 1538 francs when the printing costs 932: so she has something in hand for distribution costs. She vows never to use the profits for her personal needs, but for other little books aimed at instructing the working class.

During this period her disappointments among the workers go on. The budding friendships are short-lived: Gosset puts her in contact with a Committee of Union which shows her friendship and recognition. They are ready to sponsor the book, but they want the right to look over the manuscript.

This letter, signed by freemasons, with the three ritual dots after their initials, is addressed to Flora, calling her T.∴C.∴S.∴ and talking about Madame F . . . T . . .'s work, leading one to think she may have either belonged to a lodge (but was this possible for a woman at that time?) or, at least, promised to join one. That doesn't make her any less indignant about the right of control . . . and, in one of her rages, she dissolves the committee, which protests with many capital letters. In April, she is no longer calling the committee members her brothers, but Messieurs. The affection she showed for Gosset and Achille François, a modest and admirable militant, is shaken.

On April 16, between two visits to contributors, she goes to see Gosset and finds him with his wife.

"I don't understand you: I have only one goal, to serve you. I love humanity. I'm not asking you for justice. I have God, my love, and my conscience for me. I shall always say what I think."

"Madame, for thirty-seven years I have been working among the workers. I know their faults and vices, but also their virtues. You are condemning them unjustly. You find the people brutal and coarse."

"It is you who are unjust. I give all my time to the workers."

"But why alienate devoted men with wounding speeches? All your time? Indeed, I admire you. But our comrade Achille François works from six in the morning till eight at night and, as president of a society, stays up until two in the morning. I admire him no less."

"That one, yes, I count on him for an apostle."

"Is it really up to you alone to decide that?"

That's when Madame Gosset explodes. Flora doesn't tell us exactly what they say, but the scene must have been rough. The husband has earned almost nothing for a month, he isn't concerned with his family anymore; he is wasting his time for a woman, who bawls him out on top of it! Flora protests: they are fighting for an idea. Madame Gosset doesn't accept the idea that ideas can be represented by ladies who smell good, wear splendid dresses, talk like books and turn the heads of poor workers, only to put them down when they don't jump to their whims. Women like that . . .

The Women-Messiah tries to stay calm and asks why the blacksmith's wife doesn't come and join their struggle. Madame Gosset is outraged and lets her know, in crude terms, that she has other things to do that seem to her more suitable for women and more moral.

As recently as April 7 Flora wrote: "I have much to thank Gosset for . . . Achille François too and several others really give me all they can in time, in money . . ." And now on April 16, this scene which leaves her broken . . . but glad to have controlled her fury.

A Lady Bountiful of revolutionary thought? That's what they think. But Flora has burned her bridges. As once she left her husband, as she left Peru, she has said farewell to everything but her message. One lives only to love; she now loves only the oppressed. Her life shows her that no other cause is worth a fight to the death.

Yes, when the workers reject her she finds the people "so brutal, so ignorant, so vain, so unpleasant to associate with, so disgusting to see close up." Their fetid burnt-fat smell, the indifference, the coarseness of their conversation . . . but above all, this mistrust. . . .

And then on April 30, a letter, balm offered by this boy eleven years younger than she, this Achille François whom all his friends look on as a saint. A leatherworker come from Chartres on foot, he is a poet and president of the leatherworkers' mutual aid society (later, the police will see in him a hotheaded socialist, a champion of secret societies, and he will be deported to Algeria after June 1848). Achille François writes to Flora:

> My dear Laddy, your last letter hert me deaply first because you think that everyone is abandonning you and then you tell me that I am in collusion with the committee, I who always diffend your cause, then of the dishonesty you met with at Gosset's from his wife whaddaya want Madame theres no glory without tribulation if I told you about myself youd see how I have suffered too, well enough about me, if I wasn't afraid of being importunate I would have come to see you several times to talk about universal union for to fight the comitty

that is forming and coming numbrous I would need a lot of explanation you who are the mother of this sublime idea you could give me some advice.

Such a letter shows you that the cause is worth what you're giving to it. She went on, she certainly saw Achille François again. If his spelling is even more idiosyncratic than Flora's, he has exactly the same views as hers on himself and their struggle:

> I will never be vain but very proud [he writes "prowed"] not with personal pride, but for the cause I have embraced. Weak in book-learning, but strong in my conscience and my frankness, I am ready to fight with any weapon whoever tries to stop me in my civilizing march. For I too have my idea. . . .

The tanner's letter shows that Flora's verbal style is that of the times, not only in romantic literary circles but among the workers too.

A week before the break with Gosset, Flora gets a letter from another of the working-class reformers who aroused her.

Pierre Moreau, a locksmith from Auxerre, nicknamed "the Tourangeau," "the man from Touraine," is thirty-two. He supports his mother who is "a widow and not very happy" and ministers to the needs of brothers and sisters "who don't earn much." In his youth he wanted "to become an artisan in the ill-founded hope of climbing one degree in the arduous social scale." He was one of the first to become aware of the dignity of the working class and discover its pride, a forerunner to "we are nothing, let us be everything." In 1837, he ends his travels through France, knowing all about the moral rifts between guilds and wanting, like Perdiguier, an open guild. But he is more modern than the traditionalist Agricol. His Society of Union, founded in 1837, has thirty-two offices throughout France. In Auxerre, they call him "the founder." He starts an open debate with Agricol Perdiguier, criticizing his reformist softness, his attachment to the superannuated folklore of the guilds, and his histrionics too. He writes to Flora: "Perdiguier will do a lot of harm," and she agrees. Flora knows two of Moreau's works: *A word to workers in all professions, to all the people's friends on trade guilds, or guide to the Tour of France;* and *On trade-guild reform and improvement of the workers' lot.* She has read sentences of his that anticipate the *Workers' Union:* "It is up to us workers to teach one another." Rather strangely, she will tell the Committee of Union that "the book is very good, it will prepare minds to receive the work that I bring," but that she won't talk about it. Why? Fear of competition? Or is she, rather, put off by Moreau's rather tart polemic side? Alone in Auxerre, very isolated, he easily becomes bitter against the companions who don't understand and takes them to task, especially Perdiguier, with whom he will eventually be reconciled.

Moreover with Pierre Moreau what we call "workerism" is at its peak. He rejects "brave and devoted writers" who want to teach the people. Flora must have felt referred to here. Besides, the Tourangeau seems timid to her: instead of proclaiming the necessity for an immediate and international union, he thinks it more realistic to improve the existing mutual societies, in which the Woman-Messiah has no faith.

She accuses him of coldness; he holds himself aloof. Yet, as soon as they meet, they will discover they have the same motto: "Union which gives strength is the daughter of Love."

His letter of April 9, sent after reading the first chapters of the *Union,* restores her confidence. He promises to collect contributions, to involve all the offices in it, but he is afraid of Perdiguier: the carpenters, who are very numerous, have confidence in him. "The apathy of some ... the fanaticism of others is capable of discouraging the strongest spirits." Flora admires the firmness of the statement, perhaps also the perfection of the spelling. But she is disappointed: she proposes to work as a team with Florimond, alias Pierre Moreau the Tourangeau, and here he is pleading a frail constitution: "I haven't the firmness and self-control that is needed for my mission." He must have had troubles to explain that weren't evident from his writings.

Shortly afterward, he will come to Paris, to the Rue du Bac, where he has already sent visiting workmen to her Sunday receptions.

There he is, perhaps for the first time, in a drawing room. Modest, full of furniture bought haphazard on her limited means, but to him it must seem luxurious, with its armchairs and cushions and curtains. Flora—her contemporaries are struck by it—has a great deal of taste, with a touch of exoticism. She has always, but especially since her vocation, dressed austerely, but her living room is bursting with color. Moreau is on his guard. He must especially not give the lovely lady any excuse to make fun of him. He dreams: he goes back to Fourier's idea: if one could convince rich people to build a Workers' Union Center for children, sick people, old people? Besides, nothing is possible without equality. Universal suffrage.

"The chief goal should be the exercise of social and political rights. A perpetual battle with power would be onerous for us and would weaken the nation's strength."

Flora objects that uniting everyone should take precedence over the right to vote. But he insists: the workers must have a spokesman.

"Nothing is more crucial than the choice of a spokesman: this choice will unite or divide. It must be a man of conviction. Not only to declare the right to work but also to fight for a political goal."

Later, Flora will defend the idea she already admired among the English Chartists, of a Union spokesman: she will even propose a name: Considérant (after considering several). But Moreau sticks with the fighters for universal suffrage.

The relationship between the Tourangeau and the Parisian is rather mysterious: he constantly supports her, recommending her to his friends. When she comes to Auxerre, he is waiting for her; they certainly see each other, but Flora doesn't mention it in her diary. Well, she's keeping quiet about her private life at this point.

Whether or not there was an idyll between them, she can't have held to her first impression when she accused Moreau of coldness.

Achille François, Pierre Moreau the Tourangeau, poet, unforgettable figures in the tentative beginnings of the workers' movement, Charles Poncy, the Marseillais mason-poet, too sensitive to take an ocean voyage but brave in politics: Flora finds compensations for the mistrust and rebuffs.

23

"THE WORKERS' UNION
IS LAUNCHED"

The "little book" appears on June 1. The size of a catechism: 123 pages. On the first page are three epigraphs:

"Today the worker creates everything and possesses nothing, absolutely nothing."

"Workers, you are weak and unhappy because you are divided. Unite." (This sentence which predicts the International will disappear in the second edition.)

"Union makes strength (proverb)."

When she holds it between her thumb and index finger, insignificant-looking but explosive, a little bomb, an infernal machine that she is introducing into the bosom of society, Flora thinks she has counted her obstacles, drained her cup to the dregs, bled from every thorn. Let us not forget that the "Christ image," as we would say, dominates her, along with that, more of her era, of the damned poet or prophet. Moses:

> You made me, Lord, powerful and lonely,
> Let me sink into the sleep of the earth,

Chatterton dying of not being accepted, published, learned, recited; persecuted Hernani; Mazeppa. The superior being is always rejected by the crowd.

(This myth of the necessarily unsung innovator will wear thin during the brief period when the mass media and "science" blossom into a beatific self-satisfaction. The foes of overconsumption revive it . . . in the West, but it has never disappeared in authoritarian regimes.)

For Flora this myth is an essential stimulant. Pharisee, Boeotian, and Helot form the indispensable trilogy that bears witness to her election.

But she discovers these three figures of her crucifixion not only in the camp of power, of the "society of civilization" as Fourier said, in short, among the enemy or in the anonymous, resigned herd who must be awakened, but in her camp, among her own kind. Where does this rebellion, this contempt, this indignation, this anger characterized by words like "disgust" and "coarseness" come from? . . . Class terms, stigmata of an incurable aristocracy? But she used the same words to describe the noble, rich Peruvians who surrounded Uncle Pio. This delicate yearning for elegance in sentiments, manners, surroundings retains a strange confusion between a horror of smells and a horror of vulgarity from her adolescence, from her miserable youth. What is admirable about Flora is that she has always been able to rise above this false elegance and prefer beauty of feelings, generosity, enthusiasm.

Her book's appearance tests her afresh. First, two unforeseen blows. Etienne Cabet, the Communist, Babeuf's ex-disciple, represented by his companion Filippo Buonarroti, was then a figure in the revolutionary world. Flora has read *Voyage to Icaria* (which first appeared as the translation of an English work, then, when it was successful, republished under its author's name). She blames him—like Fourier and Considérant—for not opening up his model, for wanting a limited and closed society, in short for not from the start wanting universal union of a class instead of forming a circle of the elite. She goes to see him at the *Populace* to ask him to contribute to her book. He refuses without even seeing her. On May 23, she sends him the proofs and asks him to review *The Workers' Union*. On June 10, he publishes a jeering, waspish, contemptuous article. A guild for the workers, this utopia, this impossible scheme? Carried away by his own enthusiasm, he summarizes Flora's ideas in quotation marks. How could she have expected Cabet, this preacher of justice, this apostle of loyalty, to range himself among those who distort in order to belittle? In fury she writes to him, protesting against these false quotation marks: "As far as *style* goes, I am not for the *community:* each one must answer for himself." Cabet publishes the letter, more and more ironic: if he had praised the lady, she would have found him pertinent; he criticizes her, she judges him disloyal. Flora will pronounce judgment later in the second edition:

> Monsieur Cabet has done the workers much harm. He has paralyzed all action in them; today the workers can see only the reign of Icaria. . . . They wait instead of working actively to prepare for this happy reign.

She will no longer be there when Icaria, in Texas, fades away in sordid disputes.

This disappointment, so brutal and so unexpected, is preceded by several days by another, even more unexpected. *The Workshop* is a workers' publication, inspired by Buchez, headed by Charles Lambert who, with his sister Sophie, was a member of Enfantin's Saint-Simonian society and left it in a burst of scandal. Béranger likes the paper, Pierre Moreau writes for it. It is exactly the periodical whose support Flora might hope for. On May 31, an anonymous article ridicules both the book and the author. They attack the Irishman O'Connell in passing, and Czynski and his Fourierist *New World* which glorifies Flora. Jeering, "sexist," the article arouses in the reader the ever-ready mockery toward lovely ladies who think they are proletarian thinkers:

> O'Connell in skirts, who knows? . . . The Free Woman, the Woman-Messiah whose coming Enfantin the revealer announced to us. . . . We would like to see her up on the hustings, one hand on her chest and the other clenched, her eyes on fire, her brow knit and making us all cry hurrah, but all very nicely, like a well-brought-up woman, because a popular orator, the aristocrats say, is an ugly thing; it looks like a man of the people in a rage.

The allusion to Enfantin points straight to Lambert, who will hide behind the anonymity of the editing, whereas Buchez retreats behind his neutrality. Flora, in fact, is naïve enough to protest, an inexperienced and desperate author. Who will stand up for her if *The Workshop* takes this tone to attack her, and ridicules and negates her? A century and a half later many publications in France will hardly treat "lady proletarians" and opponents' "ladies' writings" any differently: any pamphlet praising the sweet woman's-woman and making the feminist militant seem grotesque finds readers by the armful.

The attack in *The Workshop* nets her a good article in *The Phalanx* and in *The New World*, that is, the two enemy branches of Fourierism.

On sending the proofs, in April, to various guild societies, she receives some encouragement but also some warnings. The division into little rival groups is shown in the mistrust of *The Hive, The Workshop,* the *Populace,* or in Agricol Perdiguier's bad temper. But especially, working women's consciousness of their situation is expressed in a letter of April 12 from the "Soudet woman" whose husband has his fellows' ear:

> . . . you judge [the workers] according to some that you have seen, all advanced men, but these are still weak exceptions, and it is the masses that you need. . . . I see with sorrow that you're exposing yourself to a lot of disappointments. . . . I see very few people and those I see are phalansterians and don't want to talk about anything else. . . . You don't know the workers, they're not yet ready to give women justice and have faith in them. If my husband presented your idea to his colleagues, they'd laugh in his face. . . . As for me, I can't take any part in a work that I don't believe is realizable, although I find it very beautiful, but the time hasn't come: men must learn and our children will understand better.

Yet Madame Soudet's comments are relevant to a proposition that flows logically from the Declaration of the Rights of Man to which people refer so constantly:

> Workers, in '91 your fathers proclaimed the immortal declaration of the RIGHTS OF MAN, and you owe it to that solemn declaration that today you are *free and equal men* in your rights *before the law.* Honor to your fathers for that great work! But, proletarians, a no less

great work is left for you, men of 1843, to accomplish. In your turn, *free the last slaves* who are still left in French society; proclaim the RIGHTS OF WOMAN, and in the same terms as your fathers proclaimed yours, say:

We, French proletarians, after fifty-three years of experience, recognize that we are duly enlightened and convinced *that neglect and contempt for the natural rights of woman are the sole causes of the unhappiness in the world, and we have resolved to express in a solemn declaration, inscribed in our charter, these sacred and inalienable rights. We want women to be informed of our declaration, so that they may no longer let themselves be oppressed and degraded by man's injustice and tyranny, and that men may respect in women, their mothers, the liberty and equality they enjoy themselves.*

1. Since the goal of society should be the common happiness of man and woman, THE WORKERS' UNION guarantees man and woman the enjoyment of their workingmen's and workingwomen's rights.

2. These rights are: equality of admission to WORKERS' UNION CENTERS, whether as children, injured, or aged.

3. For us, woman being equal to man, it is understood that girls will receive, however varied, as rational, as solid, as extensive an education in moral and professional training, as boys.

4. As for injured and old people, men and women shall be treated in every respect the same. Workers, be sure of it, if you have *enough equity, enough justice* to put into your Charter the lines I have just written, *this declaration of the rights of woman* will soon pass into custom, custom into law, and within twenty-five years you will see written at the top of the book of the law that will rule French society: ABSOLUTE EQUALITY *of man and woman.*

Then, my brothers, and only then, HUMAN UNITY will be ESTABLISHED.

Sons of '89, there is the work that your fathers bequeathed to you!

A grotesque misadventure will teach Flora a little more about the inevitable vanity of workers who, in a state of disorganization, despair, and ignorance without recourse to their peers, have managed to get themselves heard, educated, composed, and published. For the second edition, which she expects to appear very soon—for the first is very quickly sold out—Flora announces a contest for a song written by a worker. Since neither Lamartine nor Béranger wants to write her her "Worker's Marseillaise," let a worker compose it. . . .

Charles Poncy, the mason from Marseilles, will send her a very beautiful poem, but too late. While waiting, this contest, crowned by a gold medal offered by generous Eugène Sue, arouses the ambition of the tailor Ferrand. He presents himself in a long, admiring letter: he is a "songwriter and apostle of the people," founder of "the lyric order of templars." He writes a song. Béranger, who is supposed to judge, withdraws, to Flora's annoyance. She goes to the Belleville gate, where Ferrand is busy showing off. On Béranger's advice ("who calls himself father of the workers and is delighted to please them, but is afraid of causing discontent by deciding among four contestants") she has the songs judged by the "Songwriters Guild." Let us note that the quarrels, the scenes between Flora and her worker friends rarely lead to final breaks: Vinçard will judge this contest. When, at the "chopinette gate," Ferrand learns that they want to call off the contest, finding all the songs "unsatisfactory," he stirs his followers up to a fine riot. Down with Flora Tristan the bourgeoise, the aristocrat! Vinçard protests: it's not a question of Madame Tristan here but a jury of workers. Everyone shouts and insults one another. At that moment Ferrand seizes the prizes, a gold medal and some books, and runs away. He will eventually return them. *The Lyric Echo* makes fun of the whole business, treats Flora as a utopian, a sublime dreamer, a "feverish apostle's brain," and publishes a song-parody.

This vaudeville episode shows that in any case all the advanced workers know Flora Tristan.

The book appears on June 1. In spite of the slowness of communications, she has already received, on July 10, forty-three letters from workers and thirty-five visits, and promptly begins to collect money for the second edition, with twenty-six additional pages and the *Marseillaise of the Workshop,* by Thys. She has sent out three thousand prospectuses to Parisian workshops and a copy of the book to all the guilds with a letter meant to stir them up.

> I have dealt with the question of union among all the workers. For me, there are neither apprentices nor initiates, but only equal men, citizens who have the same rights and the same interests, unhappy brothers who must unite to demand their rights peacefully and defend their interests.

She insists strongly on "peacefully," doesn't want violence, does not think that a change of political regime would be a determining factor, and is concerned with universal suffrage only as a side issue.

Workers' societies have begun to form among printing workers for ten years now. Recently they have formed a central committee of delegates from the workers' associations: it is already a union they have there. The Philanthropic Society of Stamping Workers takes the typographers as a model. Madame Soudet, although she has declined the office of propagandist, gives Flora's book to the delegate Lièvyne. He writes her that she has come a little too soon: "A year from now we should be in contact with 500,000, perhaps a million workers." He has named his society the Union, but Flora's book means that he has to change the title, because:

> If they came to believe that you are our leader, oh! then we would be quite lost. A woman! They would fear everything about a work like ours inspired and directed by a woman; especially forced as they would be to recognize in her Strength, Wisdom and Beauty. . . .

He knows she is beautiful, as does the hatter Saive, who writes for *The Workshop* and is ashamed of the paper's attitude toward her. Jean-Edmé Leclaire, head of a painters' and glaziers' cooperative, also comes on Sundays to the Rue du Bac and admires Flora. Soon he will become famous in his field; he will replace lead oxide in paint, whose fumes kill workers, with zinc oxide. For five years he has been running a mutual aid society. Like Saive's hatters' society, Leclaire's pays its members' medical expenses.

MARX'S FRIEND

They all come to see her on Sundays: Rosenfeld; Achille François, the secular saint of the tanners; Hugont, the latheworker from Lyon, who is twenty; his friend Vasbenter, who gives universal suffrage and the political struggle top priority.

Jules Janin has described Flora for us at these meetings:

> As she spoke she gradually became animated, then, all of a sudden, she became pensive again. . . . She had very true perceptions of the outside world, but soon clouds of waking dreams and fables of castles in Spain would come to break this clear light of reason.

Often foreigners mingle with the French. One of these is Marx's friend, the young German philosopher Arnold Ruge, with whom he has been putting out the *Franco-German Annals* in Paris since October 1843. We may guess that, no doubt, after his visit, Ruge must have mentioned Flora Tristan to Marx. Which makes it all the more likely that Engels read *Walks in London* and even stranger that he never mentioned it. It is Ruge who will introduce Marx and Proudhon in 1846: Did he suggest that he meet Flora? Who knows why this meeting never took place?

Arnold Ruge is living at the time in a hotel with a friend, the poet German Mäurer. Flora hears about them and, always eager to internationalize her circle, goes to leave her little book, her card, and the information that she "receives" on Sundays. That Sunday in the Rue du Bac, Ruge and Mäurer will meet eight Germans, all socialists and most of them workers, and ten Frenchmen, of whom a good half are workers. The two philosophers are expecting an old lady or a mannish virago. They find that, in spite of her white hair, she doesn't look her forty years (at the time a woman of that age usually looked older than a fifty-year-old would today).

Her long limbs make this short woman look tall. She sits, as usual, lithely curled up in her armchair, sometimes sitting on one leg, sometimes rising to speak. It is warm: she tends to feel the cold. Visitors are installed in armchairs or—like today—on the floor, on cushions, on a padded sofa, on chairs. There is no hierarchy: you sit where you can. Except for strangers, who are put in the place of honor, in front, near the lady of the house. Ruge finds the furniture in good taste, the lamps pleasing—there aren't many. He doesn't know this is from lack of money. The workers have left off their smocks and are wearing coats or their only suit. "The workers were elegant and intelligent people." There are also "some young people who are concerned with literature," among them an editor of Considérant's new magazine, *Peaceful Democracy*, of which the first issues are appearing. Flora explains that she is starting a series of discussions.

Considérant's disciple seems to Ruge "superstitious" about the phalansterian idea; but they all are.

"Why do you want to change society and make the workers into a separate class? The world may be transformed under any form of government. Once the Phalanstery exists, the model will quickly become contagious, and thus society will be transformed."

230

Flora smiles. The others shake their heads. She brings up, without insisting, the failure of the first trial phalanstery, at Condé-sur-Vergé. The young man declares that all the conditions were not right. Then he says—as dear Czynski repeats at each interview—that he hopes to see Flora converted to their ideas, and goes away.

Then, suddenly, she jumps to her feet. Her anger bursts out. Ruge is subjugated: "Her tall stature and the nobility of her features animated by the fire in her black eyes made her speech twice as impressive." She fulminates against these utopians. . . . Does she remember that Cabet, the *Workshop*, the *Hive*, so many others, consider her a utopian and a hopeless dreamer? For every one, the utopian is someone else. And who isn't someone's utopian?

Ruge, a German-style intellectual, has most likely never heard workers argue before. What a surprise to hear them contradict this pretty, aristocratic woman!

> On the sofa next to me was seated a tall man with curly brown hair and cultivated features: he was a hatter. He dug his black hand into his portfolio, drew out a voluminous manuscript, and read a remarkable work he had written, full of method and good sense.

It is André Saive. He is known for *The Workers' Future, dedicated to the working class and placed under its protection.* His mutual aid society for hatters admits members of other societies, and even workers from other guilds. He has established a whole network across France and knows houses everywhere where he can send those who have neither work nor health to convalesce. The society is sustained by weekly contributions.

"These little sums with an eye to an immediate interest, the worker can set them aside. But to subscribe, to give a whole day's wage for a future Workers' Union Center? Suggest that they form a working class, without regard to guild? This goal is too far away for them. But let Madame Tristan make her attempt, that can't do any harm."

"But we are asking them for very little to assure their future."

"You still don't know the workers very well, Madame. The worker earns just what he is forced to spend to go on living, that is, to earn . . ."

Later Marx will analyze this truth and make it into the theory:

the worker earns only enough to maintain his strength to work; the increase in value of this work is utilized by the boss, the machine, the factory, not by him.

Saive, in a few words, gives as an example his own life as a worker: misery lies in wait for you at the end of each week. To find the time to learn, you can allow yourself neither leisure nor pleasure.

They've just been speaking of woman. Saive defends the family: "Make it so that the mother doesn't have to abandon her child to earn her bread. Get her work at home. Let the young girl work with her mother and not have to sacrifice her innocence and her future to get herself a piece of bread. Then we will no longer have the sad sight that workers' households present nowadays."

Flora protests: woman is man's equal. The family is not her only life. She has the right to a trade that interests her.

A very young man speaks. He is a latheworker from near Lyon, passing through Paris. He has written to Flora; she invited him. He is called Hugont. He repeats what he has already written her: "Education? Yes. Woman is perhaps superior to man. But his equal? No. Educating her, as you say, would give more to civilization. But for the rest, no, I do not share your ideas. Leave debate in the assemblies, hardship and toil, war and danger, to man. To woman, a tranquil and uniform life to raise and educate her children. From the savage state to the degree of civilization we have achieved, woman has almost everywhere been dedicated to the indoor life."

Flora gets up and speaks. She wants to educate the whole working class, before sending it into battle for power. Universally. And would you want to exclude women, who mold their children, and thus both sexes? You want to refuse them certain rights while claiming they are superior?

She takes fire, eyes and teeth sparkle, her voice is near tears.

On this subject, she is inexhaustible, and the men, here, listen to her.

"If you allowed woman to receive the same education, to practice the same trades as man, she would be no more constrained by misery than he. Prostitution comes from your imposing chastity for virtue on woman without restricting man likewise. You won't end prostitution by shutting women and girls up at home. It's by giving woman the possibility of living by her work and also by not rejecting the seduced and abandoned girl from society."

She goes on for a long time. Saive has shown that it is useless to institute a law against begging without first guaranteeing work for all? Well, it is equally useless to denounce prostitution. Moreover, Flora announces her tour of France, preaching for her Workers' Union in all the factory towns. She will collect subscriptions for a future newspaper, which will belong to many members cooperatively, and will have working on it a team whose sole goal is the education and universal union of working men and women.

"What a woman!" says the poet German Mäurer as he leaves. "She will seize the flag and march in front. It is only now that I understand the French."

Flora is, from then on, determined to undertake her tour of France. She has weighed the peril to her health, then she chooses a testamentary executor: Alphonse Constant, the false ex-abbé. This disdained lover, who "grumbled but marched on," already judges her as he will later describe her:

> Flora's personality was so exalted in the struggle that in her own eyes she had passed to the status of a myth: she believed she was the Woman-Messiah. After having fought like a demon, she dreamed of a martyr's transfiguration to fly away to heaven on angel's wings.

If he exaggerates, as he does in general in the portrait he draws, he still sees clearly. Flora herself explains that the new faith will be achieved only in martyrs' blood. And from now on her friends, her dearest ones, can no longer hold her back. Constant and even Jules Laure and Doctor Evrat cannot fight against her vocation in the name of her health.

Yet a first trial, in Bordeaux where she has so many memories, shows her how frail she has become. In private life, she has had a disappointment: Cousin Goyeneche refuses to see her. In public life, she cuts herself off from possible sympathizers: she refuses to see the Lemonniers, who will become her last friends, because "it has nothing to do with the Saint-Simonians." Enfantin's letter has discouraged her, along with the fact that the School asked George Sand—scarcely a socialist—to become their "Mother," which the lady of Nohant, of course, refused.

In Bordeaux, emotion and rain make Flora ill, but she neglects this warning and gives a more evident cause: she left with two bad pairs of shoes, quickly drenched in running from a workers' meeting to the back room of a suburban cabaret.

She notes with that mixture of practical determination and humor that will become characteristic of her: "My feet are continually wet and I am sick. *Well, in my position as an apostle I don't have time to be sick.*" She adds that she needs three sets of shoes and clothing and that this tour of France will be expensive for her. At least let it be fruitful for the cause. And she pursues her aim, returning to the charge: Considérant is the only one who can give her the necessary useful contacts in the provinces, besides the help of his correspondents, who are expecting her. Become "king" of the phalansterians, endlessly busy editing newspapers or with the societies that invite him, he is hard to get hold of. He likes Flora, his goodness can only be moved by this courageous woman, but at the same time she annoys him. He believes in the phalanstery: it can be achieved immediately, so it is realistic. He doesn't believe in the universal union of workers across borders, in the forming of a class. That's utopian. But he has neither Cabet's bitterness nor his sectarianism. So he replies when she writes to him:

> My dear friend, do not forget that there you are a *king* while I am still *only on the way* and as a *good brother* you must help me into the chariot.

She asks him to speak of her future newspaper: "It is good that similar blows of the pickaxe resound in your *Democracy*," and suggests some leaflets, having "great need of money" to print a second edition of 10,000 copies of her *Union:* "I need 2400 and I have only 1400." She proposes a *Daughter of Lima* which she will never write. Then she asks for an audience and adds, for humor never deserts her: "Oh! when I too am a journalist, I'll have my revenge—on the others, that is, on those who don't have the honor to be." This time the contributions amount to 1,104.50 francs. The sale of the first edition yielded 500 francs net; that left 616. Once Flora has paid for the new edition, she has 629 francs in hand for the journey of propaganda and recruitment: she wants to create circles and committees everywhere she goes. Again she asks Considérant for an article and introductions.

234

Remember, my friend, that I am leaving alone, without any support, without money to pay provincial journalists who could give me publicity, that nearly everyone is against me. Men, because I ask for the emancipation of women; bosses, because I demand the emancipation of wage-earners.

Considérant notifies his society members. And Virtue-from-Avignon, the choleric, vain, gossipy, and generous Agricol Perdiguier, sends her his comrades. Even Cabet's newspaper has to defend her against the police.

Prophets' quarrels don't mean war. The Woman-Messiah plans to go away until Christmas. In her diary she writes:

I am undertaking to rest for three months. I will try to ally myself with an individual who pleases me and I will go with him to get my daughter and take her to Italy and Spain.

"An individual who pleases me . . ." "Ally myself," so it isn't one of those with whom she is already allied, Jules Laure, or Doctor Evrat, faithful familiars, inevitable intimates. Yet, if opportunities are not lacking during the long trip and even if, once, a man pleased her, she writes truthfully, in May: "At this moment, I am not disposed to welcome anyone's love."

24

STORM LIGHT ON
A WANDERING APOSTLE

Seven months of wandering to discover workers' solidarity, that rare sun, that confidence that no acclaim can replace. She had an inkling of it in Paris. The first days, at Gosset's lodge, or while reading letters like Achille François's or young Belnot's. Sometimes, on the Rue du Bac, meetings ended in a burst of agreement about the work. But Flora had still not experienced group excitement and that moment when your voice speaks for millions. Wandering from town to town with hardly enough to live on, walking in the rain in leaky shoes, sleeping little and eating less, never allowing yourself to flag—that life is tolerable only when you know that you are bringing the world to light, that you are illuminating the cave. You can accept discomfort, anxieties, fatigue, the persecutions of police, press, and "good society," when you are bringing bread of the spirit to people starved for everything, the fire of hope to people freezing with resignation. Otherwise it would be terrible.

Flora's diary, her "notes for my work: the Tour of France," still have their caustic irony. But when she rubs the worker the wrong way, she causes suffering for herself, an apostle and thus a martyr. On the other hand she takes some good digs at the others; garrulous politicians, "liberal" bosses, rich people of good conscience: "I think I can no longer tolerate any middle-class person." The hardest is the women. When they take her for an adventuress because she stirs their husbands up. When they boo her out of incomprehension. When they say, shriveled with misery, "that there will always be rich, and a good thing, to give work to the poor," Flora is furious, then pulls herself together: "My sisters, I swear to you that I will deliver you." A hundred years later, as Hitler's soldiers are about to kill him, a Frenchman in the Resistance cries out to them: "Imbeciles, I'm dying for *you!*" The first constantly to link women's rights with workers' rights, Flora is least accepted by workers' wives. Yet her last love, maternal, moral, but more exalted than any passion, will be for a little laundress from Lyon.

Traveling for the workers, she is no longer a lovely lady with a servant and a drawing room on the Rue du Bac, albeit in the attic. Their hearts are touched by this frail wanderer persecuted by the police, the lonely woman with the incomprehensible courage, the one the press and the rich slander. They are proud of her, the one who loves them. Except for local celebrities, poets-craftsmen swollen with vanity. In spite of George Sand's unfair opinion, Flora is not vain. With Achille François the leatherworker, she could say: "I shall never be vain, but very proud of the cause that I have embraced." When, in Marseille, they acclaim her as a "beloved actress," she dissolves in sadness: don't they understand, then? But when, in Lyon, they talk about evangelism, her mission, lighting the world and ascending to heaven, she feels in tune with them. No more than the madman who thought he was God in the London asylum does she fear the Lyonnais visionaries, and is outraged that they are locked up. Isn't going crazy from and for a cause a sign that that cause touches beings more deeply than reason?

> An idea that has the power to drive a man mad through the love it engenders in him is an idea that must dominate the world.

Well—she will quickly learn—reason alone does not make for action. What can a mass oppressed to this extent reasonably do against the powers massed against it? To find courage for rebellion, you have to believe that new times are coming. Being accepted as the Woman-Messiah means ceasing to "sow on stony ground." That is what Flora will think more and more starting on April 12, 1844.

25

FROM BURGUNDY
TO LAMARTINE

It is four in the morning, dark as night, in April. On the steam-boat for Burgundy, she is enjoying the sailors' happy shouts, their familiar greetings, their gaiety. Friendly, unlike English sailors, these speak to her willingly, but barely listen to her.

A day and a half to come alongside the canal docks in Auxerre, population 12,000, on April 13 at three in the afternoon.

They are expecting her at the Union, Pierre Moreau's society. Why doesn't she mention him in her diary? His thirty disciples enchant her. Other workers, whom she meets elsewhere and thinks she can convince, seem charming to her: Burgundian gaiety. To give herself courage, she asserts that the workers are "easy to lead," if the middle class here is deaf to all progress, the clergy egotistical, and the masses, on the whole, torpid.

Running from seven in the morning till eleven at night and then, alone at last in the inn, writing up her diary, is exhausting. But "I am morally happy."

Avallon, Semur—Romanesque architecture doesn't interest her and the crusaders' descendants aren't interested in her preaching. In Saint Bernard's homeland she "sows on stony ground."

From April 20 to the 27th, she stays in Dijon. The Paris

238

newspapers, with irony or sympathy, have noted Flora Tristan's departure for her tour of France. Considérant and Agricol Perdiguier have alerted their followers, Saint-Simonians, Fourierists, the Companions of Duty members are expecting her. The local press, which she visits, talks of her "philanthropic work," her "noble foresight," her book which "makes one think."

Flora thinks she will have an ally in *The Gold Coast Journal*: Antoinette Quarré, the dressmaker-poet given her start by Lamartine, is working there right now. Flora supposes she can count on her support.

Antoinette Quarré is deformed, very sure of herself, very much the Dijon lady. Flora must have put on her charmer's air, that air of walking on the waters that generally warms people toward her.

"You know my ideas, Madame, help me propagate them. Are you not doubly concerned, as a woman and as belonging to the working class?"

The dressmaker-poet swells up like a frog.

"I can be of no use to you: I don't spend time with people of the masses."

"Are you sure that it's not they who no longer want to spend time with you?"

Flora must have wished these words unsaid the moment they were out . . . but the "new lady" promptly changes her tone and gives the Parisian the address of editors who can help her. "Vanity and baseness"; Flora leaves saddened. *The Gold Coast Journal* devotes a review to *The Workers' Union*: union in the name of material interests is impossible, decides C.-J. L., who signs it: it would never hold together without social unity: this book is not the Gospel, so why change? The editor-in-chief tells her that the Paris press is making fun of her. Flora puts on her insolent great lady air and he turns polite, humble, and pleasant . . . a typical man of the times!

The Dijon Spectator notes her presence.

Flora runs. From café to café, across from factories, in the suburbs. "I can't go on this way for three cities." The phalansterians promise to help her. The Saint-Simonians hardly budge, but "put a fine shoulder to the wheel" of History. And at last, there are "avowed partisans of woman's emancipation." The bishop ends up receiving her. Msgr. François-Victor Rivet is very frank: "You are putting a rare tenacity into the service of a cause that goes against the Church. If you succeed in forming a workers' union, the Church will fight you with all her strength."

So she has been warned. She doesn't know yet that these first stages are the calmest: the Ministry of the Interior is not yet alerted, the police aren't bothering her.

Seven days; a "clean and airy" city; friends. They tell her about monuments, museums. . . . Possessed by her idea, she looks at nothing. "I would give the loveliest church in Christendom for an intelligent worker." (This will be Lenin's point of view in the next century, but he won't dare express it so crudely.)

She meets an ardent soul, who will remain her friend through letters: Madame Mallet. "The first woman to understand me." And also a merchant, so impassioned they call him mad "like his master Fourier": Lallemant. He dedicates great speeches to her: here at last is the Woman-Messiah he has been waiting for ever since he read the Saint-Simonians!

This time, she leaves by stagecoach. Phalansterians, friends of Victor Considérant go with her to the station, carrying bundles of books, other phalansterians are waiting for her in Chalon.

As soon as she arrives, the freemasons show up. They crop up here and there to show their generally shy sympathy for their "sister in humanity." Flora seems to have been treated as an "honorary mason."

Charles Lagrange, the republican, comes to see her at her hotel. His five years in prison after the Lyon revolt of 1834 have not stifled his glibness. Broad gestures, florid phrases, Flora still finds him as ridiculous as ever, as much the third-rate politician. Workers' union? Bah, for him the Republic is the panacea. . . . He dreams of what, in fact, will happen to him one day, since he will read Louis-Philippe's act of abdication in 1848. He speaks of the meeting organized by the lodge of Perfect Equality, supports his "sister." *The Globe* will say that these two hundred listeners represent "all the distinguished people in the city." Two-thirds are bosses, petty bourgeoisie, "the tribe I like the least." Flora tells them insolently that she is accustomed to preaching only before workers. They buy

240

her book. Some of them believe in it. *The Courier* and *The Saône-et-Loire Patriot* denounce the danger of this enterprise. So that when there are fights in May and June between steamboat workers and porters and the police arrest "agitators," they recall the evil passing of the "agitatress."

From town to town, Flora, at first incautious, naïve, credulous, becomes increasingly conscious of her responsibility. Each stage, filling out her experience, gives her a higher idea of her role. The favors of the enlightened middle class, so convenient and so flattering at the beginning, are soon intolerable to her.

Mâcon is going through a bad period for workers. Small factories are competing and tottering. The workers, disorganized, cannot find jobs anymore. The bosses bring in "revolutionaries" from the country who will accept any salary, but don't know how to work. Townsmen and "revolutionaries" confront each other and fight instead of uniting. Only the coopers, organized into a powerful guild, are interested in Flora's work, although she visits all the associations. "I find the society members much better than the rest; they are already part of every body of the State": they are less narrow-minded.

She tries to speak in the taverns, as she did in Dijon. In one suburb, the revolutionaries' wives surround the café and insult her when she leaves: What can a woman be doing in a café, if not debauching their husbands?

Here two newspapers are hostile enough to print that the police will eventually have to step in. On May 4 in Paris *The Globe*, informed who knows how, writes:

> It must be admitted that it is a very odd and noteworthy spectacle, seeing women of the people insult and drive away a revolutionary bluestocking, while a deputy addresses epistles and compliments to her.

This deputy, Monsieur de Beaumont, introduces her to the *Public Good*, Lamartine's paper. There she finds young gentlemen who are interested in democratic politics as their grandfathers were interested in hunting. At least they publish a eulogistic article on the "book printed by charity": "We would like to see it penetrate the heart of the masses." The Lamartinians are such a disappointment! . . . Mâcon is so sad. . . .

What she is told about the region is even more depressing. In Bugey, at Jujurieux, at La Séauve, Lyon bonnet makers have set up workshops where they employ country girls almost exclusively. Living in, kept by the sisters under an almost monastic rule, these young girls and childless widows are cut off from the outside world. Working-class mistresses from the isolated mountain regions of Drôme, Ardèche and even Isère train apprentices brought there by their parents. The bonnet makers avoid girls from the plains: the mountain girls of Auvergne and Forez are more resigned and more docile. They are usually between fourteen and sixteen when they arrive with their trousseaus. They are taken out for exercise in a covered yard, they are taught reading and writing, and a bit of arithmetic. Their wages are between 40 and 80 francs a year, from which their room and board is withheld. They work "only" twelve hours a day. The superiors of these factory-convents "neglect nothing to make fervor reign." The farmers and craftsmen of the region are eager to marry these creatures so well trained in obedience. But they scarcely approach them: no communication is allowed with the workers at the neighboring silk mill. If a mechanic comes to repair a machine, he must work in silence and even his looks are watched closely.

After three to five years they have forcibly saved about 165 francs held by the director. Then they are presented with a suitor attracted by their virtue, the education they have received, and the dowry. Some of them even sigh that "this imprint fades only too soon."

Among the women who shake their fists at Flora, how many went through this forced-labor convent?

More enlightened workers tell how they posted themselves by the roadside leading from the mountain. To the parents who came down carrying a bundle and leading a young girl, they shouted: "Don't put your daughters in that prison: it's Cayenne!" But the peasants shrugged their shoulders at the town's bad feeling. *The Saône-et-Loire and Ain Fly* warns Madame Flora Tristan that in Lyon the police won't stand her "organization that it considers a disorganization" for long.

26

THE SILKWORKERS' REGION

The silkworkers' revolt shook France, and ten years after the 1834 insurrection still makes the middle class tremble. Yet the silkworkers were not, in spite of the song (after the fact), men who went "bare ass," but middlemen, entrepreneurs who in turn exploited sickly men and women with rickets and expressionless faces. But their rising "opened a new era for Lyon," the prefect Gasparin wrote.

Until 1830, according to him, the "leaders of commerce" took "the part of the administration." The revolution of 1830 aroused in the workers "hope for a better lot . . . [which], unfulfilled, became intolerable. Threats and provocations directed at the manufacturers, a little arrogance on their part, caused the break and hostility between the two classes: they fought because they hated and not because they suffered." So the prefect is aware of the fact: the silkworkers' revolt was a class struggle. Yet the silkworkers were an "aristocracy of master workers." They wanted to deal directly with the clients, excluding the merchants. But the workers "were already beginning to note in black chalk this new superiority trying to get organized above them."

This revolt of November 1833—the Soviet Tarlé will say in the mid-twentieth century—"marked a turning point in the history of the working class in France and in the world," because, on November 21 and 22, workers in every field rallied to the silkworkers. It was then really a class struggle, it was even the first demonstration on such a scale. It was not, as the gentle Lamartine dreamed, a hunger strike of the "tribe of European pariahs."

So Flora is right to think of Lyon as the infernal paradise of rebellion and working-class consciousness. She has read so many pages devoted to this proletariat; she knows that Franz Liszt sent the silkworkers the proceeds from one of his concerts, that Stendahl, exaggerating the amount of their salaries, commented:

> When the workers wrote on their standard: "Live working or die fighting," they were earning four francs a day (!) and there was plenty of work. Now that they have been dying of hunger for six months, from November 1836 to July 1837 and with no foreseeable end to their misery, the government has nothing to fear.

About this eight-year-old misery, gentle Marceline Desbordes-Valmore repeated to Flora, before she left, what she saw at the time:

> Thirty thousand honest, pious workers dying of misery, of cold, and searching for bread *day by day* up to the last stories of our houses which look like bleak Gothic towers. I no longer have the strength nor the means to assuage this poverty which is increasing and makes one shudder . . . in spite of their sublime virtues; for there is something sublime about these people. Some of them drop dead of hunger in the streets. This is as true as you are.

But the ten years since the revolt have seen some resistance organized, in spite of repression. In 1840, Mollard and Barallier, textile printers, organized their brothers into a real union called the Blue Ribbon Resistance Society. Louis Blanc will note:

> The men who aspired to direct the political movement had neither great enough consistency nor high enough intelligence for this role. Little known by the workers, they spoke a new language, whose violence alone could have commended it to the mob, without the prejudices that were skillfully spread among them by the rebellious leaders themselves.

Does Flora know that, especially since Mâcon and the kind

warnings of *The Saône-et-Loire and Ain Fly*, the police have begun to keep an eye on her?

Reaching Lyon on April 30, she moves into the Hôtel de Milan on the Place des Terreaux, most of whose patrons are traveling salesmen and officers. The muddy little streets, barracks-like houses, cold and dirty cafés could be discouraging. But, on the contrary, Flora feels that in this "proletarian metropolis" she will be able to find her Own Kind.

Her first meeting brings the workshop heads together at her hotel. They belong to various parties, let her know that they are always waiting for Cabet and Proudhon. They gladly repeat the latter's formulas: "What is property? Property is theft." They know that collective strength is greater than the sum of individual strengths, that simultaneity of effort creates a value greater than that given by individual effort. So in every object produced there exists a part that returns to society and that the machine owner, the entrepreneur, corners: there's the theft. The employer has not paid for all the work from which he profits. Proudhon was going to come and create his "Order in humanity." Cabet was going to come and convince them to go and found an Icaria in America.

These workshop heads—the same who unleashed the silkworkers' revolt, or their younger brothers—are educated men. They reason better than all the Parisian philosophers.

"The manufacturer's capital brings him 33 percent profit. The workshop head has the skills and rents or buys the premises, but his capital, immobilized, brings him nothing. On the other hand the skills wear out. With the dead season you get an annual deficit of 438 francs. Is that fair?"

Flora listens to them, her eyes shining . . . until the moment when she takes the floor, questions, goes further.

Then one of them confesses: "Madame, we were told that you were not the author of your book. We have read it: it is just, reasonable. We thought that only a superior man could have done it and that he pays you to front for him. Because the police aren't as hard on women."

She tries to debate and sees they are not convinced. Then she puts on her lawyer's, her poet's eloquence . . . and their eyes shine. There, she says to herself, that's what they need: in their state of ignorance and narrow-mindedness they need inspiration.

On May 29 she attends a session of the conciliation board, a tribunal where bosses and workers sit side by side. "Thus, then, one can envisage a justice where the workers, united, would have enough strength to confront the manufacturers."

Besides the society members, she knows that a friend is waiting for her there. Nearly a year ago now, when her book appeared, a workshop head wrote to her:

> Your intention is beautiful, your goal magnificent, its results important, since it can very well serve as an intermediary between "civilization" and "the integral association" proposed by Fourier, the final aim of all our various efforts. For in your centers you do for old people, children, sick people what we want to do for everyone in the phalanstery. It is good, and I see with pleasure that I can count you among our ranks, although there may still be some slight disagreement as to the means.

However, he doesn't think union can be achieved immediately, but nonetheless invites her to come and see him in Lyon: "I will show you the whole scope of the Lyonnais working class, in which I have a secret hand. But no indiscretions. If I ever have the happiness to see you I promise you some revelations face to face," and he asked for thirty pamphlets. His name is Joseph Reynier.

So she goes to see this Fourierist, who is also connected with the Saint-Simonians, "who had all the intelligent youth in their ranks." He was very prominent during the silkworkers' revolt. At the time he was twenty and made quite a stir. Since, he has founded a cooperative of true and social commerce, become a member of the "Harmonious Correspondence," in fact he has a lot of influence among the advanced workers, the very circles Flora wants to attract.

When she enters the cooperative's shed, he thinks he suddenly sees before him his feminine ideal, "the woman of my dreams, with elevated feelings, a big heart, limitless devotion, who alone can make me believe in happiness here below. . . ."

In spite of his emphatic language, the mark of Saint-Simon and Fourier, but also of Hugo and Lamartine, in spite of his great protestations of humility, Joseph Reynier is very proud of his achievements. (At the end of the century he will publish his *Memoirs*, which show him quite sure of himself and, as Flora puts it, "nuts in the area of vanity.")

246

He falls in love at this first meeting. Chazal, Chabrié, Escudero, Jules Laure, others no doubt (we know nothing about how she met Doctor Evrat), Flora seems to specialize in love at first sight. But here, there has been a year of crystallization through community of thought, and Joseph Reynier, who has surely read all her works, knows her history, her romantic imagination, her high-strung sensibility. Yet in Lyon she already feels very ill. Another admirer thinks she must be forty-five or fifty: she is just forty and has white hair.

Reynier takes her to the taverns of the Croix Rousse, a Sunday hell.

The weavers and spinners are there, sitting on long benches or wooden chairs, drinking beer without saying a word. The oldest ones made the government tremble thirteen years ago. When Lyon rocks, Paris, the Paris of the rich, is seasick. And yet they stay there for hours without moving, puny, feeble, drooping: "Under this apparent calm, a muted and terrible fomentation stirs these unfortunates whose excitement increases in proportion to the constraint they impose on themselves."

Reynier presents her, from table to table: in each tavern he knows someone. She listens and understands better that her desire to convince and argue is unrealistic. What they want is verbal escape, hope and action. A "Workers' Union Center" where they would be cared for, educated, sheltered? They would like one, they have more need for one than elsewhere: the hospitals are full, it's a favor to be admitted. Old people die of misery or eat their children's bread. The jobless beg or steal; how else can they exist? In Lyon, Flora realizes for the first time that theft is provoked by social injustice. When Chazal attacked her on the street and she got up, barely convalescent, to bring the liberal deputies her *Petition Against Capital Punishment*, she wrote:

> The individual's aggression against society is such madness that it only occurs when hunger or exasperated passions provoke it. Misery, lack of work or of a trade, such are the first causes of attacks against property.

She understands the full meaning of her own words only in these Croix Rousse taverns, one bleak and rainy Sunday in May.

In the taverns she also sees some poor girls: they lace up tight to please these taciturn men who take a little quick pleasure with them for a few pennies and don't recognize them in the street afterward. Prostitution remains, for this cerebral woman, a major enigma. How can they? . . .

Reynier organizes meetings for Flora in every district. On the Rue Luizerne, during a silence, she sees a young woman with a candid face get up and cry out that at last she hears the truth, at last she sees this Woman-Messiah whom she was told of but of whom she despaired.

"I am a laundress and own nothing. So I give you what I have: my life. Make of it whatever will serve the Cause. I want to carry your word. I know how to read and write. I can tell other women that at last our Messiah has come to free us."

From this cry on, everything changes for Flora. Why check this love that burns her, why pick it apart with arguments? What these rough, disinherited beings want is to love and to act, to spread their love and unite through love.

At the end of the meeting the young woman comes to her: Eléonore Blanc, her taciturn husband beside her, throws herself into the arms of the Bearer of the New Gospel. "You will be my St. John," Flora says, possessed by the Christ image. Around them cold and silent men begin to weep. Eléonore's husband kneels and promises to leave his wife free to accomplish her mission.

> From that moment I felt arise in me a deep and lively attachment to this noble and courageous woman, and she in turn gave me evidence of an affection which was very precious and very dear to me.

Eléonore Blanc will write, and under the awkward words, for she is intimidated by writing, one senses her sincerity. From then on she goes everywhere with Flora, the apostle's shadow, passing among the audience to sell the pamphlet and ask for contributions for the Union Center.

As a meeting rarely goes by without the police, on May 9 at ten in the morning the commissioner of the Terreaux district, flanked by four sergeants, enters the Hôtel de Milan and, followed by a good quarter of the curious tenants, goes into Flora's room, where she is writing two letters: one to Jules Laure, the other to Doctor Evrat. The commissioner shows his warrant, seizes and takes away all her

248

papers. Two days later *The Censor,* a Lyonnais paper, publishes Flora's protest: she relates the facts and notes:

> In me individual freedom is being attacked . . . I cannot guess the motive that made the authorities of the city of Lyon act in this way toward me. In the ten days I have been in Lyon, no more in this city than in any of the others I have visited, I have not committed the shadow of an offense. In my writings, in my speech, in my actions, I push to the extreme the respect due to legality.

All the newspapers in the area protest, each in its own way. *The Reform* finds it inconsistent to let a book no doubt judged harmless be published and sold, then suddenly deal severely with it. The Mâcon *Fly* recalls that she was warned. The Lamartinian *Public Good* is outraged. The *Lyonnais Charivari* talks about "a Parisian bluestocking's misadventure." In Paris, Cabet's *Populace* of July 12 gets excited: "What kind of society is it where the police can visit and seize a woman's papers and disturb her freedom like that!" It will be even more indignant on learning, on July 26, of a confiscation in the Croix Rousse. This is at a textile manufacturer's where two workers are arrested and "brochures entitled *Farewell to Rome,* made by Cabet, Brille, ex-abbé-Edouard, and Flora Tristan, Communists and Republicans," are seized. These pamphlets are a collection of articles against the Vatican.

Flora enjoys and rejoices in the incident. She runs to the public prosecutor's office, where they are friendly and embarrassed. On June 10, a month later, a nonsuit order restores her papers to her.

After the incident, the workers show her a much more spontaneous confidence and surround her with touching attentions. "This persecution has made them see that what I preach has some value, since the public prosecutor opposes it." The police occupy the next room and watch the hotel entrance, but her followers bring her new adherents every evening. Her room is transformed into a smelly steam bath. But from then on, lifted out of herself, Flora fills her messiah's part. Only her health, which is already deteriorating from day to day, troubles her: since Dijon she has had constant intestinal pains. One may suppose that she had a tumor that was spreading from month to month.

Is it Reynier or Eléonore Blanc? The disciples show so much zeal that a new edition of *The Workers' Union* is soon necessary: they come to offer her the price of four thousand copies at 25 centimes, which will infuriate "the competition." Cabet will write that Flora Tristan is making the Lyon proletariat contribute not for her great union nor for her newspaper, but for her little book.

Flora gives this Lyon edition a preface which will be published in the *Vaucluse Echo*:

> The people's way is to show its opinion through facts. It speaks little—doesn't write—it acts. The *fact*—that is its *argument*. . . . [She tells how the contributions were made.] By contributing in this way —notice—already *individuality disappears*. This time, in the contribution list, no more names: *groups*, and only groups. This fact alone *proves* that you *understand* the idea in the *little book*: UNION. Workers, it is a great and beautiful idea you have there: to form groups is to UNITE. . . .
>
> Encouraged by such a reward, I no longer fear growing weak. . . . If rivalry and hatred are already growing less, if there is already enough accord and brotherhood among all for groups to form, what can we not hope for in the future! Brothers, then let us repeat in one voice: Union makes strength—Union alone can SAVE us!

Vocabulary of the times? Undoubtedly political vocabulary, often reused since. The repetition of key words, the rhythm of the sentences will be found again a century later in Socialist and Communist appeals.

Proudhon, who has also come to Lyon, is ironic: "At the moment I don't know how many new evangelists are preaching." He lumps together Buchez, Pierre Leroux, Lamennais, Considérant, Madame George Sand, Madame Flora Tristan, Pecqueur, and adds: "I don't feel like swelling the number of these lunatics." Cabet, he says, is in Lyon, and as he prepares to leave for Texas, designates him as his successor: "I yield the succession to whoever will give me a cup of coffee for it."

Singularly, the apostle of the Union doesn't meet any of the other apostles. And she doesn't mention the feminist Eugénie Niboyet who tried, right here, to create a university for women.

In the middle of this excitement, when she is feeling more and more given over to her cause and filled by it, Joseph Reynier sends her a declaration of love . . . since Flora has announced that she is leaving for Saint-Etienne, he feels less unhappy "whatever may be the result of an avowal that is as bold as it is mad . . . than if I saw you leave without confiding in you. . . ." If she refuses "I will be fully twice as unhappy to have met you on my way; you will have shattered the illusion that sustained me. Oh! if it were otherwise, divine woman, if you stooped to me to raise me to you, this act that I would call religious would not be without reward for you, for God did not will it thus."

Very much "the earthworm in love with a star."

Flora's comments are often judged as an aristocratic disdain. According to these barbed words in the letter, she is even accused of pretending to have a love for the workers that she doesn't feel. In talking about men in smocks, with black, furrowed, calloused hands, coarse laughs, graceless ways, she has often, it is true, used the language of a disgusted middle-class woman. But we must not forget the times nor Flora's general attitude toward men. An unquestionably charming and attractive woman, going alone into cafés, workshops, guild hostels, advocating in the strongest terms the union of all, equality of the sexes, female emancipation, divorce and respect for love, how could she avoid misunderstandings? Blacksmiths, miners, weavers, in these early days of the struggle, are not at all accustomed to dealing with women as equals, friends, in short, comrades. Even if Flora isn't frigid, her own cases of love at first sight are cerebral and not sensual. Used as she is to being on guard because of her very situation, desire always finds her reticent. She can't answer with the cold simplicity of today's militant who says: "I don't care for you," or "I'm not an object."

Besides, Flora feels she is the Messiah of the working class and not a love object for one worker who doesn't attract her. So:

> Really, that's all I needed, for a worker to fall in love with me! Really, these boys have no common sense, no hardheadedness. They're all mad in the area of vanity. *And I explain: I don't want to say that a worker doesn't have the right to raise his desires as high as me.* I acknowledge this right in him as in any other man, only he ought to feel that, *at this moment, I am not disposed to welcome anyone's love.*

The time has come, as she wrote to the mysterious Olympe, when "a displacement of the senses" has taken place, when imagination has taken over her whole being.

27

BLACK CITIES

This circle around Lyon that takes Flora to Roanne, Saint-Etienne and Saint-Alban plunges her into the heart of a gray, smoky land and a proletariat at once combative and coolly determined.

Six weeks before her arrival in the region, on April 5, a violent strike broke out among the 2000 miners of Rive-de-Gier (there are 6800 miners in the whole mining area of the Loire). The 400 strikers saw troops, police, prefect, public prosecutor arrive. . . . First there was sword fighting, then suddenly the troops fired without orders. Seventeen miners were arrested for agitation, of whom seven were acquitted. The *Charivari* wrote: "At Rive-de-Gier they shoot the workers who ask for enough to give their families bread. It's an expedient way of curing them of a taste for bread."

Flora first sees the workers of Roanne in a factory where the din and the damp steam remind her of the London gasworks.

The boss, seeing her falter in the courtyard, says laughing: "It's lack of habit, my lovely lady. The human body can get used to anything."

"Even to dying," Flora answers.

A Catholic journalist, Auguste Guyard, takes her around and welcomes her into his home. Sick as she is, Flora has trouble behaving like a serene and smiling guest, nor does she dare hold too many meetings at her friends' homes. She speaks with miners who drudge underground for 2 to 2.50 francs a day; women for the same sixteen hours of work only get one franc at the most. And it's worse for work at home. In the villages, ribbon makers get from 1 to 1.50 francs but they have to deduct lighting and heat from that. "You get there by privation," they say. "You hardly see meat." The townswomen, exhausted, have no milk when they give birth and wet nurses charge ten to twenty francs per month. If they reject this lot it's "like everywhere a little work, a little stealing, a little charity and of course prostitution."

The owner of the Waters of Saint-Alban invites Flora to spend a few days with him. They like each other at first sight; they talk day and night. He is skeptical, disillusioned, and good without fooling himself. This type of man attracts Flora: what a triumph it would be to convert him to enthusiasm, to faith! A bourgeois happiness, with a man like Doctor Goin? (Maybe he suggested it to her.) They spend thirty times what a worker needs to live well. The good life? Comfort without worries, as in Peru? How could she have accepted it? How far she feels from herself of ten years ago!

> I would not consent for anything in the world. Oh! How I prefer this great and magnificent humanitarian existence that I am enjoying with so much happiness! To be alone so as to try to live everyone's life, what is greater, lovelier, happier in this world? My lover is God, it is humanity, it is love of my brothers. That is the only love worthy of me.

In Saint-Etienne, Lyon's sister city, again "all the public monuments look like prisons." The Fourierists seem to be satisfied bourgeois. The workers, disorganized and miserable, discourage and upset her. The ribbon makers work at home without a fire and by candlelight so as not to soil the ribbon. For sixteen hours a day, on old looms, often out of work, they labor for one or two francs a day. This distrust, this reserve impel her to provoke them all during her only meeting there. They call her, it seems, "a secret agent of everything." Well, let's talk about women's rights.

Lyon again, with Eléonore waiting at the stagecoach, closer now than her real daughter. Another disciple, Madame Grimaud, whispers that the middle class here too think she is a "secret agent." They are taking revenge for the caustic phrases the public prosecutor, after the seizure, took from her personal diary and allowed to leak out.

A summer rotting with rain, soaked shoes and intestinal pains. She has to run to a meeting of tailors who, alas, are singing Cabet and Icaria in every key. Fortunately letters and some Lyonnais tell her that she has changed some lives. She has no other destiny anymore: only to draw from their moral sleep those who will complete the work.

But she must tear herself away from Lyon: Eléonore and Reynier will keep the fire burning here. She still has the whole South of France to teach. If only she felt less weary. But it's July: she will be back in Paris in the fall.

The last evening, the Woman-Messiah's mission leaps the bounds of reason, reaches the same degree of ecstasy as Prosper Enfantin's audience thirteen years ago. When Napoleon came back from the isle of Elba and saw his guard rally to him, he must have felt like this. And, at the end of the twentieth century, the mystical healers, the gurus from India and America, the African prophets, or certain Marxist orators at the liberation of countries occupied by the Nazis. Outpouring, hope, ecstasy, euphoria.

It is the evening of July 7, at Croix Rousse; a session of close empathy. She says:

> Before 1789, what was the proletarian? A peasant, a serf. . . . Then the Revolution came and suddenly the wisest of the wise proclaim that the plebeians are called the people and the serfs citizens. And at once there came from their ranks generals such as Charlemagne, Henri IV or Louis XIV could never recruit in their proud nobility; then scholars, artists, poets, writers, statesmen, financiers appeared. In less than thirty years, the country's wealth tripled. What happened to the people is a good sign for women. When their '89 comes, the country's wealth will quadruple for women make up half of the human race and their strength will triple.

The Saint-Simonian Pérelle, his face flooded with tears, cries: "The Woman-Messiah. We have been waiting for her for twenty years!" Another worker, Jacob, shouts: "Kneel!" and the first rows kneel down while the *Marseillaise of the Workshop* rings out, learned from the "little book." After which the workers give Flora a banquet. Everyone drinks wine, even the apostle sworn to milk. Eléonore gets up . . . Flora cannot write down the scene that evening; she notes it on the boat the next day.

> "I love you!" she cried with looks of an ineffable beauty. "I weep with joy to feel that I am strong enough to love you so much."
> Then in her rapture she thanked me for having given her such a beautiful life. She kissed me tenderly, kissed my hands gratefully, blessed me. Oh how beautiful this rapture of sublime love made her!

Flora weeps. Reynier is so moved he can hardly give his speech. Sobs make him stop. Pérelle and Jacob clasp the Woman-Messiah in their arms and poor Reynier can, in the general embracing, hold her pressed against him for a moment. "It was as if we had all come down from heaven, we no longer knew what was going on on earth." No one sleeps. Eléonore does not go to bed. At two in the morning the Grimauds and the Blancs take Flora to the boat. It is raining so hard they can't see.

Flora remains "plunged in her superhuman state." Eléonore cries: "Oh! Mother, go in peace, your spirit remains in me!"

Flora stays in bed all day in her cabin, weeping bitterly, writing her oath: "A thousand thanks, my brothers of Lyon, for these twelve centuries of life that you have given me in twelve hours." She forbids herself ever to return to the city where her heart is, if it is not to lay the first stone of the Workers' Union Center—or to organize the provisional government: "Otherwise, never."

28

ARDORS OF THE SOUTH

Luckily, the quarrel with Virtue-from-Avignon does not prevent solidarity: the guildsmen, forewarned, welcome her. Young, vigorous, happy, there is nothing mystical about them. But the textile printers, who earn one to three francs a day and are out of work five months, are interested in the right to work. Their republican café politicians seem to her contemptible, but easygoing and pleasant company. The police note each visit, each meeting, each excursion. So we know that she visits the Popes' palace with the leaders of the Society of Glory. The architecture leaves her indifferent. But the palace is used as a barracks, and the soldiers sleep on straw: that's the important point. She also discovers middle-class people who dream of seeing the pope back in Avignon. Humanity is definitely stranger than fiction.

The bishop receives her with reticence, the mayor with goodwill. She manages to set up a committee. The workers' isolation, shut up in their region, town or village and knowing nothing of their brothers depresses her: "It's enough to drive you mad! It's really beyond human strength." As her strength declines, she magnifies the divine character of her mission. Otherwise how could she go on?

Then she is in Marseille, which astounds her. Rackets, cosmopolitan intrigues, porters who earn 50 francs a day, and from 15,000 to 20,000 Genoese, 10,000 Greeks, an immigrant work force that the Marseillais use as "white slaves." Flora agrees to have her trunk carried to the stagecoach for 1.50 francs. The porter brings a heavily pregnant Genoese woman, puts the trunk on her back and makes her walk, bent double. Then he gives her 25 centimes and, when she demands 50, hits her hard enough to knock her down. What can be done about workers who become exploiters?

It makes her fall ill and she sees that these shoemakers, bakers, and tailors love her, run around in the Southern sun selling the "little book" and getting signatures, tell each other: "Ah! my God, what unhappiness for us if this woman died!" In nine days they actually sell seven hundred copies of *The Workers' Union*. The press compares the "little book" to Franklin's pamphlets. The police make childish attempts to provoke her: one day a rich man wants to "keep her," another, a madame tells her about an opulent Greek. The workers, alarmed, promise to disguise her in national guard uniform and take her into the mountains if there is danger.

In ten days in Toulon, she discovers the arsenal workers. A doctor organizes a meeting with an audience of two hundred. (Flora is constantly meeting doctors and not one of them seems to notice that she is destroying herself. In those days they knew only one fatal illness: consumption; everything else seemed benign.) Toulon teaches Flora a lot. These workers, organized into mutual aid societies, conceive perfectly the need to form a single working class. But, since they are not afraid of unemployment, the right to work leaves them indifferent. Thus she understands how she must tie each claim to the needs of the place and time.

Friends come to her, although the mason-poet Charles Poncy, so dear to George Sand, does not appear: he has lost face, having been afraid of storms at the moment of leaving for Algeria, and he is hiding. His brother replaces him. George and Flora definitely don't have the same heroes.

The usual search in her hotel room yields nothing: she no longer keeps her papers with her. The prosecutor sends word that he wants to see her. But the Messiah is less naïve than she was in Lyon, and defends herself like an expert militant: "Tell the prosecutor that if he discovers an offense, he can send out a warrant for my arrest. Otherwise I have nothing to see him for. . . ."

She returns to Marseille, her friends organize a farewell party at which six hundred people acclaim the Messiah. Proof that Flora has no vanity: she doesn't like to be treated like a "beloved actress" and decides to sort out the friends from the curious by suggesting a contribution to the Union Circle. Yet three hundred stay, surprised to be attending a serious discussion and not an exciting sermon: these Marseillais don't understand how serious her message is.

On August 11 there is a banquet for one hundred people bringing together the members of different "Devoir" societies. The start of the Union. A young apprentice weeps as he declares he is ready to fraternize even with the old hands and even more with the second-degree apprentices. Even Perdiguier hasn't yet achieved this fusion.

A masonic lodge, guilds, even certain bosses have adopted her. When she leaves, they go along with her for a league to "give her a send-off" and applaud when she gets into the stagecoach. "Farewell, our mother, farewell!" She weeps once she is alone. In Marseille, too, she leaves tender friends, most notably Carpentras, a house-painter and poet, and an old rebellious republican.

In Marseille she discovered, in a Fourierist's house, a book dated 1583: *The Celestial, Terrestrial and Infernal Worlds,* by Doni, which Fourier, she declares, must have read—and copied without citing.

Nîmes, in spite of Victor Schoelcher the abolitionist, disappoints her. She brings away from it only one sonorous, obsessive impression: the noise of the washerwomen. They are up to the waist in water filled with toxic products from the dye works. Bent, knotted with rheumatism, with the wind in their eyes, they beat the laundry day and night, in teams. Flora gets up to look at them. One who tells her she is fifty-one looks like an old woman: she can't imagine any other destiny for her nineteen-year-old daughter.

Flora promises to the memory of these resigned women: "My sisters, I swear to you that I will deliver you."

She would have liked at least to see Barbès, imprisoned in Nîmes, but permission is refused and they can only exchange letters. "So I must live with the disappointment of not seeing you, Madame, it is cruel: we had so many things to talk about together."

Flora, identifying with his personality, answers, with a half-smile, that she would have liked to make the love of humanity that possesses her "penetrate his soul." She sends him her "little book," the law of love.

She leaves Nîmes just as she is about to be thrown out.

Montpellier is both disastrous and fruitful for her. On August 17, at four in the morning, suffering from almost unbearable pains, she is refused a room: they don't rent to single women. The hotel that takes her in is shaken by the noise of workmen who are repairing it, starting at five in the morning. "Well, there are my poor brothers who have already come to use up their lives in the service of humanity; I must get up too . . ."

In her state of excitement, a homeopathic doctor "takes away" her pains. Unquestionably, from then on, it is only her mission, her certainty that she is bringing "the word of life" in preaching for the union, that keeps her going. A locksmiths' strike leads to seven arrests: they want to work only eleven hours a day. The press and the police see *The Workers' Union* as an "incendiary publication," an agitators' handbook. *The Independent* defends Flora. A month after the strike, some locksmiths found a cooperative workshop called "The Workers' Union." Another locksmith, Vitou, who has a shop called Vulcan's Forge, wants to set up a committee. But his wife considers Flora an adventuress. Middle-class and working-class women don't easily accept it that she can talk to men, in her room, until morning without being their mistress. To apologize for this scene, the husband orders two hundred little books. Flora sighs: "This woman of the people, suffering from misery, coming to say: there will always be the poor."

At that moment, she hears from Jules Laure that the apartment on the Rue du Bac is going to be repossessed by the landlord. Where will she go, when she goes back?

For this apostle with her ruined health, sustained by the certainty of changing lives, giving a new dimension to the oppressed, this word is stifling. The confusion, the humiliation. She feels these blows deeply and it takes her many days of effort to recover from them. The eternal nomad, the wanderer in lodgings and foreign lands had finally found a "little nook," some furniture and books. And this is over? A writ can take it away from her? She envies the Jesuits "spread all over the world but always knowing where home is." Oh, well, she will lead the people. There's no way to go but forward.

Béziers, whose *Journal* welcomes her sympathetically, seems to her "a rut of intellectual and moral misery dreadful to see." Then the canalboat takes fourteen hours to get to Carcassonne. Letters are waiting for her there; circles have been founded in Marseille and Avignon. A friend of Barbès, the republican Laffitte, clever but adventurous, gives Flora's Béziers meetings too political a character for the Messiah's taste. "Political," for Flora, for Fourier, for Considérant and Cabet in their youth, has a pejorative meaning of superficial agitation. They saw the revolution swept away because minds were not transformed in depth. They weren't aiming for a change of regime, but a subversion, a basic upheaval of minds and customs. This is also what Marx hoped for. Another friend of Barbès, the lawyer Théodore Marcou, falls under Flora's spell. But above all what she sees in Béziers is that seven-year-old children work all day for eight sous and that the republicans care very little about it.

The middle class spreads comical rumors: "She is a Saint-Simonian, her husband tried to kill her, she has lovers. . . ."

A policeman warns her that she will be watched in Toulouse. He has read the "little book": "You are a saint, a liberator. I whom they despise tell you: watch out for vampires!" Flora, astonished, notes: "What a mystery humanity is!" and leaves. And yet a circle will be formed in Carcassonne, linked with Marseille. And Laffitte, always the political hustler but always efficient, has preceded her to Toulouse to organize everything.

The police in fact watch her least step: eight people at her hotel, nineteen at a meeting that lasts an hour and a half; she sends a letter; she goes out in a carriage with "three gentlemen"; she goes to the café; she talks with an editor of the *Emancipation* ("you can see that deep in his heart he still has a certain tick-tock"); she visits the director of this newspaper ("a little provincial Girardin"). A year later police interrogators will still be asking "agitation suspects": "Were you a member of Madame Flora Tristan's Workers' Union?"

The police begin again in Agen and, in the rain that follows her everywhere, Flora sees the commissioner and twenty sergeants break up a meeting of sixty workers. It is then, in this town, that she tries a strange experiment on herself. In her hotel room she finds a gold watch. To keep it is stealing. What does a thief feel? She hides the watch in her trunk, thinks about it all day, all night—and returns it to the hotelkeeper. To steal, you definitely need a real motive. She isn't poor enough and not at all kleptomaniac.

She feels better about the police harassment when she gets letters from her daughters, her daughter of the flesh and those of the spirit. Exhausting weariness? Police? Not knowing what tomorrow will bring? Blindness and deafness of those she has come to save? Too late to draw back. She must go on—Bordeaux, Nantes—after that, we'll see.

29

"... LOVED IMMENSELY ..."

September 26–November 14. Bordeaux. A city she left a pariah for the new world on her thirtieth birthday. She returns forty-one, an apostle of humanity . . . but too weary to speak, persuade, excite. When the flesh masters you, you can do nothing for others' minds. Pseudocholera, typhoid, and a stroke on top of it. She is in bed. The Lemonniers take care of her: Charles, a former philosophy teacher, Elisa, future founder of the first professional school for girls. Sometimes one meets people generous enough to help one die like this. They only know her by reputation, and yet they are at her bedside, write to Eléonore Blanc, who can come at last on October 12. Although she is lucid, Flora frightens her by her "moral sluggishness," which she shakes off to say: "If I succumb, let everyone who has loved me know that I too loved them immensely, religiously."

Eléonore goes away again, reassured by the doctors. Flora is sinking. Noises. Street vendors' cries on the Place Maubert. Jugglers' trumpets on the Pont-Neuf. Waves on the hull of the *Mexican*. Peruvian horses galloping. Carriage wheels in the Rue du Bac. In Nîmes, the washerwomen's paddles: "My sisters, I swear I will deliver you." In Montpellier, the masons' hammers: "My brothers who work, I too. . . ." A voice speaks of God, of the sacraments? She is an apostle? Sacred? Yes.

Elisa Lemonnier writes:

> On the 11th, Monsieur Lemonnier was near the bed when he saw Monsieur Stouvenel come in bringing a priest. My husband showed his astonishment. Monsieur Stouvenel asserted that he knew Madame Tristan's *intimate* feelings. . . . Monsieur Lemonnier wanted to resist until he had proof to the contrary. We asked Madame Tristan, she said no once, and then yes very decidedly. We had not known Madame Tristan at all in health, we had to respect a desire of this nature, even if it was shown during delirium.

On November 12 "there came a merchant tailor named Nau, who seems to be the head of the Workers' Union Circle" (so did Flora manage to found a circle during her short trip to Bordeaux in 1843?), "he seems to take a great and lively interest in her. He had to spend the night near her. . . ."

Thursday, November 14

"I spent her last day at your Florita's side. I saw her calm and beautiful in her painless agony, propped on her two pillows, her arms stretched out, a friend holding each of her hands. For three days she had been almost unconscious, and therefore did not suffer anymore."

At eight thirty in the evening: she begins to sob; two hours later, nothing more. "She suffered for only a brief half hour."

"I wrote to Monsieur Laure." Charles Lemonnier has a cast made of "her beautiful face . . . severe but imposing." Eléonore has the cast sent to Doctor Evrat. The caster asks Lemonnier if this lady was really—as he was told—"the mother of all workmen."

Flora wanted her body sent for dissection and then to a pauper's grave. The Lemonniers persuade Eléonore Blanc to "put up an altar to which the worker can make a pilgrimage, learn to love, to be dedicated to brothers and sisters. Isn't her work going to spread from her tomb? Let us hope for all that."

The funeral service is religious. A tailor, a lawyer, a carpenter speak. Workers take turns carrying the coffin to the Carthusian cemetery and acting as pallbearers.

When she is dead, the press all acclaim her. "Lost star of the social army . . . That noble boldness, that rough mission ended by a martyr's death were a strange anomaly in an egotistic century which does not understand the ardors of a generous faith, and which often responds to them only with irony and outrage," Victor Considérant writes. Is this conscious self-criticism? He starts a subscription for the tombstone.

30

THE PARIAH'S TESTAMENT

In the name of the Bordeaux committee, the carpenter Maigrot notifies all the Workers' Union Circles, at the same time as Considérant's *Peaceful Democracy* starts the subscription: they want a bust, a monument, a tomb, where workers can gather. The clockmaker Festeau writes seven couplets to an air by Kreutzer with the refrain: "Flora Tristan asks you for a tomb."

The first to contribute is the always generous Eugène Sue. The business will drag on until the 1848 revolution, the one Flora would have joined in so joyfully and after which she would no doubt have felt such despair. It is then, when revolutionary hopes are already snuffed out but the militants are still unaware of it, on October 22, that the broken column of white marble is unveiled in the Carthusian cemetery. The procession of militants starts with fifteen hundred, swells at each crossroads and eight thousand to ten thousand fervent listeners hear the cooper Vigier read a long poem entitled "Let us be united."

> Let us be united! Let us be united! Yes we
>   will unite! so that misery
> May sweep from our foreheads their crown of tears!

So that if our arms fertilize the earth
We may gather flowers from it.

The poem ends with a declaration of nonviolence:

Yes we will unite, but not to curse
Clemency is so sweet to the worker's heart.
No, no, we do not want to burn nor destroy,
But we want to edify . . .

The pedestal of the column is inscribed:

TO THE MEMORY OF MADAME FLORA TRISTAN
AUTHOR OF
THE WORKERS' UNION
THE GRATEFUL WORKERS
LIBERTY–EQUALITY–FRATERNITY–SOLIDARITY
FLORA TRISTAN, BORN IN PARIS ON APRIL 7, 1803
DIED IN BORDEAUX ON NOVEMBER 14, 1844
SOLIDARITY.

The repetition of the word "solidarity," the broken column, the
∴ marks made after her initials by Gosset, the father of the
blacksmiths at the time of their friendship, indicate at least a
sympathy between Flora and freemasonry. This tie, even if not
strong, would also explain the welcome she got from certain
members of the middle class.

Again sympathies, crosscurrents and diversity within the movement must be placed back in the times, not so far from the Carbonari, Masonic arches, the socialists' exalted dream, the brotherly
rivalries between Saint-Simon and the lodges. In short a whole
somewhat confused complexity of ideas and men.

Flora's journey through life was over and she probably never
knew that in Berlin, the Bauer brothers' *Allgemeine Literaturzei-*
tung was taking her, along with Proudhon, as an example of the
workerism of French socialists, who, according to them, attributed
an exaggerated creative consciousness to the worker. Even less
could she have known that in September 1844, two friends of her
admirer Ruge who were then signing themselves "Engels-Marx"
completed a work that would come out the following year under
the—makeshift—title of *The Holy Family* and that, ferociously

mocking the Bauer brothers' "critical criticism," they took up Flora's defense. Edgar Bauer said: "Flora Tristan gives us an example of that female dogmatism that demands a formula and makes one out of the categories of what exists." To which "Engels-Marx" reply that if "critical criticism" can have a meaning, it demands the organization of labor. "Flora Tristan—we find this assertion for the first time in the discussion of Flora Tristan's ideas—asks for the same thing, and this insolence of having dared to anticipate 'critical criticism' gets her treated like dirt." So, after having used *Walks in London* without citing the author, Engels gives Flora her revenge and points out that she was a pioneer. It is in relation to Flora's defense that the founders of Marxism launch their famous diatribe against Hegelian philosophy, "an old woman ... widowed and faded, who paints and adorns her desiccated body and reduces (everything) to the most abject abstraction." Thanks to this page the Marxists of following generations have at least heard of the existence of Flora Tristan, of whom no authority on Marxism ever speaks.

There were many who saw in Flora either—like Charles Lemonnier—"a woman who dedicated her life to defending the oppressed, to the triumph of freeing the people," or, more precisely—like Maigrot—a unifier of all the workers' organizations, or "a workers' saint"—like Eléonore Blanc. The disciple will carry on the Inspiration's work and in 1845 will publish a sort of hagiography full of emotion: *Biography of Flora Tristan*.

In 1846, *Woman's Emancipation or the Pariah's Testament, Posthumous Work by Madame Flora Tristan Completed According to Her Notes and Published by Alphonse Constant* appears in Paris, "At the Offices of the *Truth*, Passage Choiseul No. 39." We have seen what an ambiguous portrait he draws with it, to which he adds a physical description that is still suffused with warmth. "Ivory hands that would have tempted Phidias," Oriental eyes, vivacity, the "superb brown hair enclosed by time in a network of silvery cobwebs. Those who saw her understand why those around her yielded to her tyranny. You didn't see her? Then it's better not to talk about her 'like a coward.' " Strange term: he is aware that his description is alarming and wants it understood that the charmer's presence would rid you of all alarm and resistance.

One often has the impression that the future "Eliphas Lévi's"

(Alphonse Constant's) style is dominant. He denies it: the Catholic saints too are used to this "enthusiastic disorder," to these hyperbolic exaggerations that are customary with ardent souls. Thus, for him, his praying mantis is also a saint.

The book bears as an epigraph a sentence from Fourier which, before Marx and Engels, included woman's essential role in human development:

> Social progress and changes in the times take place because of woman's progress toward liberty, and the social order's declines come because of decrease in women's liberty. To sum up, the extension of women's privileges is the general principle of all social progress.

Flora, from the very first, appeals to "women of all ranks, all ages, all opinions and all lands," with special recommendations to rich women: that they should use their influence, their leisure, their position to "lend their powerful protection to men who have nothing going for them but the strength of numbers and the right. In their turn these bare-armed men will lend you their support." For rich or not, women fill no role in society.

To fill one, they must, whatever their class of origin, help the Workers' Union. "Women of the people, join the Workers' Union. . . . Women writers, poets, artists, teach the people and let the Workers' Union be the subject of your songs." How can woman, oppressed by the oppressed, free herself? By fighting for the liberation of all the oppressed. Flora develops her theme of woman's condition in her usual way, starting with "poor women whose price is fixed in the butcher shops of prostitution." These are the most visibly deprived of choice, and so of liberty. But right after them she puts women married without love, condemned "to a corpse's embraces," and becoming "an honest prostitute, that is, a rich, pretty, satin-clad siren." Here again, but raised to the symbolic level, are Flora's memories and inhibitions.

She castigates the rich in the manner of O'Connor the Chartist who so impressed her: "You, all the elect, well-fed and drinking too much, you flunkeys, bellies always full and always greedy, puffed up with pride and sated with infamy. . . ." The rich find that "the masses are very greedy" and "they smell bad. . . ."

Her picture of herself in fact reaches the level of the apostle's myth.

268

I was a wife, I was a mother, and society crushed my heart. I was shot because I protested against infamy, and society branded me while reluctantly condemning my murderer.

When I succumb, I will leave you this book of horrors, and they will not dare condemn it.

For I am not preaching rebellion. REBELLION IS THE CRIME OF A SEDITIOUS HANDFUL. A PEOPLE NEVER REVOLTS; IT RISES WHEN ITS TIME COMES AND DOESN'T NEED TO BE TOLD.

I write so you will know, I cry out so you will hear, I walk ahead so you will know the way.

A man dedicated himself until death, and the testament he left was the Gospel.

Well, I want to accomplish what Magdalen the sinner no doubt dreamed of at the foot of the cross.

I want to love as he loved and die as he died, so as to MAKE THE GOSPEL'S WIDOWHOOD FRUITFUL. . . .

I TOO NEED A CALVARY TO PROCLAIM WOMAN'S EMANCIPATION IN DYING.

Yes, drink, it is the people's blood. Yes, eat, it is the people's flesh. Yes, have prostitutes, they are the people's guts. And when you fall asleep, sated and indifferent, they will awaken you, they, hungry and terrible. . . .

She left these notes to Considérant with the job of getting them into order. She did not tell him that she wanted to die, but the speech, the symbols used, the cry to Calvary prove that she knew she was dying and refused to resist it. Sometimes when she was traveling, ill and alone, despair took hold of her and then she reimmersed herself in ecstatic visions such as apostles have: Jesus restored the Jewish people fallen into decline. She, Flora Tristan, will restore the Christian people. "I feel in myself a new world and I shall give this new world to the old world that is crumbling and perishing."

Her last concern is with possible successors. Flora Tristan is perfectly aware of "utopian" accusations. She heard them from utopians, she heard the "self-satisfied" attack her along with the whole array of warriors of socialism. She retorts:

Modern utopians. . . . Glory to these sublime lunatics who in other times would have been killed and who, today, we're content to jeer at pleasantly while they die of misery.

Fourier wanted to realize Swedenborg's celestial dream on earth

269

and transformed the medieval convent into a phalanx.

Saint-Simon initiated transformations of dogma and revealed the end of the Christian widowhood and the great humanitarian marriage through the moral liberation of woman.

Cabet, a man of conviction and perseverance for whom probity takes the place . . . of ideas and talents, gives in his *Icaria* the plan for a great common manna and some workshop regulations. . . .

Proudhon, a reasoner with a heavy but crushing logic, takes property as we understand it today in pincers and breaks it. His book has not been hounded by the public prosecutor's office. . . .

Victor Considérant, who revived the Saint-Simonian school and continued Fourier's work, a man of knowledge and talent, who will soon perhaps be called upon to represent in parliament the ideas of peaceful emancipation and social organization . . .

Let us note that she tries to be objective about Cabet and Proudhon who were hard on her, but dismisses them as mediocre: it is Considérant, as she said in *The Workers' Union*, who could best become the workers' elect. She doesn't know that he will go off and be ruined in the Texas phalansterian adventure.

Flora's last words show her despair at not being able, as a woman, to act without an intermediary:

An architect in Antiquity cried out: "What he has said, I will do!" Oh! If courage and dedication were enough, I would be that architect who says little but who acts. . . . *But in our unhappy society woman is a pariah by birth, a serf by condition, unhappy by duty, and must almost always choose between hypocrisy and being branded.*

Woman's liberation was the first of Flora's two goals chronologically: it came up, as we saw, when she was fighting for her own survival. Reflection on her own experience quite naturally led her to write her Declaration of the Rights of Woman.

Very much aware of middle-class egotism, she naturally asks those who must fight to free themselves to add this Declaration to their claims.

From 1831 on, the Saint-Simonians asserted: "Woman and the proletarian both need emancipation. Both, bowed under the weight of slavery, had to reveal a new language to us." Flora goes deeper, impelled by having lived through it: "THE MOST OPPRESSED MAN CAN OPPRESS ONE BEING, HIS WIFE.

SHE IS THE PROLETARIAN OF THE PROLETARIAN HIMSELF."

So everything begins "by educating women, because women's job is to raise male and female children. This preliminary rehabilitation is necessary if workers are to be themselves rehabilitated." The elements of "rehabilitation" spring from Flora Tristan's daily life:

1. Right to equal education and professional training. Elisa Lemonnier, who holds Flora's hand in her last moments, will be the founder of the "Society for Women's Professional Education." But we know that women do not actually have access to higher education until the twentieth century. We know that even today their professional training remains limited. When Madame Curie, the Nobel Prize winner, succeeded her husband as professor at the Sorbonne, the scandal reached proportions that are hard to imagine today. The first women lawyers and doctors were manna to parodists and cartoonists. Even today the Institut de France has never had a woman among its academicians. It is only recently that they are allowed on the Bench [in France], and only in certain jobs, and only in 1972 were women allowed to compete for entrance to the Ecole Polytechnique: they came in first among both French and foreign applicants.

As for equal pay for equal work, it remains a constant demand; even if the law stipulates it, employers' practices twist the law.

2. Right to free choice of a mate, outside the father's financial considerations.

3. Right to divorce, that is, to change mates if the marriage fails.

These two rights are closely linked, and also linked to the first: the one that gives economic independence. Flora knows:

> Like all women barred from almost every profession, when their children have no father to support them, they find themselves caught between prostitution, infanticide, and theft.... 500,000 men and women are annually riveted to one another forever.... Two-thirds of imprisonments, of murders, are caused by hatreds, jealousies that result from the indissolubility of marriage and woman's servitude.

The law on divorce in France only dates from 1884 and divorce by mutual consent is still not allowed.

4. Right of unwed mothers to respect and equality before the law. Right of illegitimate children to a share in their father's estate. "Infanticide is caused by the monstrous prejudice that brands the unwed mother."

A law on the rights of children born outside marriage to the father's estate, in France, in January 1972, raised an outcry, as we have said, that lasted for months. Someone wrote: "It is the end of the family." As for single mothers, if recent measures grant them equality before the law, we know how practice lags behind in considering them and their children the same as women with marriage certificates on file.

Let us not forget that the battle for divorce is barely—and very precariously—won in Italy, not at all in Spain or Portugal.

Here again, what Flora Tristan lived through still exists.

Rising above her personal case, her individual tragedy, Flora knows that it is more urgent to obtain equality for women among the working class than elsewhere. For workers to realize their situation, their membership in a class, for them to form a class and begin to struggle, there is only one way: "All the ills of the working class can be summarized in two words: misery and ignorance, ignorance and misery. Now, I see only one way to escape from this labyrinth: begin by educating woman." Is she not "the lover who is listened to, the influential spouse, the mother who molds her children"?

She wrote a lot about sexual mores, that is, freedom of choice and the need for love. Whatever her inhibitions and psychological motivations, she very rationally rejected the role of "sex object."

As for the second phase of her struggle: the association of all workers, the organization of labor, there again she goes beyond Saint-Simon's or Louis Blanc's proposals and remains undeniably the forerunner of the workers' International which her Union anticipates down to the details.

She pushes the logic of the changes she wants to an extreme. Even the penitentiary system is analyzed with a view to reform. The prisoner must repay what is spent on him? Then he should be paid so that his work becomes truly productive and so that, once the prison is paid off, he has enough to reinstate him in society. How can you punish someone who steals if you steal from him "by making him work for one-fifth or one-quarter of his salary"?

Aiming at rehabilitating the individual who has been judged

socially guilty, she very naturally takes a stand against capital punishment:

> What good has society got from capital punishment? Have crimes decreased? No, certainly not! We see man facing death for a piece of bread, to satisfy his hate, his love or revenge, his insult, and we still believe it can keep man from breaking laws? The deterrent effect of capital punishment is just about nil: it works only as a suppression.

Except for capital punishment, Flora Tristan's demands for the formation of the working class were absorbed by Marxism. That the founders of the International Workingmen's Association never acknowledged her does not prevent her from having been their forerunner. But how could those unconscious "sexists," Marx and Engels, have admitted a woman among their forerunners in theory and organization?

"Only the workers can become the artisans of their emancipation" and many of Flora's other formulas contain the seed, not only of a working-class consciousness, but of the need for a party derived from it to represent it, defend it, direct it.

It undoubtedly could be said of Flora, as it was of Rosa Luxemburg fifty years after her death, that she had too much confidence in enthusiasm, in generosity. She wasn't a scientist, but a romantic. Yet, although she was nonviolent, she recognized, we have seen, a legitimate rising of the proletarian masses. But she never dreamed of a proletarian dictatorship, isolated from the other classes: she saw the working class taking its place "at the side" of the third estate. Let us note, moreover, how the European countries that espouse Marxism are made up of technocratic, intellectual, administrative and political strata which take the place of "a new type of middle class."

Flora's feminist demands were pursued by Pauline Roland and Jeanne Deroin through the revolution of 1848. Yet, like Daniel Stern (Countess Marie d'Agoult), like George Sand, they put the accent on the right to vote and eligibility. Flora was, as we know, one of those who hardly believe in political rights alone. For her the motto "Liberty, Equality, Fraternity" took on meaning only when "Solidarity," that is, association and organization of labor, was added to it.

If the Marxists encompassed the Workers' Union's demands,

they also thought that by the same token they were fighting for woman's emancipation. Results have shown that the two emancipations don't get equal billing without effort. In fact, although the social-democratic and Communist movements have always posited woman's equality, it is still a secondary claim. In countries whose laws are inspired by Marx, legal equality is total; practical equality is not. While in capitalist countries there isn't equal pay for equal work, in noncapitalist countries the masses of women still have their traditional role. Curiously, the Communist militants especially dedicated to woman's cause were tacitly considered with an indulgent disdain: it's very important, it's not essential—unless suddenly a strike, a peace movement depends on women. Clara Zetkin constantly complained, within the Second International, of the leaders' scant understanding of her woman's movement.

After the Russian Revolution, leaders like Alexandra Kollontaï, the first woman ambassador, tried to justify woman's sexual liberation by preaching the equality of free union and marriage, the right to free abortion, that is, to free conception. Inès Armand, the militant Lenin was in love with, wanted to publish a book on these problems. Lenin dissuaded her, partly out of natural prudishness, mostly because he was afraid questions of love would divert the energy of youth from the revolution. And he ended up sending Clara Zetkin the famous letter on the danger of considering the act of love as unimportant as the glass of water one swallows. The "glass of water theory" locked the door on consideration of the sexual claim in Communist parties and countries.

The battle linking emancipation of the oppressed, the social and professional rights of women and their right to freedom of conception and private life started up again only in the mid-sixties.

In the neoromanticism of today's youth, in spite of its at times unrealistic, ill-adapted, and caricatural explosions, Flora Tristan would undoubtedly have recognized—not without bewilderment —the great impulse that drove her.

The young women of the various branches of the women's liberation movement, American, French, or any other future trend, find in the Pariah, the militant Messiah, an ancestress, a forerunner, or, better: an inspiration.

274

31

THE GAUGUINS:
MOTHER AND SON

Flora's real children follow divergent paths that only join—an obvious legacy—in a taste for the great world. Ernest, not much attached to his sister, joins the navy and is swallowed up by it.

Aline, on the other hand, is not satisfied to receive half of Flora's hair as her legacy—the other half going to Eléonore, the spiritual daughter. Perhaps in spite of herself, the child to whom Flora vowed so many dreams and disappointments seems, at several stages in her life, to have followed—in spite of herself—in her mother's footsteps.

What could she think of men and love, this girl who at ten was defending herself against incest, the major taboo? What would Freud have said about this child who came to her mother for help against the father's desire? What secrets, what shadowy distance were harbored in the unconscious of this daughter whom her parents fought over with laws, kidnappings, insults, policemen, process-servers, lawyers, slanders, and finally a pistol? What picture did Aline get of conjugal union, woman's lot, and herself? For lack of written evidence, we must base our answers on her actions.

Orphaned at nineteen, Aline inherits Flora's friends. Pauline Roland takes her to the famous Bascans school, where Marceline

Desbordes-Valmore's daughter had been a monitress and George Sand's a boarder; Aline finds a job there. Pauline also brings her to see the glorious queen of letters and progress. Let us recall George's reaction: she writes to Considérant's friend and collaborator, who edits *Peaceful Democracy* and is starting his own newspaper, which will only appear once and will be called *Humanity*. Much later, he will work on the *Socialist Review* with Benoît Malon, a great posthumous admirer of Flora's. Pompéry will also play an important role in the Teaching League; Pauline Roland and Jeanne Deroin love him. The author of *Consuelo* writes to him:

> Flora's daughter seems as tender and good as her mother was imperious and fiery. This child is like an angel; her sorrow, her mourning, and her lovely eyes, her isolation, her modest and affectionate air went to my heart. Did her mother love her? Why were they separated thus? What mission, then, can make you forget and send so far away, to a millinery shop, such a charming and adorable creature? I would much rather give her a future than raise a monument to her mother, whom I never liked in spite of her courage and conviction. She had too much vanity in her. When people are dead, one bows down; it's all very well to respect the mystery of death, but why lie? I wouldn't know how to. I have some advice to give you, my dear Pompéry, it is to fall in love with this girl (it won't be hard) and marry her. That would be a good deed, it would be worth more than being in love with Fourier. You are a worthy man, you will make her happy. And it can't be that you won't be happy, first because of that, and then because with such a face she can only be an adorable creature. The good Lord would be a liar if it were otherwise. Well! Go to the rue de Chaillot, and invite me soon to your wedding.

On receiving this masterpiece of psychological incomprehension and sanctimonious bourgeois self-satisfaction, Pompéry cannot have felt predisposed to offer Aline that sole career that Flora denounced so often. Since these literary ladies definitely have the souls of matchmakers, Hortense Allart de Méritens also gets busy finding suitors. Which has the merit of entertaining the girl and letting her get to know men.

Is it vigilant, faithful Jules Laure, or Hortense Allart, or Pauline who takes her into republican writers' circles, where her name attracts more and more attention as the figure of Flora takes on its mythic dimension, as her ideas spread?

In any case, she meets a sailor turned journalist, Clovis Gauguin. He is editor of the *National,* a political journal run by the same Marrast who was in London in 1839 at the same time as Flora: in her letter to the mysterious Olympe, the seeker of the absolute reproached this member of the opposition for spending too much time with Bonaparte in exile. Clovis Gauguin himself is a spotless republican. Of an honorably lower-middle-class family, settled near Orléans in the Gâtinais, he is smitten by Aline's heavy-lidded Oriental eyes and air of sweetness, but perhaps the memory of Flora adds to this beauty an attractive singularity. For Aline, it is a haven; but marrying a militant republican, she must have realized, also fulfils her mother's wish. The marriage takes place on June 15, 1846. Jules Laure is the bride's witness. He also draws, then paints, Aline's two children, Fernande-Marcelline-Marie, born in 1847, and Paul, born in June 1848. Paul Gauguin is a child of the barricades, who comes into the world when the revolution Flora dreamed of is already beginning to wither in the sun of a bourgeois June. The first portrait, signed Jules Laure, links the damned and glorious painter to his outcast and underrated grandmother.

The Gauguins go to live in a new district, still resounding with masons and tilers, on the rue Notre-Dame-de-Lorette. The little boy is hardly babbling yet when they unveil Flora Tristan's monument in Bordeaux. Clovis Gauguin probably attended the ceremony. In any event, he fights valiantly for the Republic and against the "Napoleon nephew," who becomes president in December. Paul is a year old—Jules Laure has just finished his portrait—when the barricades of June 1849—especially the one in the Rue Transonain, where the arrests and accusations begin—make Clovis Gauguin decide to go into exile. Then Aline's unconscious comes into play: she persuades her husband to seek refuge in Peru, near Uncle Pio, with whom she must have gotten in touch on her mother's death. A strange repetition: after his brother Mariano's daughter, here is his granddaughter demanding protection, and Don Pio invites her to come. He seems even to have promised Clovis Gauguin that he would help him start a French newspaper in Lima. The family sets out—after Aline, evidently against her husband's wishes, has her son baptized in Notre-Dame-de-Lorette. Does she remember Flora's fears on boarding a ship, her horror of ocean voyages? Does Aline have premonitions as she boards the *Albert?* The voyage is tragic for her, with a half-mad captain whose quarrels rattle Clovis Gauguin; he has a bad heart. On their arrival in Patagonia, at Port Famine with its funereal name, Clovis is laid low: an aneurism. Aline's husband is dead before he can set foot on land. So once again it is a single woman, mother of two children—but this time they are admitted to, and present—whom Uncle Pio welcomes from France. A Parisian prostrated with grief, but for reasons he knows this time. Yet how can one fail to be struck by this odd repetition? Don Pio de Tristan is at the height of his power: his son-in-law, the future General Echenique, will soon, in August 1853, become president of Peru. Aline, like her mother, takes her place among the Tristan de Moscoso "people," but this time in Lima. Paul Gauguin will later remember: "How graceful and pretty my mother was when she put on her Liman costume!" There must have been plenty, among the women of the family, to recall how Flora loved to be disguised, *disfrazada,* in dress skirt and mantle. Aline gets the ardent tenderness she gives her son from her mother. "That eye so sweet and so imperious, so pure and caressing" that Paul Gauguin will always evoke and look for among the Tahitian women is something Aline inherited from Flora. (So this angel of sweetness according to George Sand was imperious too, at least according to her son?) Does Uncle Pio feel responsible for his niece's heroic misery and exhausted death? In any case, he comes to adore the new "Francesita" who, for the second time, brings him his brother's "illegitimate" posterity. He wants to leave the daughter a large part of his estate, which he refused the mother. . . . Aline stays for five years among the Tristans and her children feel very Peruvian. Then Grandfather Gauguin feels he is dying and wants Clovis's family near him. Torn, Aline leaves nonetheless—she loves Guillaume, her father-in-law: she boards a ship at the beginning of 1855, in the midst of a Peruvian coup d'état, and arrives in time to close Guillaume Gauguin's eyes. In 1856 Uncle Pio dies too, leaving her an income that amounts to 60,000 modern francs: the Peruvian heirs rush to disinherit the Frenchwoman. That same year, 1856, André Chazal, the father Aline will never see again, is released and finds work in Evreux where he is sent on parole and where he will die in 1860. Still in 1856 the ex-president of Peru, Cousin Echenique, stripped and banished, arrives in France and proposes a deal with Aline. As intractable as her mother, she answers "all or nothing"; it is nothing—except for some 40,000 of today's francs which Guillaume Gauguin left her, not enough for the family to live on. Then Aline remembers she is a milliner ("I made workers of my children," Flora said proudly) and in 1859 moves back to Paris, to the Rue de la Chaussée d'Antin, where she opens a millinery workshop. She puts Paul in boarding school—didn't she spend nearly all her childhood in them? He wants to go to sea: why doesn't he try for the Naval School? But he fails the entrance exam and, at seventeen, joins the merchant marine: the call of the great world, a legacy from his father, but also from the traveling that possessed Flora. In 1865 Aline, on reaching forty, the age when her mother felt her final illness come upon her, finds she has no more strength. Liquidating her workshop, she moves to Romainville to a sort of community called "Village of the Future"; she dies there at the same age as her mother, forty-one, without seeing Paul, who is at sea, as Flora died far from Aline. The life of the "adorable being," as George Sand called her, seems a pale copy of the burning maternal life. Flora's violent ardor, creative restlessness, intractable pride, and even her messianic certainty, her vocation reappear, bypassing Aline, in her son. Paul Gauguin will be for some time a banking agent, a prosperous speculator, that is, socially in the system, but very quickly his genius, his demon, will tear him from the middle-class rut, from the wife married during his prosperous period, from his children. Does the urge to paint come to him from the Chazals? Or rather from Jules Laure, who exerts an unquestionable influence on him, and from his tutor and adoptive father, a speculator but a collector too? The fire burning in him, at all events, comes from that grandmother of whom he will speak with off-hand pride. One day he will write to Monfreid, his one faithful friend: "My grandmother was quite a character," will pretend, or really believe, that Proudhon "thought she was a genius," will conclude as a good "sexist" that she must have been a "socialist bluestocking." But he will show all her inability to play the social game and even the failure in marriage, the flight to far places and especially the decision to follow his vocation in total destitution rather than accept the bread of banality. Now and then he feels possessed by a violent heredity, talks about Peruvian ancestors, Spain and Montezuma; but these men of the Tristan line were hardly immersed in the ideal and only Flora could act as a model for this Don-Juanish misogynist. His contempt for money, prudent schemes, even his quarrels with the Tahiti planters and authorities recall the agonized destiny that was surely brought up before him in childhood. His letters to the cold, avaricious, demanding wife in which he begs her to let him see their children recall the drama in which his mother was the stake and which he surely knew about. The resemblance is even deeper: Flora felt that those who were called "madmen" were beings done in by the absolute and by mystic nostalgia, and madness strangely pursued Gauguin. In childhood, in Lima, he was frightened by a madman appearing before his crib; in Provence, Vincent Van Gogh cuts off his own ear after nearly cutting Gauguin's throat with a razor, and at the end of Paul's life his persecutors accuse him of madness. During his last years, moreover, the painter began to write and his quest for the absolute, his mysticism, even his defense of a sort of primitive community, the tradition of the primitive peoples among whom he lived, recall Flora's struggles against "civilized" society and the way the police persecuted her.

More than a century and a quarter has passed since Flora Tristan's death: only now can she meet her true posterity.

This romantic revolutionary who supported no party was rejected by every party after her death too. The Marxists found her too mystical, the Catholics not Christian enough, and the freemasons not political enough. She faded into inexplicable neglect. Only Jules L. Puech's admirable thesis, in 1925, tried to get her out of it. In 1953, André Breton published letters of hers in *Surrealism Itself*, devoted a quivering page to her, saw in her the supreme flowering of romanticism in her branch of society. It was the appearance of this book that gave me the desire to resuscitate Flora: I assembled documentation, in the Archives, in the National Library, and also at random from collections and sales where I was told I could find letters of hers and fragments of notes and diary. But for nineteen years or nearly so, I was constantly sidetracked from Flora by subjects which, who knows why, seemed more urgent to me.

But everything converges: one would think that Flora, that ardently consumed vine shoot, was waiting for a time when she could be understood. In this last third of the twentieth century scientific socialism has shown its faults and inadequacies; people started looking again for something: the great international explosion in the spring of 1968 was only a sign of this demand for new solutions. The women and girls of new generations have woken up, after feminism's slumbering in its illusory victories granted by parliaments and the masters of industries and universities. They have begun to struggle for woman's real emancipation, for equality of the sexes, not only in the eyes of the law but also and especially in customs, that is, in fact and in life. The joyous noise aroused by women's admission (glorious it is true) to the Ecole Polytechnique in Paris shows that intellectual equality is far from being accepted by the majority of our contemporaries. There are women governing states, in Israel and in Asia—but it is the lot of the average woman that matters for there have always been queens and artists. Exceptions are not progress. At present, with advanced laws, the most difficult part is beginning: making law pass into daily life. The most lucid, the most aware women say that the struggle for equality must not be "put off until later" when one leads a revolutionary fight, nor must women's cause be separated from the general progress of society. As in Flora Tristan's time, the struggle unites all the oppressed, and women among them—but, as in her time, the oppressed are rarely aware of the need to unite.

Today, outside the traditional parties and above and beyond them, young people are looking for those who believed in the power of *acted speech*, of ideas around which they can orient their lives —to the end. Those young people, especially the women, will find in Flora Tristan a pioneer and an inspiration.

After a century and a quarter of purgatory, Flora Tristan's time is coming at last.